D1349971

PROJECT-BASED ORGANIZATION IN THE KNOWLEDGE-BASED SOCIETY

Series on Technology Management*

Series Editor: J. Tidd (Univ. of Sussex, UK) ISSN 0219-9823

Published

Vol. 2 The Knowledge Enterprise
Implementation of Intelligent Business Strategies
edited by J. Friso den Hertog *(MERIT, Maastricht University and Altuïtion bv, 's Hertogenbosch, The Netherlands)* &
E. Huizenga *(Altuïtion bv, 's Hertogenbosch, The Netherlands)*

Vol. 3 From Knowledge Management to Strategic Competence
Measuring Technological, Market and Organisational Innovation (2nd Edition)
edited by J. Tidd *(Univ. of Sussex, UK)*

Vol. 4 Japanese Cost Management
edited by Y. Monden *(Univ. of Tsukuba, Japan)*

Vol. 5 R&D Strategy on Organisation
Managing Technical Change in Dynamic Contexts
by V. Chiesa *(Univ. degli Studi di Milano, Italy)*

Vol. 6 Social Interaction and Organisational Change
Aston Perspectives on Innovation Networks
edited by O. Jones *(Aston Univ., UK),* S. Conway *(Aston Univ., UK)*
& F. Steward *(Aston Univ., UK)*

Vol. 7 Innovation Management in the Knowledge Economy
edited by B. Dankbaar *(Univ. of Nijmegen, The Netherlands)*

Vol. 8 Digital Innovation
Innovation Processes in Virtual Clusters and Digital Regions
edited by G. Passiante (*Univ. of Lecce, Italy*), V. Elia (*Univ. of Lecce, Italy*) & T. Massari (*Univ. of Lecce, Italy*)

Vol. 9 Service Innovation
Organisational Responses to Technological Opportunities and Market Imperatives
edited by J. Tidd (*Univ. of Sussex, UK*) & F. M. Hull (*Fordham Univ., USA*)

Vol. 10 Open Source
A Multidisciplinary Approach
by M. Muffatto (*University of Padua, Italy*)

Vol. 11 Involving Customers in New Service Development
edited by B. Edvardsson, A. Gustafsson, P. Kristensson,
P. Magnusson & J. Matthing (*Karlstad University, Sweden*)

Vol. 12 Project-Based Organization in the Knowledge-Based Society
by M. Kodama (*Nihon University, Japan*)

*For the complete list of titles in this series, please write to the Publisher.

SERIES ON TECHNOLOGY MANAGEMENT – VOL. 12

PROJECT-BASED ORGANIZATION IN THE KNOWLEDGE-BASED SOCIETY

Mitsuru Kodama

Nihon University, Japan

ICP Imperial College Press

Published by

Imperial College Press
57 Shelton Street
Covent Garden
London WC2H 9HE

Distributed by

World Scientific Publishing Co. Pte. Ltd.
5 Toh Tuck Link, Singapore 596224
USA office: 27 Warren Street, Suite 401-402, Hackensack, NJ 07601
UK office: 57 Shelton Street, Covent Garden, London WC2H 9HE

British Library Cataloguing-in-Publication Data
A catalogue record for this book is available from the British Library.

PROJECT-BASED ORGANIZATION IN THE KNOWLEDGE-BASED SOCIETY
Series on Technology Management — Vol. 12

ISBN-13 978-1-86094-696-7
ISBN-10 1-86094-696-8

Typeset by Stallion Press
Email: enquiries@stallionpress.com

Printed in Singapore by World Scientific Printers (S) Pte Ltd

Preface and Acknowledgement

Successful business models do not last forever. This is common sense, but it is also a fact that a large number of companies find it difficult to extricate themselves from their successful, existing mainstream businesses. Recently, even Intel and Dell have seen a cloud pass over their successful business models.

Similarly, mobile phone businesses have rushed headlong into an era where they can no longer anticipate future profits after migrating to fixed-charge models. The mass production model is no longer widespread, even for digital electrical household appliances. It follows that companies must always be looking for new business models, even while their mainstream businesses are thriving. Forward-looking exploratory activities are a necessary condition for companies that are continually evolving through innovation and change management.

In this book, while suggesting improvements to existing mainstream businesses, I would also like to suggest a new business-creating framework that relates to strategies and organizations. A central theme organization should consider is that of "project-based organizations"? teams of practitioners possessing diverse knowledge. In this book, I consider the dynamics of knowledge creation arising from project networks formed within and outside a company through in-depth case studies from the perspective of strategies, organizations and processes.

I am an experienced project manager and project leader, in the ICT (Information and Communication Technology) field. In this book, I would like to offer readers a new theoretical framework and practical perspective regarding corporate project strategies from the findings of the latest investigations into corporate project activities, many of which I have experienced. As a practitioner and researcher in the field of management studies, my most important objective in this book is to bridge the theory and practice. My main message is to build project-based organizations within a company, and to do this, it is necessary to form relationships with existing organizations and knowledge networks extending beyond that company. I consider the ideal state of these networks and relationships from the perspective of strategic management.

This book could not have been completed without the thorough and rigorous interactions that I have had with many practitioners. I would like to extend my gratitude to these practitioners, who are of a number too great to count. Concerning the publication of this book, I wish to extend my appreciation to Ms. Juliet Lee and Ms. Sandhya of World Scientific, who provided tremendous support.

Mitsuru Kodama

Contents

Preface and Acknowledgement v

1. Project-based Organizations 1
   1.1. Why Are Project-based Organizations Necessary? 1
   1.2. The Philosophy of Project-based Organizations 4
   1.3. Community of Practice and Collectivity of Practice 6
   1.4. "Project-based Organizations" as "Teams of Boundaries" . . . 9
   1.5. Teams of Boundaries and Strategic Communities: The Empirical Background 15
   1.6. Structure of this book 19

2. Project Networks as Marketing Innovation — The Challenge of the Mobile Communications Businesses 23
   2.1. Exploration and Exploitation 23
   2.2. Case Study: Mobile Phone Business Innovation 26
   2.3. The Formation of Teams of Boundaries 49
   2.4. Network Competencies through Leadership Teams 52

3. Boundary Innovation through Project Networks — J-Phone and Sharp Take on the Challenge of Camera-Loaded Mobile Phone Development 57
   3.1. The Fusion of Organizational and Technological Boundaries 57
   3.2. J-Phone's (Vodafone's) "Sha-mail" 58
   3.3. Joint Development by J-Phone and Sharp 61
   3.4. J-Phone's Incubations with Specific Corporate Clients Collaboration between Businesses in Different Industries 67

3.5. Sharp's Technology Integration 70
3.6. Establishing Competitive Dominance with Networked ToBs 77
3.7. Conclusion 82

4. Radical Innovation through Integrative Competencies of Project-Based Organization: Case Study of Mitsubishi Electric 83
4.1. Introduction 83
4.2. Visual Communication 84
4.3. Trends in Global Visual Communications 85
4.4. Changes in the Product Architecture and Market for Visual Communication Systems 87
4.5. New Challenges for Mitsubishi Electric 95
4.6. New Framework Resulting from the In-depth Case Study 109

5. Business Model Innovation through Boundary Management: Case Study of PlayStation by Sony 115
5.1. Innovation by Means of Corporate Ventures 115
5.2. A Case Study of Sony 116

6. Boundaries Synchronization: Case Study of Matsushita Electric and Canon 151
6.1. Project Strategies Flexible to Changes 151
6.2. Innovation by Matsushita Electric 152
6.3. Project Network by the Formation of a Flat Hierarchical Organization and ToB Network 168
6.4. Canon's Innovations 170
6.5. Boundaries (ToB) Synchronization 187

7. Use of Project Formation to Stimulate Innovation in a Traditional Big Business: Case Study of Communications Businesses in Japan 193
7.1. Management Change in Corporation 193
7.2. Digital Communication Revolution at NTT 194
7.3. New and Practical Insights into this Case 207

8. Innovation by Project-Based Organizations 211
8.1. Exploitation and Exploration by Project-Based Organizations 211
8.2. Strategy By Project-Based Organizations 213
8.3. The Strategy Dynamics of Project-based Organizations and Project Formation Dynamic Chain Reaction 220
8.4. Knowledge Integration through ToB Network 224
8.5. ToBs and ToB Network as Macro-Micro Linkages 242

9. Implications and Conclusions 247
9.1. Trigger Business "Chemical Reactions" Both Inside and Outside the Organization! 248
9.2. Building a Foundation for a Project Culture 250
9.3. Form Project Networks for New Innovations! 254

Bibliography 257

Index 269

1

Project-based Organizations

1.1. Why Are Project-based Organizations Necessary?

In the knowledge-based economy of the 21st century, diverse human knowledge has become the source of product, service and business models with a new competitive value. Many companies are discussing a move away from the mass-production, mass-consumption business model that thrived in the 20th century. They are rushing into an era where they must search for businesses that are as yet undiscovered. In the former business environment, certain level of profits could be made through management methods such as cost-cutting by investing in IT to boost business efficiency in sales and production divisions; strategic outsourcing; and rationalization of personnel. However, in an economic environment with an over-abundance of goods and services (especially in industrialized nations), rapidly developing Asian economies, and globalization, companies can no longer make a profit simply by developing and producing goods and services efficiently, and then supplying them to customers. The revolution in ICT (Information & Communication Technology), moreover, has led to great changes for the consumer, as well as the company. Because of this, companies must continually come up with creative and competitive products, services and business models, and must always deliver new value to the consumer. The larger the company, the greater the need to develop innovation and efficiency, while simultaneously pursuing economies of scale, scope and speed.

Meanwhile, the advance and diversity of technology and the rapid evolution of IT are adding complexity to the business models that companies ought to deliver. Companies urgently need to fuse and integrate different technologies and product, service development and business models across industries (see Kodama, 2002, 2005). Previous technology innovations involved an exhaustive pursuit and development of specialist knowledge, but the unprecedented concepts behind the new products and services have led to frequent cases of fusing technologies from different fields. In high-tech business fields such as IT, telecommunications, e-business and content, automobiles, electronics, FA (factory automation), precision instruments and biotechnology, the best core technologies have been dispersed, which have led to innovation globally. In the knowledge-based economy, many companies are finding it difficult to keep innovations in these cutting-edge business areas under the full control of the company, as they did under the conditions of hierarchical organizations and closed, autonomous systems of the mass-production era (see Sawhney and Prandelli, 2000; Chesbrough, 2003; Haour, 2004).

Accordingly, in an era where valuable knowledge produces wealth, open systems in which the management integrates advanced knowledge from multiple viewpoints dispersed within and outside the organization (including customers) will become increasingly important. This is not to go so far as to say, however, that one company should encourage another to sustain and develop the first company's hard-to-copy core competences as its own (see Hamel and Prahalad, 1994). Put another way, in the knowledge-based economy, it will become increasingly important to develop and accumulate in-house the core competencies that confer a competitive advantage, while undertaking external core competences, and creating new product and service business models from knowledge integration among one's own and other companies.

One question is the kind of management that companies creating a competitive edge in this kind of knowledge-based economy should possess. One of the solutions is the message of building project-based organizations within the company, as I emphasize in this book. In recent years, the most advanced high-tech and multinational corporations (MNCs) (see Forsgren, 1997; Bartlett and Ghoshal, 1989; Nohria and Ghoshal, 1997) have been transforming their traditionally hierarchical organizations to flatter, speedier, and more flexible and horizontally-integrated structures based around teams and projects (see Child and McGrath, 2001; Child and Rodrigues, 2003). In an environment with such dramatically changing markets and technologies, flexible and autonomous project-based organizations are also optimal organizational structures to integrate knowledge both within and outside the company, and to generate business models for new products and services (see Lundin and Midler, 1998; Hobday,

2000; DeFillipi, 2002; Lindqvist, 2004). Project members target shared objectives and collaborate, while promoting business within set time frames (see Henrie and Sousa-Poza, 2005).

The structure of project-based organizations has come to be applied to a range of industries, especially construction (Gann and Salter, 1998), IT, communications (Kodama, 1999), automobiles (Clark and Fujimoto, 1991), the media (Windeler and Sydow, 2001; DeFillippi and Arthur, 1998), and consulting and professional services (Alvesson, 1995). The mission of the project-based organizations is to generate results in response to specific client demands by structuring projects around temporary assemblies of in-house specialist staff and executing business within a fixed time limit. The entire company can also be thought of as an assembly of project-based organizations where the routine business that goes on at a consulting firm is almost non-existent.

A great deal of research has accumulated around project management and project-based organizations (see Turner, 1999; DeFillippi, 2001; Sydow, Lindkvist and DeFillippi, 2004). Definitions of project-based organizations vary, but a key point is that project-based organizations possess all internal and external resources, as well as individual functions such as development, production and sales, and established organizations are structured to execute business as individual projects (Hobday, 1998, 2000; Prencip *et al.*, 2001). Another point is that in order for large companies to implement the most important themes, such as projects to enhance management efficiency or develop new products, an organizational structure should exist to build the project after members of temporarily existing organizations have ended their participation, and to have the project carried out by specialist members (see Midler, 1995; Keegan and Turner, 2002). A third characteristic is that a matrix form exists for members to participate in projects in addition to following their primary business in existing organizations (see Galbraith, 1969). The fourth characteristic is that there are cases where members of existing organizations form informal project networks within and outside the company (cases of Japanese companies working to maximize these features are analyzed in this book) (see Kodama, 2005). As you can see, the term "project-based organizations" has several meanings. In this book, I have used the same term to define all these variants.

In this book, I also identify new knowledge generated from the boundaries of inter-organizational networks (between disciplines, projects and existing organizations, among projects, and between project networks within and outside the organization), centered on project-based organizations, as a source of innovation. The dynamic view of strategy comprising the development of diverse organizational and knowledge boundary networks existing within and outside companies (including customers and external partners) demonstrates the creation of new organizational capabilities to generate innovation. In this book, I use detailed case studies from hi-tech Japanese companies to analyze the mechanisms by which the development of diverse-boundary networks, formed through project-based organizations and project networks, dynamically integrate diverse knowledge within and outside the organization, and create new innovations and strategic positions. In this chapter, I propose frameworks for project-based organizations that form the core of this book.

1.2. The Philosophy of Project-Based Organizations

The recent shape of project-based organizations has been defined in the following ways.

A project is a temporary organization to which resources are assigned to undertake a unique, novel and transient endeavor that involves managing the inherent uncertainty and need for integration in order to deliver beneficial objectives of change (Turner and Miller, 2003, p. 7).

Project-based organizations refer to a variety of organizational forms that involve the creation of temporary systems for the performance of project tasks (Sydow, Lindkvist and Defillippi, 2004, p. 1475).

Clearly, a project-based organization incorporates the meaning of an organizational structure specially formed for a temporary period to enable a project-based organization execute a specific task. The project-based companies of Japanese companies are not simply playing the role of organizations that execute temporary functions, but are also positioned as specialist, official organizations that execute specific functions.

Some companies, for example, adopt project-based organizations as organizations specializing in exploratory activities (March 1991) to promote future strategies. This book examines the cases of NTT DoCoMo in Chapter 2 and NTT in Chapter 7. Japanese companies, moreover, are structured simply as official project organizations. There are cases in which each functional organization builds projects through temporary responses from informal networks (see the cases of Sharp in Chapter 3 and Matsushita Electric in Chapter 6). Moreover, these organizational forms do not exist simply as project-based organizations enclosed within a single company, or between company and client, which are perceived as a project-based organization, but rather as wide-ranging inter-company networks incorporating clients, group affiliates and partner companies (see cases of Mitsubishi Electric in Chapter 4, Sony in Chapter 5, and Canon in Chapter 6). Accordingly, in this book, I am not looking at project-based organizations from the viewpoint of projects as temporary systems or systems sealed within a single organization. Rather, I want to view them as optimized organizational forms to achieve specific work targets, and to formulate and implement future strategies through the adjustment and integration of resources and capabilities within and outside organizations (including customers).

Next, I would like to mention the differences between projects in US and in European companies on the one hand, and Japanese companies on the other. In the academic research centered on the US and Europe, projects have come to be perceived as a favored methodology adopted to achieve innovation (see Hobday, 2000; Lundin and Midler, 1998). Because the project itself is a temporary organization, however, it has been pointed out (see DeFillippi, 2001; Keegan and Turner, 2001; Grabher, 2002; Newell *et al.*, 2003; Prencipe and Tell, 2001; Middleton, 1967) that the accumulation of knowledge within the project is insufficient, and that knowledge transfer to other projects and existing organizations and organizational learning through knowledge sharing is problematic. What happens with projects at Japanese companies? My conclusion, derived from qualitative data[1] through ethnography, participant observation and interviews, is that Japanese companies tend to promote more mutual learning, knowledge transfer, and knowledge sharing among projects and between projects and existing organizations. I will describe this when I discuss the project-based organization framework.

---

[1] This book is based entirely on inductive research from qualitative data. Over the past decade, I have acquired considerable insights from semi-structured interviews and informal dialogues with a total of 308 people including project leaders, project managers, technical staff, strategy division managers, marketing and sales division managers, and production division managers in high-tech Japanese companies (companies featured in this book's case studies and 23 other companies). I graduated from a Japanese Graduate School of Science and Engineering (majoring in electrical engineering), and have come to acquire a defined framework concerning the state of Japanese companies' distinctive project management, including knowledge gained from 20 years experience as a project manager and project leader, strategy division manager, planning division manager, and personnel training division staff of an IT company.

1.3. Community of Practice and Collectivity of Practice

Before I explain the project-based organization framework that forms the core of this book, I would like to consider the existing research. Recent research regarding the organizational behavior of temporary projects involves analyses from the viewpoint of the typology of knowledge work (Lindkvist, 2005). As Wenger (1998) mentions, a project clearly differs from a community of practice. The latter involves a group of actors rooted in the community within a company, who have the same specializations and job functions. A community of practice has the character of a "learning community" (Lave and Wenger, 1991; Brown and Duguid, 1991; Orr, 1996) comprising a group with the same basic specializations (actors possessing fixed domain-specific knowledge in fields such as management, development and production).

Vital knowledge in the community of practice resides in practice as "decentered" knowledge, in the system of activities and the tacit, communal background knowledge contained in the practice and narratives of the community. In the community of practice, vital knowledge resides in practice as "decentered" knowledge, in the system of activities and the tacit, communal background knowledge contained in the practice and narratives of the community. The community of practice does not rely on specific individual knowledge. Members create a communal and coherent knowledge platform through sustained cooperation and coordination over an extended period of time. It has the merit that the knowledge thus accumulated through sustained learning is oriented toward organizational growth. Since the actors in the community of practice are working in the same functions and specialist fields, the members possess similar "thought worlds" (Dougherty, 1992), and the knowledge boundaries between them (Brown and Duguid, 2001) are not great. Since the work revolves around the daily business routines, the project-work elements of novelty and uncertainty do not figure large in the project-work. It follows that there is little conflict and abrasion among the actors. In the community of practice, new meaning is created amidst the daily business routine, and incremental improvement is promoted through the learning of these members and sharing the depths of their knowledge.

Community practice project members come from various specialist groups. Lindkvist (2005, p. 1190) considers the organizational behavior of projects as follows:

Typically, such temporary organizations or groups within firms consist of people, most of whom have not met before, and who have to engage in swift socialization and carry out a pre-specific task within set limits with respect to time and costs. Moreover, they comprise a mix of individuals with highly specialized competences, making it difficult to establish shared understandings or a common knowledge base. Such a transient group, I suggest, operates more like a "collectivity of practice".

Projects are highly autonomous within goals set, in terms of time, money and outcome qualities. In particular, projects have strict time limit targets, and project members have no time to take on the new behaviour of the community of practice, share new meaning and context, and accumulate sufficient communal knowledge. It follows that the project tasks depend greatly on the knowledge and competence of the project members. In the project, members do not rely on decentered knowledge (as in the community of practice), but must be able to operate on knowledge that is radically dispersed, distributed or individualized, being impossible to gather or comprehend for any single, overseeing mind. For the project leader, moreover, individually held domain-specific knowledge and coordination targeted at competences, integration (well-connectedness) has become especially important. So when projects are completed, the membership breaks up and the expertise gained as the fruit of the project is accumulated individually by the project members (effective as individual learning). It is difficult, however, to effectively engender transfer and sharing to other projects and other existing organizations.

With "collectivity of practice," moreover, since actors have different job functions and specialist fields, the actors each have different thought worlds (Dougherty, 1992) and large knowledge boundaries (Brown and Duguid, 2001). Moreover, the novelty and uncertainty elements from new project work become greater. Accordingly, new knowledge differences and business dependencies arise among actors. As a result, conflict and abrasion frequently occur within a project.

The community of practice and collectivity of practice can be positioned figuratively on a knowledge-based axis as in Figure 1.1, showing the extent of knowledge boundaries among actors, abrasion and conflict among actors, and the "thought world" possessed by the actors. In the community of practice, the actors from the same disciplines with the same specialist knowledge (knowledge boundaries among actors are small) possess similar "thought worlds," and embed new knowledge as a group or organization through the practices of far-reaching dialogue and collaboration (little conflict and abrasion among actors) on the foundations of context and meaning.

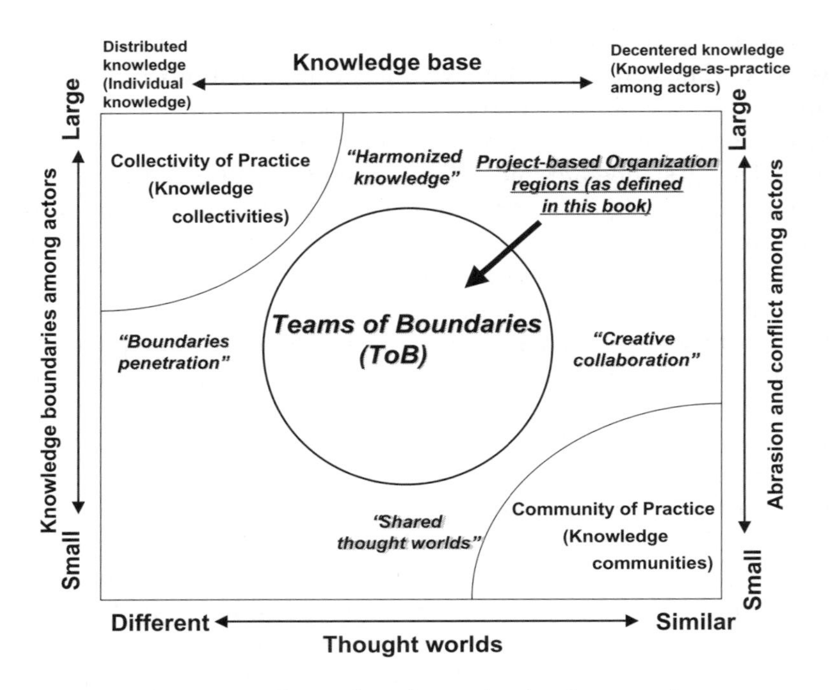

Figure 1.1: Project-based organization framework.

With collectivity of practice, on the other hand, actors with different specializations (large knowledge boundaries among actors resulting in serious abrasion and conflict among actors) possess different thought worlds, and undertake collaboration and coordination on the basis of minimal communal and common knowledge.

So, with the collectivity of practice, the integration of individuals' specialist capacities creates the fruits of the new goal of explicit knowledge. The features of the community of practice and collectivity of practice can be an extreme way of thinking. Organizational classifications can be simplified by saying that a divisional, departmental, or product line group operating in the same work function and specialist area within a company is a "community of practice," while a group working on a temporary project is a "collectivity of practice". In reality, however, can all corporate projects be described as collectivities of practice? From my experience as a project manager and project leader, I believe that actual organizations, including project-based organizations that implement diverse strategies, are still more complex than that. Now, I will itemize and consider these points.

1.4. "Project-Based Organizations" as "Teams of Boundaries"

I can clearly recognize, from my experience both as a project manager and project leader, and from informal dialogues with a large number of corporate practitioners, the existence of the collectivity of practice aspect as project behavior. However, I believe that the character of the projects differs considerably according to the culture of the country or company concerned. The behavior of the project members also differs according to the content of the goals of individual projects including the complexity of the business model, ease of new model development, and specific requests from clients.

One point about these different national and corporate elements relates to training methods for project managers and leaders. In US and European companies, career paths are defined more by segmentation of job function and specialization than they are in Japanese companies. US and European companies, for example, clearly define job categories of specialist management personnel, such as project managers, and the engineers and scientists who specialize in science, engineering, and product development.

This US and European personnel training system, known as the "dual ladder system," is backed up by a large body of research (see Bailyn, 1991; Maccoby, 1999; McKinnon, 1987; Allen and Kats, 1986; and Kochanski, 2003). Until now, there have been numerous reports of this system functioning well, especially in the US and Europe (see Gunz, 1980; Omta and van Engelen, 1998). The US 3M Company, for example, famous for its innovative products, provides a dual ladder system to promote innovators.

Project managers confirm the project's progress management and milestones, and take charge as coordination specialists aimed at individual task management and issue resolution. Accordingly, they rarely understand the project's technological details, commit themselves to the field, or discuss progress. The project management mechanisms of Japanese companies, however, differ on these points. In these companies, almost all project leaders and managers go beyond the role of project management to involve themselves in technological details.

A diversity of specializations is required, especially, among the project leaders and managers of the appliance manufacturers, IT manufacturers, and communications companies that feature as case studies in this book. Japanese companies offer a varied career path where new employees joining the company after graduating from university or postgraduate studies are given experience in a range of job functions and specialist duties. Among appliance manufacturers, graduates and postgraduates from technological universities can follow a path to cultivate engineering skills, which might start, for example, with research into component technologies, move on to system technologies and design, and then proceed to micro- and macro-technology. Among these, there are frequent cases of personnel changes between the factory, product planning, marketing and sales divisions. The project leaders and managers get experience of multiple job roles and specialist fields at the least, and with each promotion, they take on work and gain junior management ability, while refining their ability to make adjustments between relevant divisions, including external partners (this situation was based on discussions with a large number of practitioners and with colleagues working at appliance manufacturers that I first came to know during my postgraduate days). I have had the experience of working at a communications company and followed a career path similar to that of an appliance manufacturer, with experience in a large number of job roles and specialist fields.[2]

I believe that, in this way, project leaders and managers in Japanese companies cultivate more flexibility to grasp matters from the viewpoints of different job functions and specialist areas. For example, project leaders

---

[2] Among Japan's leading communications companies that I have served, technology employees are assigned, either to the business or the research divisions, after they join the company. Engineers assigned to the business division are rotated to various job functions within the division every two or three years.

An example of a career path following graduation might be to join the technology division with responsibility for the development of communications machinery and services; proceed to the plant as chief clerk or section head of the equipment division; become development manager of the technology division; become general manager of the sales, equipment, or other division at the plant; become general manager of the technology division; become director of the plant; and finally, become director of marketing and sales. Different individuals follow different career paths, such as becoming R&D manager after transferring from the business division. Engineering staff assigned to the research department, meanwhile, might set out by mostly pursuing individual R&D projects and taking over R&D manager duties following the promotion.

Then there is the specialist career path of the scientist or engineer. There are many cases of lively interactions between the research and business divisions where researchers transfer to the technology arm of the business division, or to the marketing and sales division. After gaining experience of the business division, the engineer returns to the laboratory he or she was originally attached to. This is consistent personnel training oriented to research and development directly connected to business, and thereby avoids the "death valley".

and managers from a technology background can propose new technologies from a marketing perspective, while those from a sales and marketing background have a strong desire to learn in general about the technologies and prioritize cooperation to discover connections between the market and technologies. Accordingly, project leaders and managers possess a "thought world redundancy" regarding individual job duties and specializations on the basis of cross-over career paths, which I term as "shared thought worlds" in this book.

Project leaders and managers in Japanese companies, moreover, need wide-ranging specialist technical knowledge, together with management skills, for the resources of people, goods, and money. For project management, especially, project leaders and managers must coordinate and collaborate with existing organizations, and rely on different corporate cultures, while implementing inter-project collaboration. Essentially, projects at Japanese companies are structured formally and informally with participants in "communities of practice" as organizations with multiple existing job functions. The participants share knowledge and expertise with the existing organizations, and mutual knowledge transfer becomes very important. In many cases, the project members might be old friends, or would have worked together in the past as colleagues, superiors and subordinates. In project organizations among Japanese companies, there are relatively few project structures where most members appear for the first time (Lindkvist, 2005, p. 1, 190). In many cases, project members execute project tasks within a framework of a pre-existing shared understanding, mutual knowledge (Cramton, 2001), and common knowledge (Carlile, 2002).

Thus, I feel that knowledge acquired on a project platform in a Japanese company is not simply the domain-specific knowledge of individuals or individual competences reliant on individual skills and expertise, but is also a complete fusion of localized, embedded and invested (Lave, 1988; Wenger, 1998) "knowledge ability" and "competences in practice" as practice within the organization until now. In other words, it is also a fusion of "distributed knowledge," relating to decentered knowledge and connectivity of practice, as a community of practice. In this book, I will call this a project's "harmonized knowledge".

Next, I will discuss the behavior of project members. The greater the subject of the project becomes, the greater the novelty and uncertainty of the project's content, and greater the various issues and problems with the process of execution. Conflict and abrasion among project members naturally arise, and in many of the cases where time is limited, project members come up with compromises and trade-offs. This is not the only way that a project should be selected. As seen from this book's case study, behavior is observed where project members aim not to compromise, but to reconcile and synthesize seemingly contradictory elements through a thoroughgoing discussion. The practical, yet creative, conflict or abrasion (Leonard-Barton, 1995) and the productive friction (Hagel III and Brown, 2005) among different types of members can also be a resource for the creation of new knowledge. Some senior managers describe projects as "battles".

In Japanese companies, there are many cases of support from other projects and organizations along the lines of having a "lively meeting" and "let's lend a hand". The organizational behavior of this kind of project fuses the rivalry of knowledge relating to this "connectivity of practice" with the harmony of knowledge relating to the "community of practice". I call the simultaneous pursuit of these elements a project's "creative collaboration".

Next, I would like to mention features of the knowledge boundaries necessary for innovation-oriented project management. It goes without saying that knowledge is the source of a company's competitive edge (Kogut and Zander, 1992; Nonaka and Takeuchi, 1995; Leonard-Barton, 1995). I believe that human knowledge is the starting point of strategy formulation and implementation. The tacit knowledge of skills, expertise, and core competence is embedded in individuals (Brown and Duguid, 1991). For the knowledge integration so necessary to project management, in particular, the knowledge held by diverse individuals inside and outside a company transcends organizational boundaries, and needs to be gathered and integrated.

The creation of new knowledge (innovation) has a strong tendency to arise from the boundaries between disciplines and specializations (Leonard-Barton, 1995). Companies are split into various work function organizations and specializations, and numerous boundaries exist, some visible and others invisible, including geographic boundaries as globalisation, industry boundaries as strategy, organizational boundaries as theory of the firm, and human cognition as bounded rationality. As mentioned previously, however, abrasion and conflicts arise in the project, hindering knowledge integration among actors (Leonard-Barton, 1995). Knowledge boundaries, that arise not just from the sectionalism of organizational boundaries between company actors, but also from each actor's values, background and specialization, also exist (Brown and Duguid, 2001). The reason is that actors with different backgrounds and experience are dominated by fixed mental models (see Markides, 1999; Spender, 1990; Grinyer and McKiernan, 1994) and path dependencies (Rosenberg, 1982; Hargadon and Sutton, 1997), and actors may feel uncomfortable and resist when faced with expressions of this new and differentiated knowledge from organizational boundaries (Carlile, 2002). History tells us that companies and organizations dominated by fixed mental models cannot avoid competency traps (Levitt and March, 1988; Martines and Kambil, 1999) and core rigidities (Leonard-Barton, 1992, 1995), while path-dependent knowledge may result in loss of innovation opportunities (Christensen, 1997).

It follows that in industries subject to changing markets and stiff competition, many companies aiming to create new knowledge and innovation must cross multiple internal and external boundaries (including those with clients), and actors must integrate diverse knowledge and implement strategies. As mentioned, the case studies of this book, companies like Sharp, Canon and Matsushita Electric are responding to rapid technological and market changes in the mobile phone and digital appliance businesses by implementing a range of close collaborations. These collaborations are aimed at technology integration by transcending technology division boundaries, while implementing market-beating strategies through successive new products, which embed marketing, sales, technology and manufacturing divisions simultaneously.

Project members are also sharpening views and thinking from different specializations, and are constantly transcending divisions to share technology and project development roadmaps. Moreover, with innovations that bring about not just technological change, but also new business models, projects must be structured as project networks with various partners (including customers), which transcend the boundaries of organizations, industries and one's own company. The project network formations of NTT DoCoMo mobile telecommunications and Sony games businesses featured as case-studies in this book are good examples of such structures. I will call the organizational behavior of projects that create new knowledge-crossing boundaries as "boundaries penetration".

The project-based organization with the four elements of shared thought worlds, harmonized knowledge, creative collaboration and boundaries penetration will be termed "Teams of Boundaries (ToB)" in this book. Figure 1.1 compares ToB, community of practice, and collectivity of practice. ToB is positioned as an intermediary between communities of practice and collectivity of practice. I interpret it as the formation of projects having the characteristics of both types.

In this book, from observations of case studies and other fields, ToBs are formed in space and time around the focus of different organizational and knowledge boundaries. Four types of such pattern formations can generally be considered (see Figure 1.2). The first is where the project-based organizations have ToB features (pattern 1). The second is where ToB network development exists in the process background of each job-function organization when members of established job-function organizations form informal project networks in-house (pattern 2). The third is where ToBs are formed among projects, and among project and existing organizations, from the angles of the implementation process for new strategic policies inter-project learning (Prencipe and Tell, 2001), (pattern 3). The fourth is where ToB networks crossing industry boundaries form project networks (pattern 4). I will describe these individual patterns through case studies from Chapter 2 onwards.

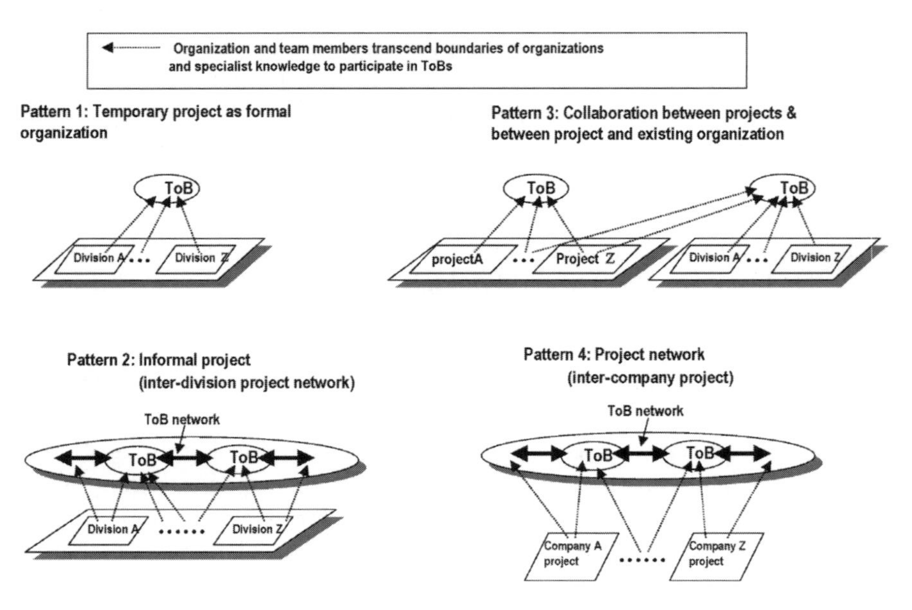

Figure 1.2: Teams of Boundaries (ToB) patterns.

1.5. Teams of Boundaries and Strategic Communities: The Empirical Background

I have presented the notion of "strategic communities" (SCs) through previously-conducted fieldwork. In this chapter, I would like to focus on the relationship between SCs, ToBs, collectivity of practice, and community of practice. To state the conclusion, SCs possess aspects of the two notions of ToBs and collectivity of practice. I want to consider ToBs and collectivity of practice as they relate to two case studies (Kodama, 2002, 2005) previously published in *Long Range Planning* journal.

The first concerned a new product development case of a communications system incorporating world-class technology (Kodama, 2005). It involved the process in which Fujitsu, one of Japan's leading communications equipment manufacturers, rapidly developed a new, improvised system in collaboration with telecommunications carriers. Corporate actors centered on Japan and the US, with globally-advanced technology in relevant fields, shared the time and space parameters of SCs; integrated knowledge in different technological areas including communications, computers, image and voice processing, and software; and had content that achieved a new architectural innovation (Henderson and Clark, 1990).

In this case, under time constraints oriented to communications carrier clients and to goals, the issue was how to integrate competencies held by individual company actors. Actors were already grouped according to specializations in their relevant fields, and promoted collaboration with a minimum of common knowledge through improvised mutual learning. The development process involved multiple SCs formed in chronological order (aggregate of participants from each company's engineers). Task execution within the SCs relied strongly on the knowledge of individual actors' skills and expertise. The development process involved looking at several technology issues and searching for the optimum solution aimed at technology integration through trial and error. These SCs were closer in character to collectivity of practice than to ToBs.

The second case involved the business development of one of the world's most advanced mobile internet services (i-mode) by NTT DoCoMo, a leading Japanese mobile communications carriers (Kodama, 2002). Compared to the new product development cases mentioned previously, this case had few problems with regard to limited time for learning and improvised decision making. The i-mode development project within this large company involved forming SCs from established organizations and external partners, and aimed to share value, while building a business model and learning from a technological angle (Kodama, 2001). The project members transformed the internal and external conflicts and abrasion into productive and creative outcomes. In other words, creative collaboration functioned very well in the SC. Then the new project team, composed of heterogeneous members gathered from within and outside the company, formed a "project network" through "boundaries penetration" across industries and businesses. "Harmonized knowledge" advanced with the i-mode development project. In other words , project knowledge depended strongly on the knowledge and competencies of individual team members. At the same time, the project team possessed elements of "knowledge in practice" comprising learning among members with the same specializations in the project and established organizations. NTT DoCoMo is a company that has grown from an in-house venture (see Chapter 2 for details). The sharing of information and knowledge from different work functions and specializations was always permeating from large companies, and was established around a core of original members of the "shared thought world" transcending these work functions and specializations. The character of the i-mode development project embedded within and outside the company approached that of a ToB, not "collectivity as practice".

As can be seen, a project's character is multi-faceted, and cannot be explained as a single pattern. We can think of models other than those displayed in Figure 1.1, such as the following cases from actual projects. It has been shown that when the project tasks for specific clients are completed and the project is dissolved, organizational learning through these processes within the project, among projects, and between the project and established organizations, becomes problematic (see DeFillippi, 2001; Keegan and Turner, 2001; Grabher, 2002; Newell *et al.*, 2003; Prencipe and Tell, 2001; Middleton, 1967).

This does not mean, however, that once the fruits of the project are introduced to the client, the client and project-side companies are happy to wrap it up. IT and other large-scale systems, for example, involve a great amount of responsibility regarding subsequent maintenance and upgrades, and realistically, some of the project members who participate from the start must continue to be involved in this business, since they know the project details and possess the required technical skills and expertise. The project stages move from initial exploratory activity to exploitative activity. Business priorities will determine whether the project continues as it is, or whether its duties are transferred to existing organizations. The handling of the project also depends on the shape of a company's organizational activity and its personnel resources at that time.

Moreover, as mentioned above, the characters of the projects vary as a result of matters such as the complexity of the business model targeted by the project, the ease of new product development, and specific client requests.

Of late, new product development has become path-dependent as a result of past technologies. Even if there is a strong tendency to develop new technology elements, it is because of the members who possess the required technological details and skills.

As the scale of system development grows larger, the system is developed in layers such as customer demand specification analysis, whole system settings (architecture), detailed settings (subsystems, components, hardware and software), and branching out to specialist technical fields. Moreover, the radical and architectural innovations (Henderson and Clark, 1990) are accompanied by several business themes. With the development of this kind of large-scale systems, I do not believe that project structuring among technology members who have met for the first time is a realistic policy. If it becomes possible to build large-scale systems combined with module devices with clear technical interfaces, new specialist teams may be able to undertake rapid development. Generally, product competitiveness hides the contents of individual module devices, module and subsystem connections, fixed software, and the entire system architecture, as in a black box. Engineers who have accumulated expertise as a black box are existing organization members who have studied past path-dependent technology.

With existing research accompanying the dramatic reform of architecture and components, the emphasis should be on new organizations including members possessing new skills, rather than on established-member organizations for new product development (see O'Reilly III and Tushman, 2004; Tushman and O'Reilly, 1997; Utterback, 1994; Tushman and Anderson, 1986).

I believe, however, that these depend on conditions considered from technology viewpoints, such as new product groups in individual industries, scale of development, scale of the development organization, corporate culture, and country. I also believe that architectural innovation is key to achieving technology integration. As you will see in the Sharp (Chapter 3) and Sony (Chapter 5) cases, the way in which in-house members with different specialist technologies were assembled for a project first of all is important. The creation of new organizations with new members is not a priority. Moreover, cases of radical innovation that greatly transform architecture and components must lead to new concepts from the viewpoint of a range of technologies. In this kind of case (see Mitsubishi Electric in Chapter 4 and Sony in Chapter 5), it is pertinent to activate existing personnel resources, while further introducing external knowledge and competencies as necessary (Leonard-Barton, 1992, 1995). Activating existing personnel resources means accumulating scientific and technological knowledge through daily learning, and emphasizing the experience and expertise of the engineers. This kind of path-dependent accumulation of technology makes it possible to clear the high hurdles of creative radical innovation (in other words, the specializations of science and engineering are fundamentally important).

My philosophy, developed against a background of the conventions of Japanese companies, turns to existing resources and existing organizations. Compared with companies in the US and Europe, the fluidity of the external labor market is low, and an employee's career path as a graduate or postgraduate can offer an experience of diverse responsibilities and specialist technologies.

Moreover, the Japanese company features of lifetime employment and a "crossover" career path, in addition to implicit and internalized control mechanisms for the group and organization, are established among employees by means of a company's common tacit knowledge, norms, values and culture. At the same time, organizational structures based on informal and control mechanisms have come to be structured in-house (see Ouchi, 1980: Nonaka and Takeuchi, 1995). It follows that the project-based organizations of Japanese companies have a strong tendency to be formed from an extension of existing organizations, regardless of formality. As mentioned above, the features of the "community of practice" for existing organizations are more likely to be embedded in a project than they are in the US and Europe. In other words, since common employee behavioural norms and personnel training systems are firmly established in Japanese companies, the thinking around the formation of projects aimed at new product and business developments is, first of all, to prioritize reliance on the resources of existing in-house personnel and organizations. These people have the advantage of being able to quickly establish a project and implement a task.

Various case studies exist on the form and execution process of the project-based organization, including the state of US and European companies' project management. Further research may be necessary in the future. In this book, I would like to analyze distinctive ToB frameworks as project management, which are centered on case studies of Japanese companies.

1.6. Structure of this Book

In Chapter 2, I will take up cases of marketing innovation through the formation of project networks among Japan's fast-developing mobile phone businesses. The introduction of special-duty project organizations that are separate from existing bureaucratic-function organizations, and the formation of exploratory networks that cross industry boundaries, centered on projects within and outside the company, are seen as dynamic processes that have led to the radical innovations of future business strategies.

Moreover, in order to disseminate, reform, improve and establish new business by forming project networks, we consider the exploitative practice as a sustainable routine activity through networks of bureaucratic-function organizations. In other words, this is the incremental innovation aspect of the expansion of existing business and the execution of growth-oriented strategies through exploitative networks. I will also discuss the dynamics whereby the practices arising from the formation of dual exploratory and exploitative networks created dialectically recursive interplays (Giddens, 1984; Barley, 1986; Barley and Tolbert, 1997) between the environment and market (structure) on the one hand, and the organization and individual (practice) on the other, which greatly enlarged the mobile phone business market.

In Chapter 3, I will consider the innovation processes involved in the Japanese development of camera-loaded mobile phones, a world's first, by Vodafone and Sharp, in the context of technology integration crossing organizational and technological boundaries. Further, high-tech companies demanding new business model structures through the fusion of diverse technologies and services must synthesize boundaries existing inside and outside the company from multiple viewpoints, and continually aim to create new knowledge. I will also suggest that the integration of many of the boundaries inside and outside an organization, in other words, the networked ToBs, can promote knowledge integration and transformation, and create the capability for competitive advantage, while at the same time securing a dominant position in the marketplace.

In Chapter 4, I indicate the basic framework for creating new knowledge from the integration of various organizational and knowledge boundaries crossing different organizations inside and outside the company. Through an in-depth analysis of Mitsubishi Electric, I will consider the dynamism of integrating diverse knowledge from the simultaneous absorption of external knowledge through the horizontal integration of ToBs from strategic alliances among companies, and knowledge integration through the creation of vertical integration networks of ToBs within a company.

In Chapter 5, I will analyze and discuss frameworks for successful project management as corporate ventures among large companies from a viewpoint of knowledge integration and technological innovation. I will take up the game business centering on Sony PlayStation as a case study. Then I will suggest new insights from a new business model relating to large companies' corporate ventures and an in-depth case study regarding an enabler promoting technological innovation.

In Chapter 6, I will consider project strategies in industries in rapidly-changing markets and competitive conditions. High-tech companies that take on the IT field and digital product mass market must simultaneously implement technological reform in response to changes in customer needs and change the market structure in response to technological reform. In this chapter, I will discuss business strategies for digital appliance products as the expansion continues worldwide. Case I will look at Matsushita Electric and Canon's digital appliance strategies, and offer a new viewpoint of common development processes for each company's new products. Each company's vertically-established strategy maintains its dominant position in the global market through the execution of a time-pacing strategy. In this chapter, I would like to indicate the concept of boundaries synchronization for project networks enabling the execution of this time-pacing strategy.

In Chapter 7, I will consider conflict and abrasion between projects and existing organizations, and synergies among projects. I will examine NTT, Japan's largest telecommunications company, as a case study and look at examples from new product and business developments. First, I will consider the process by which new project-based organizations overcome the conflicts and abrasion relating to large companies' various business customs, and execute new product development. Second, I will look at the integrated management of existing projects aimed at new business development.

In Chapter 8, I will discuss new insights acquired through case studies. One point is the relationship between the project-based organization, the strategy-making process, and implementation. I will consider how project-based organizations are built and mobilized as corporate strategy from the viewpoint of leadership, network strategy, and strategy as action. A second point is the relationship between boundaries and knowledge integration (technology integration and new business model formation). Innovation as an aspect of corporate competitiveness arises from boundaries and the integration of boundaries. I consider the formation of these ToBs (boundaries innovation resources) and ToB networks from the viewpoint of the knowledge integration process. A third point is the relationship between the project and organizational learning. I will consider the state of project management promoting company-wide organizational learning and innovation.

In Chapter 9, amid managerial implications and conclusions, I would like to offer new, practical viewpoints aimed at the structure of the project-based organization.

2

Project Networks as Marketing Innovation — The Challenge of the Mobile Communications Businesses

2.1. Exploration and Exploitation

For a company to maintain competitive dominance in a market, it must simultaneously establish practices to grow existing business and address the theme of future business development aimed at the acquisition of new strategic positions (e.g. Markides, 1998; O'Leiley and Thusman, 2004). Organizations aiming to grow their existing business (perhaps by improving existing products and services, and expanding profits through improvements and upgrades) must formulate and implement business planning in a short time frame. Actors in organizations of existing business activities can learn to predict business change and modify their practice to a certain degree. Actors with a base of tacit knowledge accumulated from such sources as path-dependent technology and sales are promoting exploratory practice as daily routines (Nelson and Winter, 1982; March, 1991).

Exploitation refers to the routine behavior involved in refining current organizational capabilities and improving the performance of current organizational routines. With exploitative practice, daily organizational learning aimed at incremental innovation (Nelson and Winter, 1982; Tushman and Anderson, 1986; Bridge and O'Keef, 1984) is required of the organizational actors.

In their future exploratory practice, companies must go beyond new scientific research and technical development to construct new business models through marketing. Actors must boldly face market uncertainty and risk, and seek out new business by means of experimentation, incubation, and trial and error.

Actors promoting exploratory practice must emphasize architectural innovation from technological knowledge to effect radical change in technological design (Henderson and Clark, 1990), and radical innovation from scientific knowledge comprising the development of core technology based on new theories and principles (Fleming and Screnson, 2004). But it is important for actors and organizations in practical businesses to emphasize new knowledge from a marketing focus that looks beyond technological and scientific knowledge in order to radically transform existing business systems. In other words, new marketing knowledge is needed to dramatically transform the existing value network (Christensen, 1997) and value chain (Porter, 1985), and to create new business models. Marketing knowledge that brings the customer close has the important capability of creating radical innovations leading, for instance, to new business creation or lifestyle changes. I would like to use the term "marketing innovation" for innovation driven by marketing knowledge (the mobile phone business case in this chapter is an example of marketing innovation that brings the customer close).

The thinking of organizational leaders aiming to acquire marketing knowledge with a customer-oriented viewpoint must incorporate the following: freeing themselves from existing mental knowledge models (see Spender, 1990; Banker, 1993); a temporal and spatial system in which diverse, heterogeneous knowledge intersects (Johansson, 2004); new concepts to leverage and stretch existing resources and capabilities from a strategic intent (Hamel and Praharad, 1989); avoidance of competency traps (Levitt and March, 1988; Martines and Kambil, 1999) and core rigidities (Leonard-Barton, 1992, 1995); destruction of the organization's information filter (Henderson and Clark, 1990); destruction of the organization's power structure and "creative destruction" of vested rights and resources; breaking down the organization's structural inertia (Hanna and Freeman, 1984); breaking down successful personal experience and promoting strategic policies for future aims (Ackoff, 1981); and building a hierarchy of imaginative capability (Hamel, 1996; Mintzberg, Ahlstrand and Lampel, 1998). Individual actors, moreover, must deliberately shake up their "thought worlds" (Doherty, 1992) based on individual backgrounds and specialization from the viewpoint of the customer. Organizational leaders also need the element of "disciplined imagination" (Weick, 1989; Kodama, 2003) to select the many exploratory strategies that have been discovered and make decisions appropriately.

With exploratory practice, an organization's actors are required to look beyond acquiring knowledge from daily organizational learning (as with exploitative practice), and to display still more challenging innovative behavior aimed at radical innovation (Nelson and Winter, 1982). As explained above, a company must simultaneously establish the elements of exploration and exploitation in order to acquire sustained competitive dominance from innovation.

In this chapter, I will take up the case of marketing innovation through the formation of project networks in the mobile phone business that is developing rapidly in Japan. The following three points contain the gist. First, I will introduce communications carrier NTT DoCoMo Inc.'s special-duty organization projects that are detached from existing bureaucratically-functioning organizations. I will also consider the dynamic processes whereby the formation of exploratory networks crossing industry boundaries and centered on projects within and outside the company achieved the radical innovation of future business strategies.

Second, I will consider exploitative practice as sustained routines from networks of bureaucratically-functioning organizations with the purpose of establishing, improving and distributing new business that has been put into practice as a result of the formation of project networks. In other words, it is an aspect of the strategic practice of incremental innovation aimed at the expansion and growth of existing business through exploitative networks.

The third feature is that these two types of network (exploratory and exploitative) are effectively linked by the central means of a communications carrier (DoCoMo), and the actors' practice arising from the formation of these dual networks will greatly expand the mobile phone business market as a result of dialectical recursive interplays (Giddens, 1984; Barley, 1986; Barley and Tolbert, 1997) between the environment and market (structure) on the one hand, and organizations and individuals (practice) on the other. Corresponding to these dual network nodules is the existence of ToBs comprising leaders and managers of project organizations and functional organizations, which transcend boundaries within the organization of the DoCoMo communication carrier. The ToBs that have the task of joining the dual networks possess strong "network connectivity."

But these network formations and the creation of an environment are not limited to Japan's mobile phone business market. The world's mobile phone markets are developing similar behaviors from the best practices of DoCoMo's domestic and international development of the "i-mode" mobile Internet service (Kodama, 2002) and business models similar to those adopted in Japan.

2.2. Case Study: Mobile Phone Business Innovation

This case involves DoCoMo's i-mode innovation and its third-generation FOMA mobile phone service that DoCoMo aimed to develop and distribute as a global pioneer of Internet and multimedia-related mobile communications services.

What is notable about this case is that while DoCoMo was restricted by the limitations of the market environment, dual networks (project and functional organization networks) holding diverse knowledge formed spontaneously within and outside the organization. Here, I will analyze the dynamism involved in building a new market environment as a result of integrating dual networks by means of creating and distributing new services in Japan and overseas, as well as new services for the next-generation system.

2.2.1. *DoCoMo's innovations*

The main driver behind the expansion of mobile computing's potential and its usability is data communication from mobile phones. Today's mobile phones have progressed from "portable handsets" to "information terminals" thanks to Internet-accessing technology from mobile phones represented by DoCoMo's "i-mode." When it comes to mobile Internet use, Japan is reputed to have at least a two- to three-year lead over the US and Europe. US journalists, moreover, suggest that Japan's wireless Internet access system, that people in Japan are wildly enthusiastic about, has the potential to control the world.

At present, i-mode has achieved the figure of 40 million subscribers in Japan, while the i-mode business model is spreading throughout the world. Moreover, Japan has launched the fast i-mode service through the pioneering FOMA third-generation mobile phone service centered on DoCoMo, and the new system is being further developed for the global market. I will describe the three phases of this DoCoMo innovation process chronologically.

2.2.2. *Mobile phone phase one (1992 to 1998): the challenge of voice communication (See Figure 2.1)*

In 1992, the mobile communications business of NTT (Nippon Telegraph and Telephone Corporation), Japan's largest telecommunications enterprise, was spun off to ensure a fair, competitive telecommunications market. That was the birth of NTT DoCoMo. The government's objective was for DoCoMo to split from NTT, and to launch into the competitive market with its parent company barred from support of any kind. The first fiscal year, however, returned a deficit, as net sales fell below the figure for the previous year due to poor sales of mobile phones. Although it is hard to believe now, at the time of DoCoMo's launch, nobody thought mobile phones would sell, and nobody predicted a rosy future for DoCoMo. DoCoMo's US and European rivals also found them hard to sell, with the exception of the northern European countries bounded by the Arctic Circle in the north and the Baltic Sea in the south, where the laying of cables is problematic.

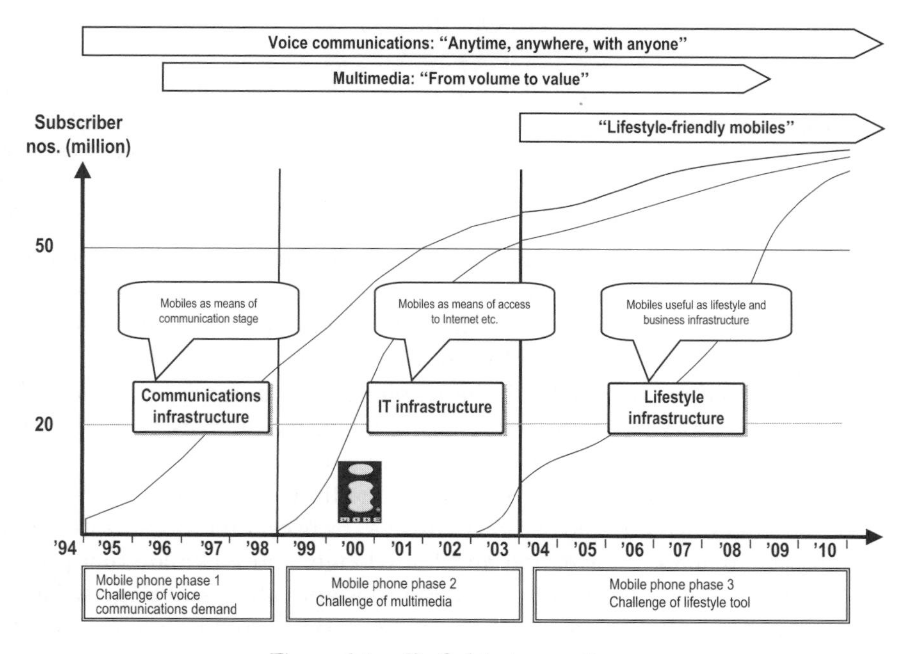

Figure 2.1: DoCoMo innovations.

The first CEO of DoCoMo, Kouji Oboshi, remembers:

Having risen to managing director under NTT, I looked on DoCoMo as a second, relaxed phase to my working life. Soon after arriving at DoCoMo, however, 20 colleagues around the age of 30 gathered together and chatted over beer, and they all began to express anxiety over the company's future. Everyone was saying that the company could hardly be secure if it continued to operate in the red. What struck me is that they these people were weak and maudlin drunks.

These people were under the thumb of their wives, who were saying to them, "Why on earth did you join a strange company no one has heard of, when you should have been working for NTT, the world's largest firm of its kind, number one in Japan, and a company that will never go bust?" Hearing such talk made me mad. I hit the desk and said, "I'll make sure that five years from now, you'll walk down the middle of the road, proud that you're working for DoCoMo!"

The first job for the new CEO was to provide a place where the employees could work securely. Oboshi says:

I would say I was like the president of a small- or medium-sized company, and the employees were my family. I had to protect them. I could not just lie back. I felt that I would dedicate the rest of my life to DoCoMo.

This episode shows Oboshi's true feelings that formed the basis for DoCoMo's later progress. Oboshi broke the cycle of negativity created by the mobile phones' failure to sell, and cultivated new values and a sense of unity by bringing the employees together to create a community. DoCoMo aimed to share with all the employees its intention of reversing losses and creating new markets. Sharing the sense of crisis with all the employees heightened the sense of a new business challenge.

DoCoMo was launched as a small- or medium-sized business. It created a climate where individuals always transcended organizational boundaries to share information and knowledge, and a climate that promoted business oriented toward a shared sense of values and targets. The employees transcended organizational boundaries in individual communities of practice such as sales, development, technology, maintenance and planning, and in-house communities developed to deal with urgent topics, which consisted of informal projects, task teams, or the company as a whole.

In this book, I will use the term "community knowledge" (Kodama, 2001) for the knowledge created by this cross-functional, in-house community comprising employees from various backgrounds and possessing specialist skills transcending organizational boundaries in this way. An important view is that the dynamic knowledge-creating practice in the company community is a dialectical process synthesizing structure (market) and action (organizations). This community knowledge is not a static, but a dynamic process that has been observed (see Kodama, 2002) as a large number of organizational activities (which I call the "community knowledge creating cycle" in this book) in a series of spiral processes of sharing, creating and accumulating. As mentioned above, the behavior of DoCoMo employees in the mobile phone's first phase could be the stage of knowledge-sharing among all employees (as shown in Figure 2.2) from the viewpoint of the community knowledge-creating cycle.

Escaping further from the negative cycle, Oboshi's first task as CEO was to create informal, cross-functional project teams from each division, including marketing, sales, technology and equipment, which transcended organizational boundaries. Moreover, the leaders and managers of the development and technology divisions that supported the mobile phone platform undertook joint development, (through a trial-and-error approach) with a mobile handset manufacturer aimed at surpassing Motorola by developing highly-functional phones lighter than any others in the world. (Figure 2.3 illustrates the organizational structure of the mobile phone's first phase.)

In response to the question, "why don't mobile phones sell?", Oboshi gathered user data at the points of sale, and directly and thoroughly analyzed the issue himself. As a result, he identified the following causes. The first was a problem of network equipment. The network is the life-blood of mobile communications. Car phones were miniaturized to become shoulder phones, and could be carried around outside. Ignoring the changing usage scenario, the networks had continued to follow the route of the car-phone era, and it became necessary to modify some development concepts.

The second point was the usage charge. Charges were nearly three times as high as they were in the US. That is to say, lowering the price was sure to bring price elasticity into effect and the mobile phones would begin to sell. Once they began to sell, economies of scale would make them cheaper, which was sure to create a vicious cycle whereby lower prices would lead to still larger sales.

The third point was the hurdle of subscriber applications for new mobile phone users. The pricing system's entry point was set higher than those in the US. Accordingly, lowering the initial burden of entry for new subscribers, which included deposits, would make it easier to sign up.

The fourth point is the publicity strategy. Consumers paid little attention to DoCoMo because they had never heard of it. So in the first stages, it was important to conduct a concentrated, large-scale advertising campaign aimed at brand saturation within a short space of time. From the viewpoint of a community knowledge-creating cycle, the behavior of these employees can be an inspiring stage oriented toward the creation of new knowledge, as in the first phase of the mobile phone in Figure 2.2.

DoCoMo employees took swift action to address various themes acquired at the knowledge-inspiring stage. The expansion of the communications network especially created strategic knowledge networks with communications equipment manufacturers (as strategic partners), group companies and affiliated companies (construction companies), and aimed to build equipment and develop networks that took into consideration a balance of timely demand and supply (see Figure 2.3 for the organizational structure of the mobile phone's first phase).

Concrete measures were implemented to solve the issues one by one, with the result that sales quickly rose threefold, and sales of the world's lightest mobile phone (developed by DoCoMo's technology group) took off. As the phone began to sell, economies of scale kicked in and the mobile phone grew cheaper. The mobile phone "rent back" problem arose, and Japan's Ministry of Posts and Telecommunications regulating authority sensibly demanded the adoption of a sell-out approach (1994). As a result, competition intensified.

While the sales take-off was a relief for DoCoMo, the net increase in numbers (share of new subscribers) was gradually falling. When it reached the warning mark of 40 percent, DoCoMo analyzed the differences between itself and its competitors. The cause turned out to be sales channels. During the NTT era, Oboshi saw the fixed cost of personnel as the cause of the company's deficit. He segmented his targets by business use, and narrowed them down to efficient "business streets" as sales bases. The sales vicious cycle rapidly brought down the phone prices, so that they could be purchased by individuals. This prompted DoCoMo to recognize the need to extend sales bases to the suburbs.

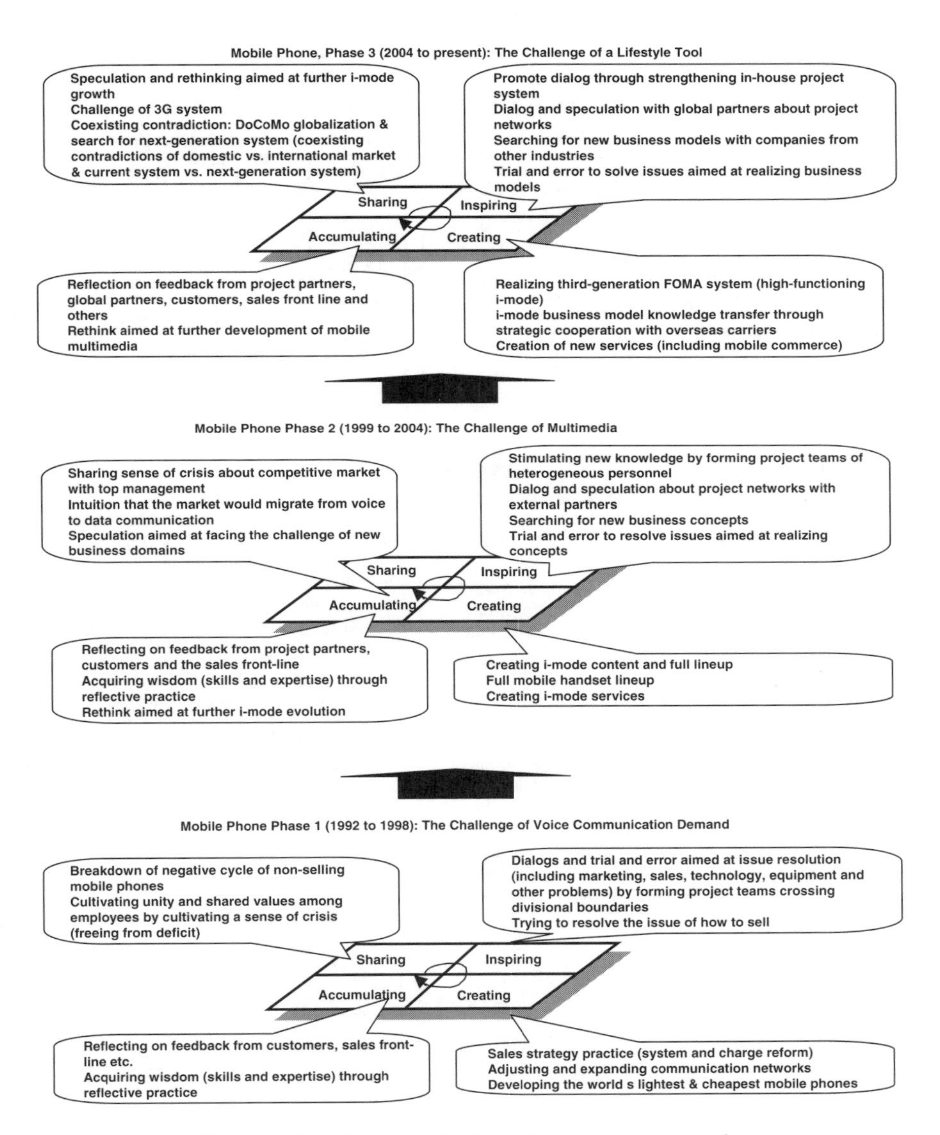

Figure 2.2: Community knowledge creating cycle.

Considering, however, that increasing the number of company stores would gradually become less efficient and adversely impact the balance sheet, DoCoMo built its sales network by outsourcing to existing electrical goods outlets as agents and distributors (Figure 2.3 shows the organizational

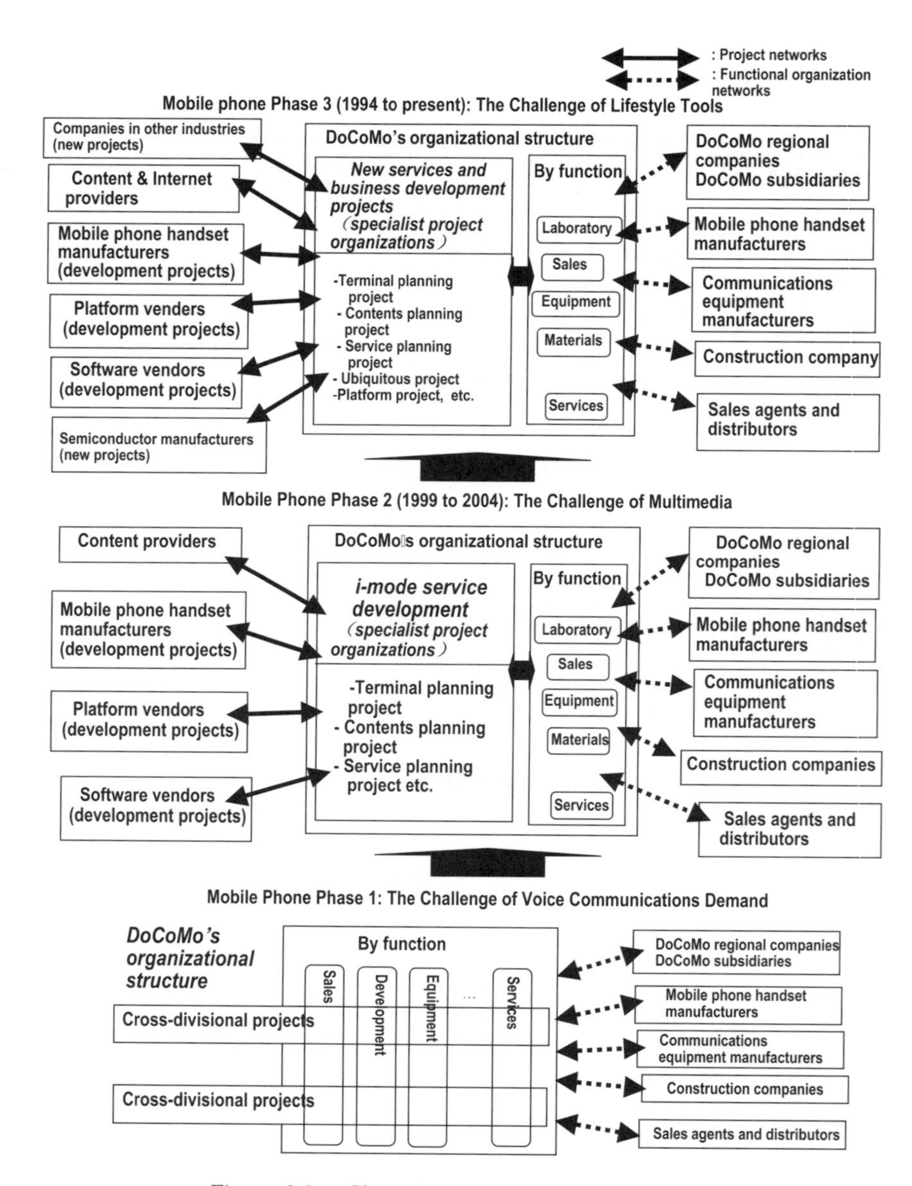

Figure 2.3: Changing organization networks.

structure at the mobile phone's first stage). This enabled DoCoMo to expand sales channels in a relatively short period of time, and to both recover market share and create new demand. Through this kind of strategic outsourcing and sales channel expansion, DoCoMo succeeded in growing the market from the conventional business to the personal use layer and creating new demand. This employee behavior is shown from the viewpoint of a community knowledge creating cycle in Figure 2.2 as the new knowledge-creating stage of mobile phone phase 1.

DoCoMo experienced rapid growth as "demand creation" swelled the size of the pie, but Oboshi believed that complacency without change could become a risk factor, and in 1996, at the peak of the sales curve, he was quick to predict the next crisis. First, Oboshi calculated the potential size of the mobile phone market from figures such as the size of the population, the number of vehicles, and the number of machines using wireless devices. He predicted that sales would grow by around 30 percent a year for the next 13 or 14 years.

At this point, however, the effect of price elasticity reduced prices several times within a year, and sales growth accelerated to nearly 100 percent. Oboshi, head office managers, and middle managers recognized with a sense of crisis that since the growth rate was three times the predicted speed, market saturation would soon be reached, and unless the next wave of new demand could be created quickly, growth would soon stop. Although it was good to see the rapid rise in user numbers, user layers at first centered around the heavy user, especially the business user. Later, the rapid fall in the prices of mobile phone handsets from the economies of scale added to the individual user layer. It was, naturally, a light user layer that paid a lower tariff. This layer expanded, lowering the average revenue per unit. Successive price falls ensued, and the income that exceeded 10,000 yen per user in the initial phase fell below 9,000 yen. A crisis was predicted whereby the increase in users would saturate the market, rapidly halting the net increase (share of new subscribers), and absolute income would decline. The need to create new value-added services became urgent.

From the get-go, DoCoMo recognized the importance of the communications network and quickly established a dominant lead in network expansion and digitalization. Over a two-year period, however, DoCoMo's competitors caught up. The next stage was to take a lead in jointly-developing miniature handsets with handset manufacturers, but this lead also disappeared after about two years. By around 1996, there was little difference between the services of DoCoMo and its competitors. The fact that users were offered very similar services for mobile phone use naturally drove users to base their purchasing choices on the criterion of price alone. A fierce price war ensued. DoCoMo and other mobile phone businesses procured mobile phone handsets from handset manufacturers, and sold them on commission from sales agents under their own brand name.

Competition for sales commissions grew intense, until handsets were selling for just a few yen, a ruinous figure well below cost price. The only way to climb out of this morass was to quickly create differentiation of service.

In this way, Oboshi and the other DoCoMo leaders and managers acquired practical business experience of the mobile phone market, where both market and technology changes rapidly. The sales and technology expertise accumulated both in the individual and the organization. The behavior of these employees can be shown stage as experience in the mobile phone phase 1 in Figure 2.2 from the viewpoint of the community knowledge-creating cycle.

To recap, the DoCoMo startup at the mobile phone's initial phase found itself in an environment where restrictive conditions made it unable to sell. A new market (structure) for mobile phones arose through practice resulting from the formation of cross-departmental projects and functional organization networks arising from a sense of crisis shared among the whole company. Meanwhile, newly-created structures were driving competition, and led to new innovations and strategies in organizational networks, especially for NTT DoCoMo (see "Mobile Phone Phase 1," Figure 2.4).

Then from the knowledge gained from direct experience, Mr. Oboshi embarked on a bold strategy turnaround aimed at cultivating new markets. In July 1996, he announced it to the world in a newspaper advertisement, and immediately carried it out. DoCoMo launched its new vision under the slogan *"Value from Volume."* First, it succeeded in developing wireless packet communications as a network infrastructure. Then it offered a service connecting mobile handsets to laptops. Since the Internet began to spread around this time, loading a simple browser into the mobile phone and enabling Internet access rapidly led to a rise in user numbers. Within two years, DoCoMo succeeded in creating an explosion in demand that created more than 20 million subscribers. In the next section, I will discuss the challenge of bringing mobile multimedia to the mobile phone through the IT infrastructure in the mobile phone's second phase. This was the beginning of the development of the "i-mode" mobile Internet service.

2.2.3. *Mobile phone phase 2 (1999 to 2004): the challenge of multimedia (See Figure 2.2)*

As I described in the phase one section, Mr. Oboshi predicted as early as 1997 that the mobile phone subscriber growth curve based on the use of voice communications would soon reach saturation point. As a result,

Mobile Phone Phase 3 (2004 to present): The Challenge of Lifestyle Tools

Structure
· Creating new markets (from domestic to international/creating mobile phone culture as a new lifestyle)
→ communications traffic besides phone & email (including image, music, gaming and e-commerce)
· Creating new industries (financial and distribution revolutions from mobile phones)
· Changing competitive environment →fixed price system, falling prices, new entrants intensify

Practice
· Disruption of constraining conditions (saturation of domestic markets)
· Breakdown of current business models (volume based communications charge business model) → Creation of ubiquitous mobile services
·Innovations from expanded project-based organizations
→ Collaboration from expanded project networks including those in other industries

Mobile Phone Phase 2 (1999 to 2004): The Challenge of Multimedia

Structure
· Creating new markets (creating mobile Internet culture)
→ Expanding data communications markets
· Creating new industries (creating mobile content industries)
→ Forming inter-company networks of comprising content providers, platform vendors, communications carriers, communications infrastructure manufacturers and mobile terminal manufacturers
· Changing environment conditions → diversification of service strategies

Practice
· Disruption of constraining conditions (voice communication business model)
Business model migrationfrom voice-to-data communications, and volume-to-value
· Innovations from project-based organizations
Collaboration from project networks with DoCoMo, content providers, platform vendors and mobile phone manufacturers

Mobile Phone Phase 1 (1992 to 1998): The Challenge of Voice Communications Demand

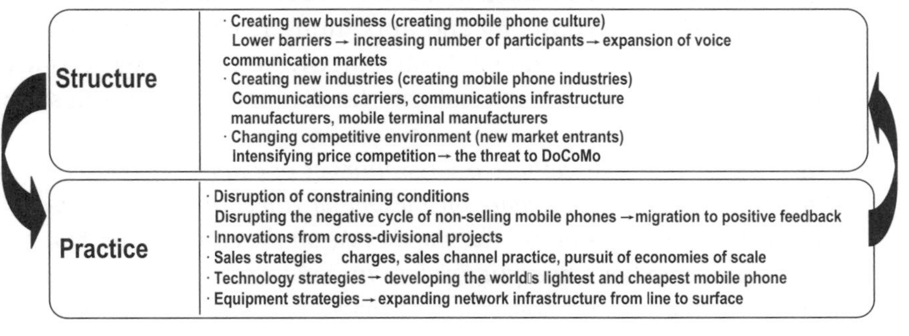

Figure 2.4: Recursive interplay of structure and practice.

DoCoMo's profits would fall at some point, creating a sense of crisis that DoCoMo's growth would be endangered. This prompted Mr. Oboshi to turn his attention to the data communications market, a new market displacing that of voice communications.

When I started at DoCoMo, I predicted that Japan's mobile phone market would grow to 12 million people — 10 percent of the population — by 1999. That prediction was considered extremely bullish. The actual speed of distribution, however, saw this prediction come true in mid-1996, three years earlier than expected. Seeing that mobile phone use was spreading like wildfire and believing that market saturation would be reached in the not-too-distant future, I felt that there was a need to create new markets outside that of voice communications. Mobile computing was a promising field. Thinking that it had applications beyond business use for text and data communication, I determined to put our efforts into creating a non-voice domain service for the general market on the basis of moving from "volume" to "value" (Oboshi, 2000).

Oboshi developed this vision of creating a new market in his head out of the sense of crisis that the Japanese mobile phone markets he had established would reach saturation and DoCoMo's growth would stop, and on the basis of the knowledge he had built up from experience. Then he engaged in dialectic thinking to resolve the mutual contradiction of both maintaining existing business and establishing new business.

In January 1997, Keiichi Enoki, who worked as division head of NTT DoCoMo (formerly NTT DoCoMo's managing director and general manager of i-mode, currently CEO of NTT DoCoMo Tokai, Inc.), was instructed by Oboshi to develop mobile multimedia services using mobile phones for the general user. Oboshi also instructed Enoki to gather talent by scouting outside the company and appointing from within DoCoMo, and to build a new organization. Oboshi empowered Enoki with control over personnel and resources to establish the new services. Oboshi said:

> *I knew from talking directly to a large number of employees that creating a new field depends more on individual capability than on the organization. So I considered who should take on the vitally-important areas of new product conception, planning and development. Large numbers of individuals came up with novel and striking concepts. Then the organization had the capacity to cultivate the ideas through circulating them in the market, processing them and refining them (Oboshi, 2000).*

Enoki both empathized with and was galvanized by Oboshi's way of thinking. But he was a complete novice when it came to informational content for the mobile multimedia service. On the other hand, he could not refuse a direct order from the CEO. So he set about laying the groundwork with a condition that he could use his discretion over budgets and personnel.

Until then, from his experience of working for DoCoMo with Oboshi, Enoki was aware of the crisis that hit voice communications business model that was then limiting DoCoMo's business activities and the sluggish mobile phone markets, and he had seen the need to develop new markets. Then while thinking about how to break down DoCoMo's current environment (structure) for future growth and develop the new mobile multimedia services, he began to have new belief as he recalled his past business experience (at NTT, he had had sales experience with an information terminal named Captain, a video-on-demand service aimed at the home market) and his joint experience with Oboshi in DoCoMo's mobile phone business. In this way, Enoki had implicitly acquired the basis for new concepts by integrating the knowledge of all concerned, while incorporating his own internal environment.

Enoki gathered capable and remarkable personnel both from within and outside DoCoMo (including the recruitment of content specialist Mari Matsunaga and Takeshi Natsuno from an IT venture company), and launched the project (in charge of Gateway) with a staff of around 10. By August 1997, a new organization had been launched with a staff of around 70 (Gateway Business Division: below, GBD). Then GBD undertook the development of the new i-mode service as a project-based organization under Enoki's leadership. GBD employees, especially Oboshi and Enoki, shared their visions and individual thoughts about the development of the new service. This behavior can represent the employee knowledge-sharing stage from the viewpoint of the community knowledge-creating cycle as shown in mobile phone phase 2 in Figure 2.2.

Making a success of the i-mode service required positive feedback, that is the sustained provision of appealing digital content from Content Providers (CP) caused the number of end users with i-mode compatible mobile phones to increase, which in turn increased CP content provision to appeal to still more users. Achieving this kind of positive feedback involved the hardware issues of developing a user-friendly, i-mode supporting mobile handset and a content distribution network system (including server systems). A second, software-related, issue was how to acquire CPs with appealing content.

Enoki thought that solving these two hardware and software problems and realizing a new service required the fusion and integration of knowledge resources such as new ideas and views from the implicit knowledge of the outstanding GBD personnel, the superlative technological and sales skills and expertise that DoCoMo's functional organization (existing organization lineup excluding GBD) had accumulated over many years, and the content possessed by the CPs as external customers. The new knowledge created from this fusion and integration became an important element in the construction of the new i-mode business model.

Forming teams of boundaries (ToBs) within DoCoMo

The development of the i-mode mobile phone handset and server required cooperation among the development, technology and equipment divisions of DoCoMo's functional organization. To begin with, however, the opinion about the services within these organizations was negative, and disagreements arose between personnel in the GBD and other divisions arising from differences in thinking about the services. Enoki stood at the front line of these contradictions and conflicts between GBD and the other organizations, and he resolved them constructively and productively by steering the divisions in the direction of tenacious dialectic debate and collaboration.

Enoki's leadership in gathering together all GBD members with the strong aim of making a success of the i-mode service, on which they had staked their professional pride, provided the driving energy behind the in-house organization.

Enoki displayed strong leadership aimed at realizing the i-mode service, acquired the understanding and agreement of the functional organization's leaders, and launched a liaison group to promote the introduction of an in-house mobile gateway service. This liaison group comprised all the leaders of the DoCoMo division including the CEO and Enoki, and was positioned as a ToB to share information and knowledge at the top management level aimed at realizing i-mode services, and to offer dialog and the time and space for decision-making aimed at business promotion.

Meanwhile, the project leaders, centered on Enoki, launched a total of seven working groups comprising of middle management from the GBD and other organizations. These groups covered network servers, mobile phones, equipment construction, equipment maintenance, systems and sales, and content and application. These ToBs discussed specific issues and themes aimed at realizing the i-mode service. Every Tuesday, moreover, a task force specializing in i-mode handset development and i-mode servers (the Gateway Service Specifications Investigation

Committee) would assemble to decide on service and technology specifications aimed at realizing the i-mode service. Moreover, in order to promote discussion and collaboration within its own organization, the GBD held a regular meeting of all members each Tuesday to share information and knowledge, and to share values and feelings about realizing the i-mode project.

Enoki and Natsuno seized on the following strategies aimed at a dramatic expansion of the i-mode. First was a portal strategy for developing attractive new content using i-mode. Second was a terminal strategy for the product development of new i-mode mobile phone terminals, including the addition of new functions. Third was a platform strategy to cultivate subscribers who use the handset as a platform, as well as a mobile phone. These three business strategies were mutually-connected and created considerable synergies.

Promoting this kind of business strategy requires promotion of project networks from strategic cooperation among various external partners and by creating specific results. The organizational behavior that we should focus on here is the resonance of DoCoMo's new business strategy proposals with external partners and the establishment of projects with individual partner companies. DoCoMo deliberately built its projects into project networks with external partners. In other words, the focus was on the creating the phenomenon of the project formation leading to a chain of project networks. With these project networks, a creative dialogue was always taking place, which was oriented to the formation of a new environment (structure) that spread and established mobile Internet culture. Then various problem areas and issues were dialectically synthesized, and i-mode's new business concepts were created. A major feature of these formed project networks in the second phase, was their greater expansion outside the company.

Forming project networks with CPs

Meanwhile, the GBD content planning project was concerned with acquiring CPs with appealing content. The strategy adopted by content planning project leaders Matsunaga and Natsuno was to build a win–win relationship leading to the success of both CPs and DoCoMo. When creating the i-mode content lineup, DoCoMo unilaterally bought content from specific CPs, but instead of taking a "tenant fee" from the CPs, both the CPs and DoCoMo thought of opposed standpoints, and shared the concepts of risk and profits, creating a win–win relationship. DoCoMo's first step was to have the CPs create first-class content and provide a platform to collect a content service usage fee as an agent, thus acquiring a service profit from the end user.

Matsunaga and Natsuno explained the concept of the win–win relationship to a large number of CP representatives. DoCoMo and the CP values resonated, and project networks aimed at establishing new business were formed. With these project networks, DoCoMo and the CPs jointly addressed the issue of developing content to make the end-user, who pays the content service fee, while paying a content service fee truly happy. They discussed the speed, accuracy and sustainability of content, and the viewpoint of end-user satisfaction and then went ahead to create appealing content that the end-user would not tire of. Driven by Matsunaga and Natsuno, the GBD content planning project acquired a succession of effective CPs including mobile banking, credit card, airline, hotel, news, newspaper and magazine providers. By the time of the i-mode service launch in February 1999, DoCoMo had acquired 67 CPs.

In this way, Enoki, Matsunaga and Natsuno deliberately formed ToBs of top and middle management within DoCoMo, but centered on GBD, external project networks with CPs, and project networks for technology discussions with mobile phone handset manufacturers, thus building up positive and constructively-creative dialogs aimed at forming the new environment (structure) for the i-mode mobile Internet market. From the viewpoint of the community knowledge-creating cycle, this DoCoMo employee behavior can represent the inspiring stage of new knowledge-creation shown in mobile phone phase 2 of Figure 2.2.

With these project networks and ToBs, the gaps between the knowledge possessed by individuals and the present environment (structure), as well as the conflict and contradictions among individuals, were dialectically synthesized, and the i-mode service concept was created. Aiming to launch the i-mode service, the GBD and DoCoMo in-house functional organizations cooperated effectively and took the service concept toward a higher strategic and analytical level. Specifically, the knowledge of i-mode-compatible mobile handsets, i-mode server specifications, sales manuals, operation manuals and content lineups was created and consolidated. The construction of the i-mode promotion system and the detailed specifications of the i-mode service were also initiated in-house. These can be represented as the new knowledge creating stage in mobile phone phase 2, Figure 2.2.

The distribution and establishment of new services, however, cannot be realized solely by exploration networks (project networks) as exploration practices. Moreover, exploitative networks formed from in-house functional organizations (including sales, technology, equipment and maintenance) as exploitation practices must function well. DoCoMo firmly consolidated these dual networks of exploration (project networks) and functional organization (exploitative networks) in-house through ToBs. DoCoMo also integrated the individually-differentiated knowledge in dual networks through ToBs. I call this ToB-inspired knowledge integration and organizational capability "network competencies".

The i-mode service was launched in February 1999. By August 2000, i-mode subscriber numbers exceeded 1,000, and the world's first mobile phone Internet market was born. DoCoMo had created a new market (environment/structure) (see mobile phone phase 2 in Figure 2.4) Through i-mode, the user had access not only to mobile phone online services, but could also send and receive email, connect at will to the Internet (on a PC), and obtain desired information "easily," "anywhere," "at any time." By realizing the concepts of "need for a mobile phone handset" and "easy availability," i-mode took the first step toward developing mobile multimedia.

The widely popular i-mode system mainly comprises the following system elements (see Figure 2.5). The first is the i-mode compatible

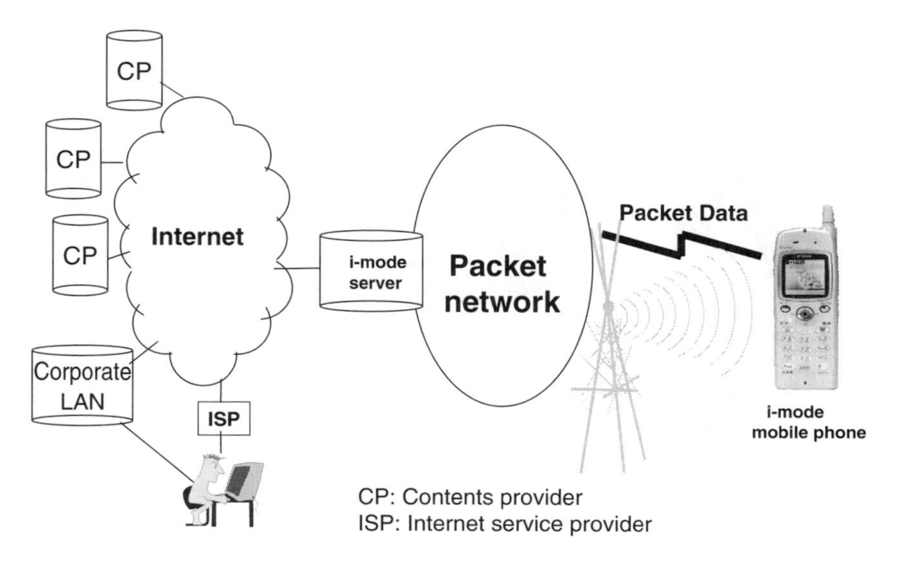

Figure 2.5: i-mode system.

mobile phone handset. This is loaded with a web browser (using a subset of HTML), enabling users to enjoy high-speed access through the current third-generation FOMA system. The second is the packet communications network. The packets are used to connect the i-mode server. The third is DoCoMo's i-mode server network and web-connection functions. It executes content distribution, the sending, receiving, and accumulation of email, and user and CP administration. The fourth is content. CPs provide content to mobile phone users using the Internet and dedicated lines.

The following factors explain why i-mode was such a great hit (see Figure 2.6). First was the feature of sending user-friendly email from the mobile phone and meeting the needs of young users who grew up in an environment of text communication. Moreover, the generation that mastered the pager began exchanging messages using mobile phones and Personal Handyphone System (PHS) handsets around 1997. Around this time, exchanges of short messages, names and emails were limited to mobile phones or PHS terminals from the same company. The i-mode handset was open to calls from other companies, and enabled email exchange via the Internet with mobile phones and PCs from other telecommunications companies.

The second phase was responding to user needs with rich content. i-mode created a diverse content menu lineup including transactions such as mobile banking and ticket reservations; databases such as restaurant and passenger guides; information for daily life such as news and weather forecasts; and entertainment such as program information and online

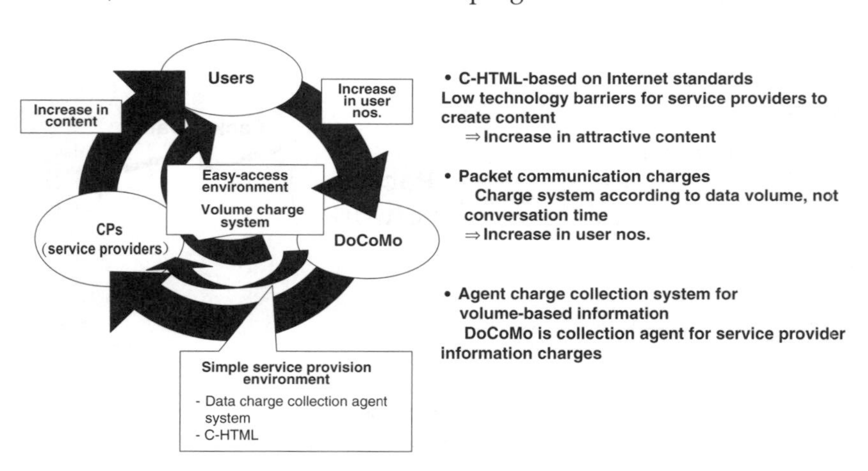

Figure 2.6: i-mode's positive feedback.

games. (On March 31, 2002, 2,020 CPs were hosting 2,994 websites. In addition to i-menu sites, there were 50,000 sites prepared by ordinary users for viewing on the i-mode.) This kind of rich content contributed to the increase in the number of i-mode users.

Third was the building of a win–win relationship with CPs. i-mode boldly adopted an improved version of HTML, using words to record Internet content.

HTML was already the *de facto* Internet standard. A large number of CPs were able to use improved c-HTML to easily distribute HTML content. So the CPs were able to participate easily in the i-mode service without excessive investment in equipment. Moreover, DoCoMo constructed a content fee collection system as an agent for the content providers. As a result, CPs were able to collect small service fees from a huge number of mobile phone users. Put another way, the CPs and DoCoMo created a win–win (profitable for both) relationship, whereby CPs providing attractive content for mobile phone users grew in a positive cycle.

The i-mode portal offers a number of representative services including advertising distribution businesses and sophisticated financial services from Internet banks; development of new java-enabled mobile handsets (the i-appli service); the i-area service; game machine links (such as PlayStation); the c-mode service (links to vending machines), convenience stores (Lawson); links to AOL email; links to car navigation; and other services.

In December 2001, DoCoMo achieved 30 million subscriber contracts. i-mode was a great hit in Japan and had become a popular topic for discussion. A new mobile Internet culture lifestyle was established, especially among the youth. Moreover, the hitherto non-existent market of mobile content distribution using mobile phones was growing rapidly (the digital content market for ringtones, mobile screens, games and other features increased to 120 billion yen). Around 3,000 CPs including Cybird, Index and Bandai (the number of officially-recognized CPs is soaring rapidly) entered the market.

The progress of this group of companies has created a wider new environment. i-mode has brought about great changes in the digital content market for PCs. The success of i-mode has also had a great impact on the world's mobile telecommunications businesses. In January 2000, the US magazine, *Business Week*, ran a feature on DoCoMo, in which it described its sudden user expansion in Japan and suggested that "the Internet services supplied by DoCoMo are widely popular in Japan and may take over the world". Foreign media and DoCoMo employees are once again recognizing DoCoMo's power and potential. They are motivated to work towards further innovation.

Centered around the GBD, DoCoMo members have dealt with customers' (end-users and CPs) reactions and complaints, taken swift action to deal with i-mode server crashes caused by the sudden increase in communications traffic, and in other ways benefited from diverse practical experiences, while accumulating new wisdom (skills and expertise) as tacit knowledge among individuals. The behavior of these employees can be represented from the viewpoint of the community knowledge-creating cycle's knowledge-accumulating stage (see "mobile phone phase 2" in Figure 2.2).

As shown above, in DoCoMo's second mobile phone phase, the i-mode mobile Internet market (structure) was created with the aim of migrating from "volume" to "value" under the restrictive conditions of voice communications and plummeting prices, and as a result of practice through dual networks of project networks, extended outside the company and functional organization networks. Meanwhile, the newly-created structure encouraged competition with rivals, and led to new reforms and strategies for the organizational network centered around DoCoMo (see mobile phone phase 2 in Figure 2.4).

DoCoMo re-formed (re-produced) a new environment that differed from that of phase 1. DoCoMo employees acquired diverse wisdom by providing i-mode services in a variety of sales locations.

2.2.4. *Third phase (2004 to present): the challenge of a lifestyle tool (See Figure 2.2)*

KDDI, Vodafone, and other DoCoMo rivals have also entered the mobile Internet Service market. Although DoCoMo was the first to enter the market, Enoki and Natsuno were alert about possible competition. The mass media predict that i-mode will soon reach saturation point on the S-curve. Enoki and Natsuno felt that issues like constantly-changing environment, creating mobile Internet culture and facing competition can be addressed through their skills and expertise acquired through years of experience.

DoCoMo's approach to these subjects was swayed by the thinking that the market was driven not by technology, but by the market principle. In other words, it was the thinking that the motive power was positive feedback created by the perfect balance (dialectical synthesis) between the conceptions of mutually-contradictory market and technology trends. This notion also drew on the tacit knowledge that Enoki and Natsuno had acquired from past experience.

The next challenges for DoCoMo, as a company that achieved 40 million i-mode subscribers, were first, to expand i-mode distribution to foreign markets; second, to migrate from the current second-generation system to third-generation system; and third, to identify a mobile phone "lifestyle tool" represented by a mobile e-commerce service (the "mobile wallet" service).

Regarding creating a new business model for i-mode's further development, Enoki and Natsuno always welcomed the spirit of innovation without being complacent about the environment (structure) they had created. Furthermore, besides the project-based organization (the products and service division of i-mode's business headquarters) that Enoki and Natsuno belonged to, DoCoMo that took the credit for i-mode's success developed the vision of creating a new communication culture and realizing a new knowledge society for the 21st century mobile phone culture gained.

The knowledge (experience, skill and expertise) Enoki, Natsuno and the other employees that led to i-mode's domestic success with a second-generation system was due to knowledge sharing among related divisions of each management level, including DoCoMo's functional organizations.

Two major challenges that faced DoCoMo-during this phase were the growth of the domestic market as a result of the profitability of the current system, and the interaction of new business risks from foreign markets and new-generation systems. Another challenge was to establish a new mobile phone service as a lifestyle infrastructure. This behavior can represent the employee knowledge-sharing stage shown in mobile phone phase 3, Figure 2.2, from the viewpoint of the community knowledge-creating cycle.

DoCoMo's project-based and functional organizations formed global project networks both within DoCoMo and with external partners aimed at supporting DoCoMo's globalization and next-generation system, while creating further lifestyle tools. The first challenge was to form project networks aimed at the overseas development of i-mode and third-generation systems with European, Asian and US communication carriers.

The second challenge was to form project networks with different industries as a new service strategy aimed at creating a mobile phone lifestyle tool. Specifically, this involved forming project networks with different industries such as banks involved in settlements and commercial transaction domains, credit card companies, convenience stores, various kinds of shops and railway companies in order to realize mobile e-commerce services. Collaboration with Sony to realize the "mobile wallet" service was especially important. Sony had already worked on the development and sale of an IC chip (the "FeliCa chip"), that was not very profitable: Sony also faced the challenge of risk and displayed a forward-looking attitude by forging strategic alliances with DoCoMo to realize e-commerce through mobile phones. As DoCoMo project leader, Natsuno displayed skillful "tipping point leadership" (Kim and Mauborgne, 2005). He finally established a joint venture between Sony and DoCoMo named FeliCa Network Inc. through top-level negotiations with PlayStation creator, Mr. Kutaragi (currently the CEO of Sony Computer Entertainment) and then-Sony CEO, Mr. Idei.

FeliCa Network made use of jointly-developed mobile e-commerce platform, and DoCoMo came to offer full-scale mobile e-commerce.

In the broadcasting domain, the joint venture formed project networks with leading broadcasters, targeting a service fusing mobile phone connection and terrestrial digital broadcasting. In the content and the Internet domain, it established strategic cooperation and joint ventures, and dynamically formed project networks with internal and external development partners (such as the US company, Texas Instruments), which were aimed at the joint development of core technology (hardware and software) for mobile phones (see Figure 2.7).

The development of the central LSI (Large Scale Integrated Circuit) system (Kodama, 2005) with the help of semiconductor companies is the need of the hour for DoCoMo, given the short life cycles and high functions required of mobile phone development. DoCoMo will share its mobile phone development roadmap with handset development manufacturers and semiconductor manufacturers, and enter the market for mobile handsets loaded with timely and rhythmical new functions. With the i-mode mobile phone business creating successive waves of S-curves, creative dialogue was promoted to form a new environment (structure). From the viewpoint of the community knowledge-creating cycle, this DoCoMo employee behavior can represent the inspiring stage of new knowledge creation shown in mobile phone phase 3 of Figure 2.2.

With these project networks, various problems and themes were dialectically synthesized, i-mode and roaming services were realized overseas (specifically through i-mode licensing contracts with communications carriers in Germany, the Netherlands, Taiwan, Belgium, France, Spain, Italy and the US, and the launch of i-mode services abroad), and the "mobile wallet" was created (see Figure 2.8) as a key lifestyle tool service. "Mobile wallet"

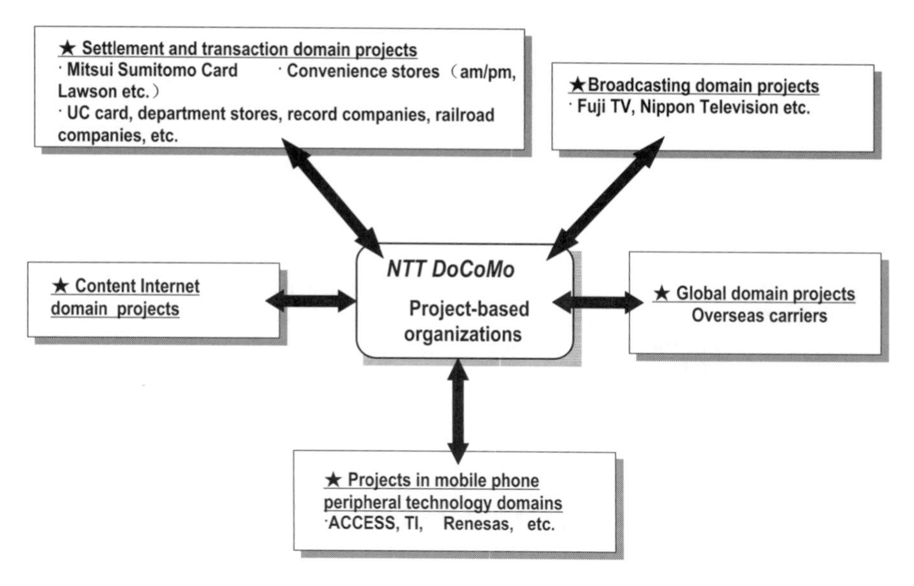

Figure 2.7: Project networks for creation of new business.

services enable the acquisition of shopping, all kinds of coupons and members' cards with electronic money and mobile credit. Of late, the mobile phone is being used to verify employee status for corporate security management. Further expansion into the areas of global scope, different industries, and expanded technologies are major features in phase three project networks when compared to those for phase two. Moreover, it has become possible to develop and provide mobile handsets as "lifestyle tools" loaded with various new functions (ubiquitous communications functions beyond phone and email) (see Figure 2.9). By May 2006, DoCoMo had 46.70 million i-mode subscribers and 25.36 million FOMA subscribers. This is the new knowledge-creating stage shown in mobile phone phase 3 of Figure 2.2.

By providing service in various locations, DoCoMo employees at stage three acquired diverse and high-quality knowledge. From the viewpoint of the community knowledge-creating cycle, this behavior can represent the stage of accumulating knowledge as experience in mobile phone stage 3 of Figure 2.2.

Under the restrictive conditions of domestic market saturation, DoCoMo planned to switch from a domestic to an international focus, migrate to a new generation system, and create a mobile phone culture

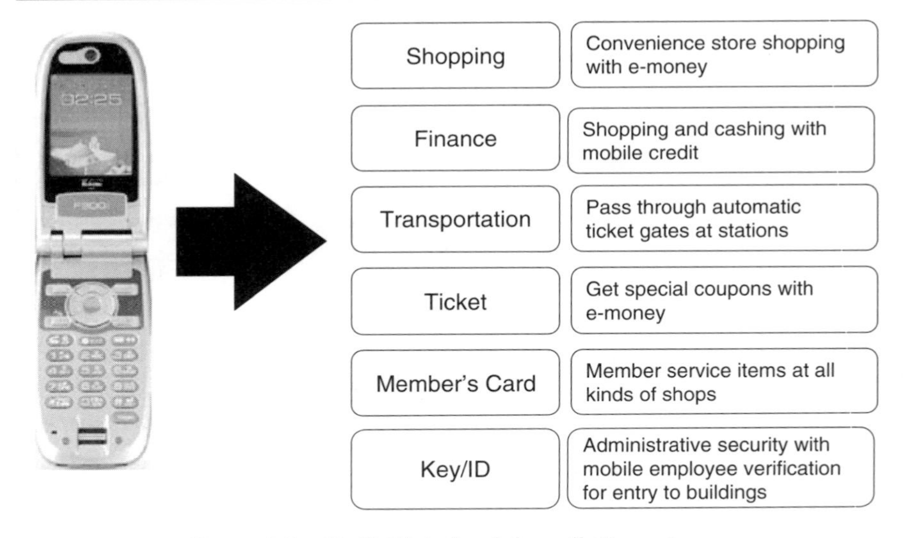

Figure 2.8: DoCoMo's "mobile wallet" service.
Source: DoCoMo IR data

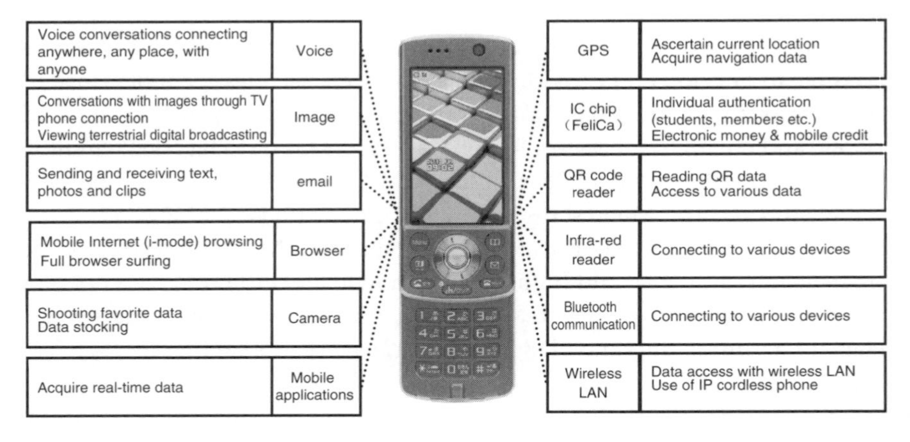

Figure 2.9: Mobile phones as individual lifestyle media.
Source: DoCoMo IR data.

with new lifestyle tools. In this phase, DoCoMo created new overseas and "lifestyle tool" markets (structure) through dual networks — more extended projects and functional organization networks. Meanwhile, the newly-created structures are facing competition from rivals, thus leading to new innovations and strategies in organizational networks, centered around DoCoMo (see mobile phone phase 3 in Figure 2.4).

The behavior described above is not exclusive to DoCoMo. The Au (KDDI) and Vodafone mobile phone carriers are also working simultaneously to create new markets, and establish and disseminate existing markets through dual networks — exploratory practice from project networks and exploitative practice from functional organization networks.

2.3. The Formation of Teams of Boundaries

At the time of its split from the major player NTT in 1992, NTT DoCoMo was a small organization consisting of 2,000 people. The first challenge faced by DoCoMo was to foster unity among the employees. The company had transferees from NTT, employees hired by DoCoMo, outside staff, temporary employment agency staff and others. The then-CEO Oboshi and other management staff established practical, simple and clear management objectives under the slogan of "*good, cheap services,*" and created a sense of unity among employees. Adopting a top-down leadership style, the founding CEO Oboshi also emphasized a bottom-up approach with direct communication between CEO and employees, and gathered opinions and news from users and sales locations. Typical of this is the "communication post" that enables anyone to contact the CEO directly at any time with questions, opinions, or suggestions. Twice a week, the leaders in sales and maintenance divisions held a "taking order" teleconference involving head and branch offices. This mechanism enabled a two-way communication between head and regional branch offices, and contributed greatly to the smooth sharing of information and knowledge.

At first, DoCoMo employees were transferred from NTT divisions and contracted from outside companies. Colleagues who did not know each other were suddenly working together. This resulted in employee participation regardless of their hierarchical levels. This led to the formation of cross-functional project teams that were both flexible and adaptable.

DoCoMo's top and middle management layers shared a corporate vision of quickly establishing a Japanese mobile phone market and building a new mobile communications environment, differentiated from Japan's public fixed phone services, where communication could be enjoyed by "anyone, anywhere, anytime." To rapidly expand the new mobile phone market on the basis of this vision, top and middle managers positively implemented swift decisions through information and knowledge sharing among leaders at each management level, and through thorough discussion aimed at mobile communications infrastructure management and the expansion of new services (development of new mobile phone terminals and services). In this book, I will call the ToBs formed from leaders and managers at each management level and across organizational boundaries as "leadership teams."

Leadership teams were split into top and middle management layers to absorb the expansion of DoCoMo's mobile phone market and corporate growth (both earnings and scale) together with the expansion of organizational scale in July 1998. To strengthen the linkage between top- and mid-level leadership teams, top management leadership teams with middle management representation thoroughly discussed important topics proposed by middle management leadership teams before the top management executed prompt and appropriate decisions.

At its launch as a new company, DoCoMo set out a corporate vision of its basic values, behavioural standards and "corporate philosophy" criteria. At the core of this concept is the thinking that mobile communications liberate people from the confines of time and space. This mobile communication engenders new business styles and lifestyles, and creates a new communication culture unprecedented in terms of time, space and form. In other words, the mobile communications services has triggered the development of a new type of knowledge society. DoCoMo had a large role to play in realizing this society, and energetically took on issues such as rich service functions, the expansion of service areas, development of more detailed, higher-quality services, and the setting of low fees aimed at enabling any user to access mobile communication anywhere. A large number of people who transferred from NTT at the time of the split maintained and migrated the positive elements of the traditional organizational capabilities (such as a high-quality, disciplined business system in a disciplined organizational culture) from their time at NTT, including research and development, network design and construction, high-speed network operations technology, and a nationwide sales force, while at the same time nurturing a creative, youthful corporate culture capable of maximizing the capabilities of all its employees. At the time of the start-up,

DoCoMo became a symbiotic organizational structure of functional organizations with assets inevitably hidden during the NTT era, and project-based organizations possessing a new corporate culture (quite different from that of the NTT era) that later became the driving force behind new marketing innovations such as i-mode development. These ToBs leadership teams have become dual network (exploratory and exploitative) nodules. In other words, they are positioned as hubs or nodes in a network (see Figure 2.10).

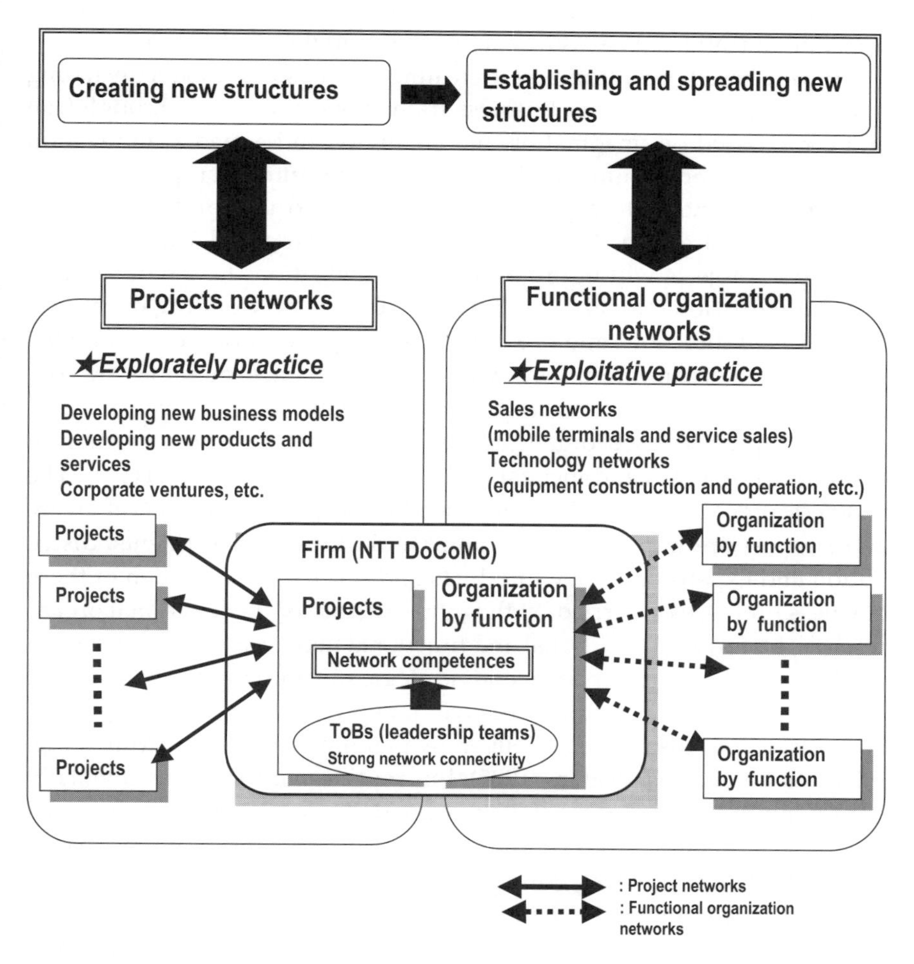

Figure 2.10: Recursive interplay of structure and networks

2.4. Network Competences through Leadership Teams

As mentioned above, DoCoMo's corporate activities are supported by the 21st century vision of pursuing long-term positions, and the creation of absolute value by realizing a new communications culture and knowledge society through mobile technology. Continuous knowledge-creating activities take place, which are aimed at realizing the corporate mission and business domain based on this vision. Major characteristics of DoCoMo are continuous innovation and the dialectical synthesis of project-based organizations possessing new, heterogeneous knowledge assets with functional organizations possessing expertise acquired over the years.

Project-based organizations are creating new business model (including new products, services and business frameworks) concepts through trial and error, based on imagination and creativity, and aimed at innovation in an uncertain environment. They are forming multiple project networks (exploratory) with external strategic business partners, and implementing emergent strategies (Mintzberg, 1978; Mintzberg and Walters, 1985). Individual projects within project-based organizations take independent distributive action (Nonaka and Toyama, 2002) as network organizations. The business directions and objectives are regulated, however, among the project-based organizations as a whole, whose business activities are constantly monitored by the organization's top level.

These project-based organizations constantly lead to the creation of concepts, prototypes and incubations for new products and services. The business processes of equipment assembly, sales, distribution, aftercare and support are important for prompt and efficient investments, distribution and expansion of new products and services. The burden of these business processes is carried by the infrastructure of the functional organizations, by forming traditional and functional networks (exploitative networks) with group companies and strategic outsourcing partners based on knowledge assets accumulated over many years. Functional organizations draw up disciplined, deliberate planning strategies (Mintzberg, 1978; Mintzberg and Walters, 1985), but routines aimed at incrementally improving business process efficiency are daily occurrences. So the fruits of innovative new product and service concepts from project-based organizations are promptly, surely, and efficiently invested in the market, and then distributed and expanded.

These two types of organizations (project-based vs. functional) and network (project vs. functional organization) are general classifications.

They possess paradoxical elements such as creativity and independence on the one hand, and efficiency and tradition on the other, and disagreement and conflict usually break out between the organizations. These elements are a major hindrance to the integration of actors' knowledge in each organization. It is the duty of the ToBs' leadership teams to promote this integration. Leadership teams comprise leaders (CEO, executives, division heads, departmental heads and project leaders) and managers (project managers and assistant managers) at each of DoCoMo's management levels (including top management, middle management, and mixed management teams at project-based and functional organizations, informal cross-functional teams and task forces).

"Leadership teams" possess strong network connectivity to bind the dual networks. "Network connectivity" is the mutual connection capability of networks possessing heterogeneous characters and knowledge. "Leadership teams" fuse and bind each piece of knowledge from the dual networks, and creatively and systematically establish the strategic methodology of establishing coexisting contradictions of opinion, giving rise to DoCoMo's general "network competences" (see Figure 2.10).

With leadership teams, each leader must display dialectical leadership (Kodama, 2005) aimed at fulfilling DoCoMo's vision and mission. At the same time, leaders must thoroughly appreciate problems and issues through constructive debate, and expedite them through shared dialectical dialog. Each leader must also communicate and collaborate in order to recognize the role and value of each job. This way, leaders can engineer constructive outcomes from the various conflicts. Meanwhile, the CEO, as the final decision-maker in the leadership teams, must display top-down leadership when necessary, and strengthen communication linkage with individual leaders, by positively creating time and space for dialog and debate within leadership teams, and maximize the coherence of each leader's dialectical leadership.

In DoCoMo's case, strategy implementation has created a spiral of unprecedented new markets by forming project networks (exploratory networks) with content provider clients, strategic partners and players in different industries such as finance and distribution. Project-based organizations centered on the products and service division have launched successive new products and service concepts aimed at realizing mobile phones as "lifestyle infrastructure," such as mobile e-commerce from handsets loaded with prepaid and credit cards, and those loaded with digital terrestrial broadcasting functions.

New services marketability is first confirmed by analyzing the processes of concept making, marketing, trial development and incubation at project-based organizations. The distribution and embedding of these services in new markets that are swiftly commercialized by functional organizations (including equipment, maintenance and sales divisions) is then promoted spirally. Functional organizations are promoting a series of efficient business process management cycles. These include efficient and accurate equipment investment planning policies in response to predicted demand for new services; the introduction of network operation systems to maintain high-quality services; nationwide sales and maintenance systems from functional organization networks (exploitative networks) as a result of strategic collaboration and outsourcing of group companies and sales branches; and the establishment of aftercare support systems.

DoCoMo's project-based and functional organizations discuss issues of emergent strategy and the planning that supports it such as timing, type of strategy, tactics, mechanisms and resources, and making decisions. This takes place through the leadership teams comprising leaders from each project and functional organizations in each business including marketing, research, service development sales, equipment, investment and maintenance services. The leaders of these leadership teams select the strategies and tactics that could result in true marketing innovations after thorough dialog and discussion, and each leader moves to specific execution through dialectical leadership. The synergies of dialectical leadership through the collaboration of CEO and leaders from each management level, including executive staff, emphasize dialectical dialog, promote detailed, deliberate strategies for carefully selected emergent strategy issues, and realize the synthesis of knowledge and strategy from different networks. These "network competencies" launch spirals of new market (environment) creation and growth.

DoCoMo's network competences created by its leadership teams resulted in the launch of the prototype FOMA in Tokyo in May 2005. This was the world's first third-generation mobile phone service, and enabled the launch of full-scale services in October 2005. By the end of May 2006, DoCoMo had signed up 25.36 million subscribers.

From the viewpoint of the strategy-making process described above, DoCoMo's dynamic view of strategy, centered on these leadership teams, could also be the realization of an integrative strategy from the coexistence of emergent and deliberate paradoxes (Kodama, 2003a, 2003c). A more important focus, however, is the process of dynamic, strategic knowledge formation at the root of realizing integrative strategy. In other words, it is the viewpoint of the synthesis of thought (strategy) and action (practice) promoting the spiral conversion of the community knowledge-creating cycle's knowledge creation process (see Figure 2.2). What is required of leadership teams is to accurately grasp the state of the market, build up common recognition as an organization, and have the capability to form dynamic, strategic knowledge that is flexible and adaptable. The basis of this methodology is neither deduction nor induction, but the transcendentalist thought and practical methodology of "abduction": a concept that enables the search for the unknown. "Abduction" is a method of thinking advocated by Charles S. Peirce, the US originator of pragmatism.

In other words, it is a knowledge methodology that (i) grasps potential factors and mechanisms created by new opportunities through sharing tacit knowledge of the market (environment), (ii) reviews the shared potential market and creates specific models linked to practice, and (iii) modifies the hypothesis through this process, and justifies and theorizes as knowledge to solve problems. The essence of this emergent and deliberate integrative strategy-making process is for the members of leadership teams to open up dialectic dialog as the basis of creativity and imagination, and repeat the self-modification of the formulated transcendent hypothesis. Then finally, it becomes truly possible to reliably and systematically realize the transcendent hypothesis through abduction. Leadership teams exhibit network competences, and create and practice dynamically and strategically through the abduction of new knowledge from dual network integration with external strategic partners, including customers (market).

3

Boundary Innovation through Project Networks J-Phone and Sharp Take on the Challenge of Camera-Loaded Mobile Phone Development

3.1. The Fusion of Organizational and Technological Boundaries

Innovation is always demanded in industries where markets and technologies change frequently. In the ICT and home automation fields, led by the mobile phone, engineers are required to fuse and integrate different technological domains (see Tidd, 1994; Kodama, 2005). In other words, in the distinctive technology domain, it is the creation of new technologies by expanding towards the horizontal domain (integration) of different technologies, while pursuing the vertical. This innovation from technology integration is not just distinctive module development, but is required of architecture development (see Chapter 4 of this case study for details) for the entire product design. Engineers need a great deal of knowledge to integrate technologies. This knowledge can have the capability, however, to combine these diverse technologies (whether modules or products) into one. Engineers need the knowledge (capability) of different technology domains (or fields of study) to discover the mutual effects of different technologies on one another.

Under the conditions of a rapidly changing competitive environment, companies in every industry are focusing on core competencies, while searching for new business models in an attempt to survive and emerge winners. The fusion of different technologies and diversification of business models require companies to integrate diverse, distributed knowledge internally and externally. The process of this knowledge integration is an important corporate theme (Kodama, 2005, 2006a). The task of the top management is to bridge and fuse the technological knowledge of engineers from different specializations.

Factors such as the acceleration of Internet-related business, the specialization and fragmentation of technological boundaries, and the specialization of organizations further complicate the organizational boundaries within and outside the company. Innovation, however, arises from different knowledge boundaries and organizational boundaries (Leonard-Barton, 1992, 1995).

Boundaries can be places of conflict among organizations, and of opposition and contradiction, regarding an individual, and specialized knowledge. At the same time, they can be places of innovation. It follows that enlivening communication at boundaries can be a strong driving force for the invention of new technologies and products. In this chapter, I will consider the innovation processes of the development of the camera-mounted mobile phone, a Japanese invention and the world's (knowledge) first such product development, through a case of technology integration crossing organizational and technological boundaries.

3.2. J-Phone's (Vodafone's) "Sha-mail"

In November 2000, J-Phone (later acquired by the UK's Vodafone, and in May 2006 acquired by Softbank. In October 2006, the name of the company was changed to Softbank Mobile) launched a phone model with a built-in digital camera. The 74-gram device, the first cellular mounted with a camera, enabled users to transmit color photos to other mobile phones. The phone was launched from J-Phone's home base of Japan. In addition to the transmission of 256 color images, users could attach photos to e-mail messages sent via the phone. Its screen also allowed users to display photos stored in memory, and caller photos could be set to appear when they dialed the device.

J-Phone was a leading mobile operator in Japan and a member of the Vodafone Group, the world's largest mobile community. J-Phone offered sophisticated mobile services including high quality voice telephony, "Sha-mail" picture messaging, "Movie Sha-mail" video messaging, "J-SKY" mobile internet and e-mail access, and Java applications. Sha-mail is a service that allows people to take pictures with a camera-mounted mobile phone

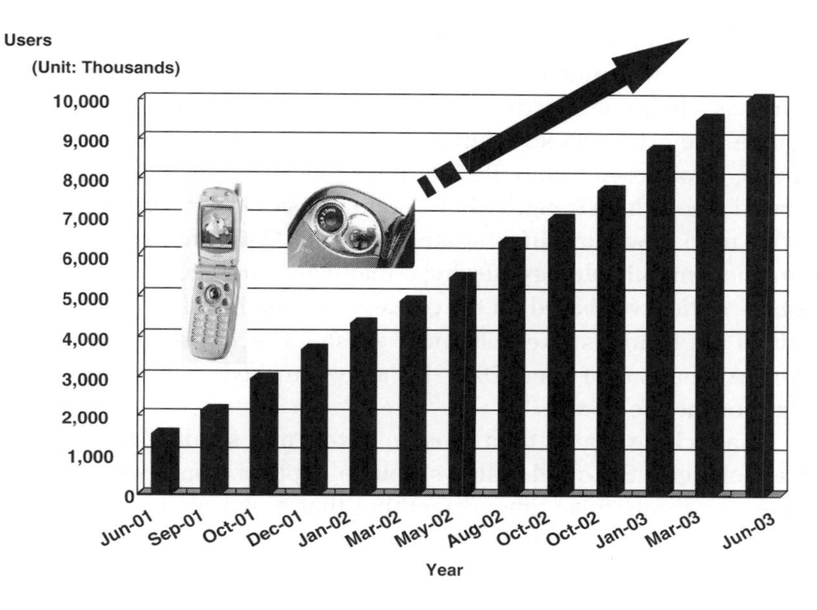

Figure 3.1: Number of "Sha-mail" users.
Source: Based on press release by J-Phone.

and send them as e-mail attachments. Encouraged by its ease-of-use, more and more customers have recognized and adopted the Sha-mail brand, resulting in rapid expansion of the product. After introducing its first camera-mounted mobile phone in November 2000, J-Phone reached the milestone of 10 million Sha-mail users in approximately two years and seven months. See Figure 3.1.

In December 2001, J-Phone adopted the J-Phone/Vodafone dual logo to visually promote its membership in the Vodafone Group. By adopting the Vodafone brand, J-Phone aimed at creating stronger brand presence in the Japanese market by combining Vodafone's association with reliability and global services, and with the former J-Phone brand's reputation for innovation, as exemplified by the pioneering Sha-mail picture messaging service. As a member of the Vodafone Group, J-Phone strove to offer its customers richer communications that were global in scope and advanced high-value-added products and service. Vodafone rolled out Sha-mail in Europe as Vodafone Live, capturing more than 380,000 users by December 2002.

By around 1999 to 2000, Au, a competitor of J-Phone, was running a network with a higher speed (64 kbps) than J-Phone's (9.6 kbps), while both DoCoMo and Au were planning the launch of a third-generation system[1]. J-Phone was under a tremendous pressure to do something to offset their overwhelming disadvantage in data transmission speed. However J-Phone knew that its strength lay in e-mail and other communication aspects, as opposed to mobile Internet services like i-mode, and decided to build upon that strength. So J-Phone's basic policy for promoting the mobile market was to differentiate itself from DoCoMo and Au by developing new mobile phones offering e-mail-based mobile services. The new mobile service was based on the concept of e-mail, and offered customers various applications like "Sha-mail — shoot, send, see-mail — begins here." At the end of June, 2001, J-Phone launched its new service campaign for mobile phones.

By attaching digital data (image) to text and sending to a partner as an attachment, Sha-mail "allows you to capture a face's expression or scenery at a particular time, something that a text mail alone could not express, by taking a photo and sending it to a partner" (Keiji Takao, J-Phone's mobile phone development project leader). The company set the goal of building a market for Sha-mail. Takao was transferred to J-Phone from automaker Mazda in 1992 (he was transferred again in 1996). During that time, Takao was inexperienced with mobile phones, but he and his colleagues undertook to develop the service progressively, and Sha-mail finally blossomed.

The concept of the Sha-mail arose from the incident described below. Takao's parents were visiting Tokyo from Kyushu. Wanting to relax and spend time with his parents, Takao went with them on a trip to nearby Hakone, a famous holiday destination.

The three of them rode on a cable car, and enjoyed the fabulous view. But another sight also caught his eye: a woman talking into a mobile phone and saying "hello? hello? oh, there's no connection. Okay, now how do I send a message?" She was trying to communicate her feelings on seeing this beautiful view from the cable car through e-mail, but the operation seemed to be very complicated. She did not seem to have a camera either, and was unable to take a photograph. Takao had a revelation: "of course! if mobile phones came with cameras, we could soon send our

---

[1] Although current mobile phones and portable terminals are capable of high-speed transmission, these are next-generation mobile and portable video terminals that can interactively transmit video, as well as voice and text. W-CDMA and cdma2000 are next-generation mobile telephone systems proposed by the Swedish company Ericsson and the US company Qualcomm, respectively.

feelings to a partner with a photograph!" This episode gave birth to the concept of "Sha-mail".

3.3. Joint Development by J-Phone and Sharp

At first, three employees, including project leader Keiji Takao, set to work drafting a development plan for establishing an e-mail-based image communication market. Their vision was to create a new form of image communication out of conventional text-based e-mail in Japan. They encountered innumerable technical and business problems including the following:

- Developing a low-cost, high-quality, digital camera-mounted mobile phone.
- How should J-Phone promote the camera-mounted mobile phones?
- How should J-Phone create and provide service for customers?

Keiji Takao believed that collaboration with a mobile phone manufacturer would be important for developing the camera-mounted mobile handsets. In Japan's mobile phone industry, communications carriers do not just provide a mobile phone service, but also supervise mobile handset marketing, product planning (they determine the handset's functions and usage — in other words, its specifications), and sales. Mobile phone manufacturers design their mobile phones on the basis of the specifications provided by the communications carrier, and supervise the apportioning of parts development and manufacturing. Mobile phone brands are also sold with communications carrier brands (such as Vodafone, DoCoMo and Au). The contract requires communications carriers to buy phones in bulk from manufacturers (the relationship between communications carriers and mobile phone manufacturers in Japan differs from US and Europe, and is characteristic of relations among Japanese companies).

Japanese household appliance manufacturer, Sharp (its large liquid-crystal Aquos TV is known throughout the world), entered the mobile phone market much later than many other Japanese manufacturers (including NEC, Fujitsu, Matsushita, Mitsubishi and Toshiba), but bagged the (mobile phone shipping figures within Japan in the fiscal year 2005) number one slot through its pioneer product camera-mounted mobile phone.

Before Sharp entered the mobile phone market, it focused its business resources on the PHS (Personal Handyphone System). However, problems arose when PHS users migrated to the mobile phone. In June 1998, Katsuhiko Machida, who was the CEO of Sharp, predicted the future profitability of the mobile phone business and concentrated business resources on the mobile phone. To begin with, he promoted collaboration with J-Phone, which was centered around Sharp Communications Systems business headquarters in Hiroshima.

Taking the opportunity of the launch of J-Phone's SkyWeb content distribution service in December 1998, the first mobile phone incorporating Sharp's core liquid-crystal technology (SH-01) was launched. Sharp had exploited this unique technology through close collaboration with J-Phone. The phone that incorporated a liquid-crystal panel (large for its time) became a great hit. In December 2000, J-Phone launched a mobile camera mounted with a color liquid-crystal panel. By this time, however, NEC, Fujitsu, and DoCoMo (for i-mode) had completed the development of their color LCD-mounted mobile phones, and Sharp began to lose its dominance in the market. The leaders of the personal business division product and planning team, and technology team, at Sharp Communication Systems' business headquarters felt a sense of crisis, and were impatient to grab the number. They strongly felt the need to anticipate other companies' actions and to strike one slot back with a new product.

Sharp wanted to incorporate a camera module into a mobile phone and to create a mobile phone with a "print club" (a photo booth found in malls and other places that creates photo stickers of the user with backgrounds of flowers or cartoon characters), which was then popular among Japan's junior high and high school girls. The idea was to make the new phone a "portable print club." This idea was further supported by the stages in the evolution of mobile phones. Looking at the evolution of mobile phones, a progression could be traced from voice communication to e-mail and text, then to mobile Internet such as the i-mode service, then to ringtones and image download services. Considering this evolution of mobile phone technology and customer usage structures, the customer would naturally prefer a camera that could take photographs. Contrary to the customer evolution, however, the camera-mounted PHS, developed and sold by Kyocera that was bulky and expensive did not sell well.

Sharp felt that the camera-mounted phone did not sell well as it did not suit the life style of the customers. The TV phone was ahead of its time, in that the culture of seeing someone's face while talking had not yet developed. The situation for still images, rather than the moving images of the TV phone, was different. The digital camera was becoming popular, and if pictures could easily be taken with a mobile camera, they could then be saved for later enjoyment or attached to an e-mail and sent to a friend or family member. The leaders believed that such a phone would sell well.

As mentioned above, J-Phone's Keiji Takao was thinking of exactly the same idea. J-Phone's and Sharp's expectations coincided exactly.

Around this time, Sharp approached DoCoMo with its idea for a camera-mounted mobile phone. DoCoMo, however, was at the peak of its success with the i-mode-loaded mobile phone, and sales were on rise. DoCoMo's priority at that time was to maintain i-mode's distribution and expansion, and DoCoMo felt that adding a camera would raise the price of the handset. DoCoMo also predicted that even if users took photographs with the camera, they might save the pictures on the mobile phone, but few would use DoCoMo's communications circuits to send photographic images. Since DoCoMo would not be able to charge a fee as a communications carrier unless the photographs were transmitted, the company saw no merit in the proposal, and responded negatively to Sharp's proposal. Sharp had seen this as an opportunity to land the coup of developing a camera-mounted mobile phone, while establishing a partnership with DoCoMo, but unfortunately, it was not to be. DoCoMo's logic had been impeccable.

It became clear, after the camera-mounted phone became popular, that users preferred to save and enjoy the pictures, rather than sending them by e-mail. Also, a mobile phone would not sell unless it was accessorized with a camera. Sensing that it was behind J-Phone and Au, in June 2002, DoCoMo decided to sell camera-mounted mobile phones in collaboration with Sharp. Later, DoCoMo used its brand strength to surpass J-Phone in camera-mounted mobile phone sales.

For Takao, who was project leader for initiating the joint development of camera-mounted mobile phones with Sharp, it was important to cooperate with the in-house functional organizations of business planning, sales, equipment, maintenance and other divisions, while strengthening collaboration with Sharp's development project. During this time, Kyocera's camera-mounted "Visualphone" was an influencing factor. Negative opinions about the development of the camera-mounted phone were heard within J-Phone. Takao had the support of his immediate superior, however, he required strong commitment from the leaders and managers in related divisions, and he managed to gain their consent for the

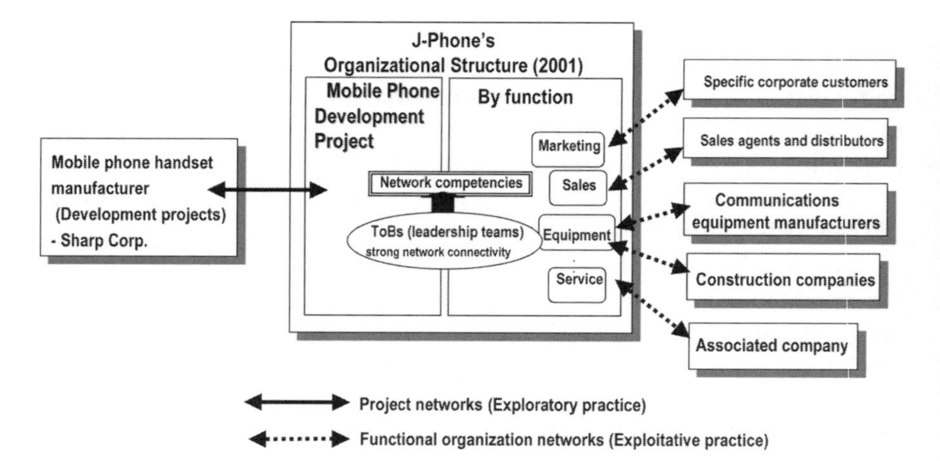

Figure 3.2: Functional networks centered on J-Phone.

new development. During this time, J-Phone sensed the pressure from DoCoMo and Au. This prompted J-phone employees to face the challenge of developing a camera-mounted mobile phone. Leadership teams were formed within J-Phone as ToBs between Takao's project teams and functional organizations (see Figure 3.2).

Meanwhile, Sharp, which J-Phone had contracted to develop the phone, was forming a development project involving various divisions within the company aimed at small-camera module development and camera mounting (see Figure 3.3). The frequent meetings with Takao's project in Tokyo were attended by the product planning team of Sharp's personal communications business division in Hiroshima, design and technology leaders, and Tokyo's sales team leaders. These groups engaged in discussions about the concept and idea of camera-mounted mobile handsets. The ToB-0 (Sharp) in Figure 3.3 accurately takes on board the needs and ideas of the J-Phone customer. It is a ToB that appreciates the product's specific functions and specifications, and shares, inspires and creates context and knowledge regarding user needs.

At Sharp's personal communications business division, the ideas and specifications discussed with J-Phone were consolidated to specific design data (overall system architecture, hardware and software, and individual module level elements). Then designers and members were involved and exchanged their views (see ToB-1 in Figure 3.3: this ToB shares, inspires, and creates context and knowledge related to product

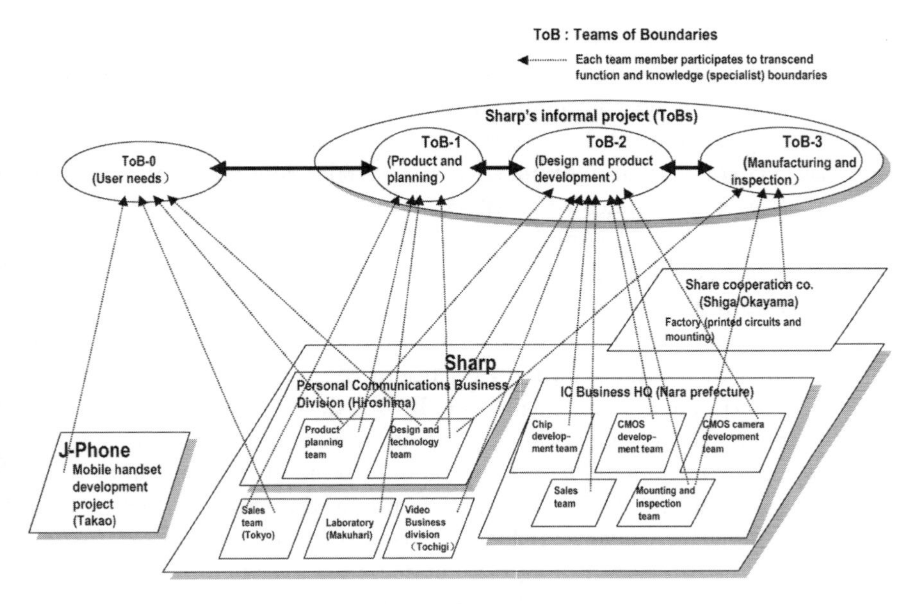

Figure 3.3: J-Phone & Sharp's project networks.

planning). The focus of the new development was the small camera module. The engineers in the personal communications business division were an expert group with regard to mobile phone communications technology, but they had no specialist knowledge of lenses or image processing. Realizing a camera-mounted phone, however, required the fusion of heterogeneous technologies including communications, lenses and image processing ICs. Fortunately, Sharp had acquired image and camera technology from the Zaurus PDA hit product and the liquid crystal Viewcam video camera. Without further delay, the Hiroshima engineers accessed the CCD division of the IC business division in Tenri, Nara Prefecture.

In Tenri, technology members from the personal communications division and the CCD division held numerous meetings. The subject of these meetings was "how to develop a small camera module (unifying image elements, lenses and image-processing ICs) and load it into a small mobile phone, while maintaining the phone's size". The investigation progressed energetically through discussions that included the new development of low-energy IC chips dedicated to image processing, development of small CMOS camera modules, and methods for loading the new components (see ToB-2 in Figure 3.3: a ToB that shares, inspires, and creates context and knowledge relating to design and component development). During the development period required by the J-Phone customer, Sharp's engineers faced development process issues, such as CMOS sensor noise correction and miniaturization of the lens-integrated CMOS sensor. Many of the issues were solved, however, by transcending organizational barriers and sharing individual specialist skills. In this way, they succeeded in reducing the thickness of the camera module compared to the one used in the Zaurus PDA (a hit product for Sharp).

The next step was to develop technology to mount more than 50 new components, including a miniature camera module and a dedicated IC chip onto a compact circuit board. The IC business headquarters' mounting and inspection team outsourced the volume manufacture of the circuit on which the components would be loaded to one of Sharp collaborators known as Sumitomo Electric Printed Circuits in the Shiga prefecture.

A flexible circuit board for loading components was adopted for the first time in the industry. But a problem occurred in which the circuit pattern, or electronic wiring, could not be seen clearly after surface processing, and the percentage of good-quality boards was an atrocious 20 percent. With predicted sales figure of 10,000 units a day, this kind of situation was unacceptable. To deal with this issue, the IC business head office's mounting and inspection team, and Hiroshima's Production Control supervisor, gathered at the partner company in Shiga prefecture, reconsidered product standards, and reviewed circuit patterns and surface processing, while implementing a trial and error approach. The quality ratio rose steadily.

New problems arose, along the way. After manufacturing the printed boards, loading a large number of components onto the boards' small surface area caused an interruption of the circuit pattern during the mounting process. The heat of the soldering caused the circuit board to undulate. These major problems were solved through division-crossing cooperation (in this case with support from a mounting technology specialist in Hiroshima) within Sharp, and highly-precise mounting became possible for the first time ever in the mobile phone industry (see ToB-3 in Figure 3.3: a ToB that shares, inspires and creates knowledge relating to manufacturing and inspection). In this way, it became possible to surmount obstacles and develop a camera-mounted mobile phone. A key point for the formation of cross-organizational project teams is that teams sharing various contexts aimed at problem-solving should be formed informally with regard to boundaries between generally different organizations, and among individuals possessing different specializations (knowledge). Then context and knowledge can be shared among the informal teams (ToBs). In Sharp's case, both Sharp and J-Phone were benefitted by Sharp's project networks and J-phone's technological expertise in camera-mounted mobile phone.

After surmounting the problems, Sharp, in a joint development project with J-Phone, launched a Japanese-developed, world- and industry-first, camera-mounted mobile phone (J-SH04) in November 2000. J-Phone gave the name "Sha-mail" to the service that enabled a picture taken with the mounted camera to be sent out as an email attachment. The camera-mounted mobile phones sold in a flash. The J-Phone marketing and sales teams did not just focus on consumers, but carried out numerous application development tests exploiting Sha-mail for practical use with targeted corporate clients from different industries, then publicized the product promptly widely, and acquired good sales. The marketing and sales divisions as functional organizations (see Figure 3.2), as described in the following section, propelled advertising and sales strategies to publicize Sha-mail widely through the formation of networks with specific corporate customers. Regarding the opinions on and technological support for the functions of camera-mounted mobile phones, the functional organizations became the hub of a system constructed a round first-rate technology and after-sales service.

3.4. J-Phone's Incubations with Specific Corporate Clients Collaboration between Businesses in Different Industries

3.4.1. *Accelerating the popularization of "Sha-mail" applications in the medical field*

Collaboration is based on interactive relationships between businesses and customers in other industries, with the goal of finding new markets and expanding existing markets for products and services generated in the strategic creation of new businesses. The leaders and managers must discover and search out key people in businesses in other industries, and then work with them to create and expand new markets. This is also essential for improving the quality of the products and services generated during strategic business creation, so as to create value for customers (Kodama, 2002b). Having customers as strategic partners and working with them to improve the quality of products and services, helps in creating new businesses and expanding markets. J-phone, in the course of increasing the diffusion of the "Sha-mail" into various medical institutions and companies (representative among which are universities) has moved forward with a business strategy of winning over medical institutions throughout Japan.

J-Phone's task was to exploit Sha-mail and mobile networks to realize an environment in Japan, which would allow large numbers of patients to overcome the limitations of space and time, and apply to the emergency medical field, anywhere, any time, and without inconvenience. The key to achieving this goal lay in popularizing Sha-mail among medical institution customers. For this purpose, it was important to create strategic partnership-based business teams with medical institutions and companies, and succeed with a Sha-mail-based medical information network as part of a one-point penetration strategy.

It was important for J-Phone to apply the knowledge, expertise and new ideas gained in creating its first team in the business it would create with its second strategic partner. This, along with innovative leadership on the part of leaders and managers to further popularize Sha-mail, provided important knowledge for the company.

The strategic collaboration that J-Phone promoted in the field of medicine could be seen in the business expansion the company achieved through a series of consecutive strategic partnerships with universities and large medical institutions and technical companies, such as the following:

May 2001: Partnership in the joint development of mobile medical systems with Philips Medical Corp. and Infocom Corp.

October 2001: Launched CT and MRI image transmission experiments with several medical institutes and companies through Sha-mail.

January 2002: Partnership in the emergency medical field with Kyourin Medical University using Sha-mail.

In this manner, J-phone has created and succeeded with Sha-mail applications in the medical fields. The new virtual medical services that combine these types of multimedia technologies and services in the medical fields can be viewed as a new form of knowledge-based service (Davis *et al.*, 1994; Kodama, 1999).

New business model combining communication and broadcasting services

Other J-Phone challenges were to collaborate with TV broadcasting companies, and to create a strategic partnership with TV-Aichi Corp. regarding the trial service combining Sha-mail and TV programs. This trial service enabled Sha-mail users to interactively participate in live TV by sending an image, pictures or text information through Sha-mail in advance. While enjoying a program on television, for example, a user would be able to participate interactively by using a Sha-mail mobile phone after going to J-Phone's web site (J-SKY) and sending image, pictures, or text. In addition to the strong entertainment value of the trial service, broadcasters would be able to obtain basic demographic information about their interactive viewers, such as their age, gender and location for marketing purposes.

3.4.3. New business model promoting the creation of consumer communities

Sha-mail is a service that allows people to take pictures with a camera-mounted mobile phone and send them as e-mail attachments. Its user-friendly features resulted in increased popularity and expension. In addition to being able to send pictures to other J-phone users, the Sha-mail service allows users to send photos to other mobile operator subscribers. J-Phone further enhanced Sha-mail communication possibilities by introducing the "Sha-mail album," a service that allows users to save and upload photos and create and display original photo albums online. This service enabled subscribers to display all their Sha-mail pictures on J-Phone's web site (J-SKY). Users can create their own original "Sha-mail album" on J-SKY by sending their pictures to a user address issued at the time of subscriber registration. The completed album can be viewed not only on J-Phone handsets adapted to J-SKY, but also on other operators' handsets and PCs with Internet access. This service can promote and enhance the user communities and contribute to the further growth of Sha-mail.

As described above, Sha-mail was driven by close collaboration between functional organizations at J-Phone, such as the Takao-led project and the marketing and sales division. Within J-Phone, each division's leaders and managers (including top management) were formed into leadership teams as ToBs. Then the leadership teams established a strong business process linkage among development, marketing, sales, publicity and advertising, equipment and after-sales service for its camera-mounted mobile phones. DoCoMo's organizational system was described in Chapter 2, but J-Phone as a communications carrier promotes new business development as a project, and has the functional organizations to promote exploitative practice to establish and distribute new business effectively and efficiently (as with Takao's project). These functional systems build individual independent networks. They then create markets as new knowledge through knowledge-sharing (see Figure 3.2), that arises from network competencies engendered through leadership teams formed among organizations.

3.5. Sharp's Technology Integration

This case study makes it clear that the development of the camera-mounted mobile phone is a result of technology integration that utilizes the abilities of engineers who possess the knowledge of various specialist technologies. In other words, the phone is the result of fusion of core technologies possessed by Sharp's various technology organizations including communications, information, liquid crystal, image processing, and semiconductors (IC, CMOS and other technologies). Current mobile phone technology has advanced still further. As shown in Figure 3.4, mobile phone system architecture comprises range of hardware and software. Software technology such as applications, middleware and operating systems processes fast game distribution, music distribution, image distribution, TV phones and other rich content. Dedicated LSI systems are required for this software to execute high-speed processing, and different hardware technologies are required to execute high-speed mobile communications processing. The accessories of high-functioning cameras, colour displays, and high-functioning batteries require further development. As with far-reaching innovations in specialist technologies, technology integration increasingly requires the fusion of multiple technology fields. At the same time, in individual hardware and software fields, engineers with varied, in-depth knowledge in specialist domains have come to need high-tech companies, as Sharp did in the ICT field.

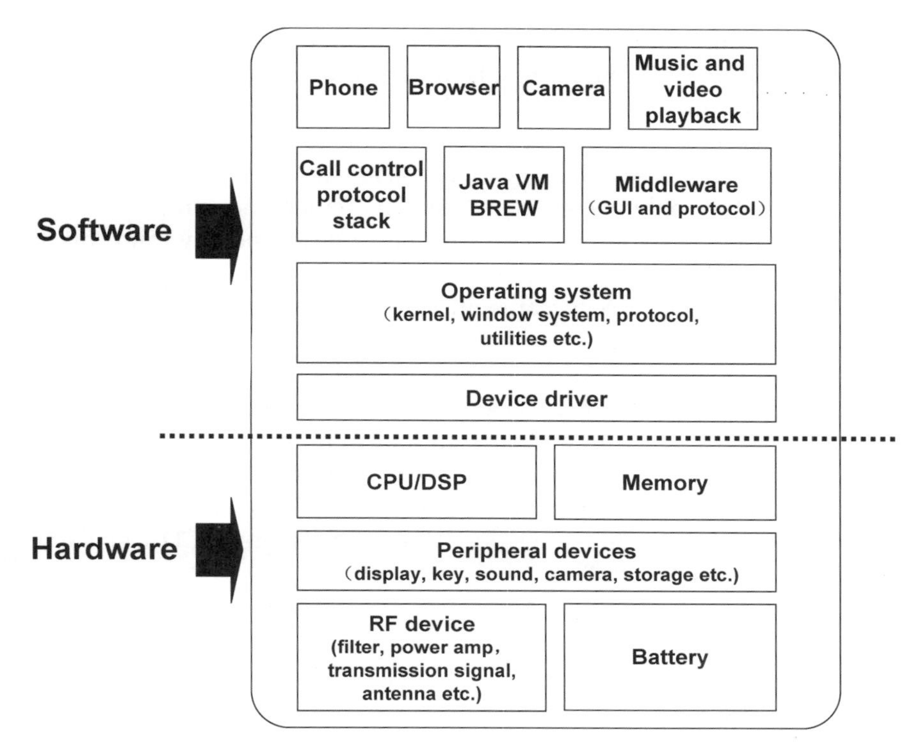

Figure 3.4: System architecture for mobile handset (example).

It follows that the key to revolutionary technological innovation and independent products lays emphasis on fusing multiple technology fields. In addition to the vertical fusion arising from "only one product" with high value-added from "only one device," horizontal fusion integrating the core technologies of inter-device technology, image, communications and information is also required. While Sharp has always effectively exploited its accumulated technology resources, it can be deemed an outstanding company that accurately grasps the changing times and competitive environment, and is not prepossessed with the frame of individual technology fields, but unites people who surmount divisional barriers by crossing organizational boundaries, and unites specialist technology. The organizational capability for this technology integration could be termed Sharp's DNA. According to founder Tokuji Hayakawa, who rapidly found success with radio and TV commercialization, it is the "manufacturing mindset". Hayakawa's DNA that led to "creating products that rivals copy" continues to be inherited by Sharp's engineers, and the drive for "only one technology that other companies cannot copy" and a "black box strategy" has a connection to current management. Sharp's distinctive research and development, and commercialization trials rooted in the "only one strategy," lie in its "emergency project teams". Sharp's product development based on "only one technology" and "black box strategy" did not happen overnight.

The emergency project teams are controlled by the CEO. They are chosen and formed from special priority lists and draw personnel from various specializations and development divisions. The aim is to launch an important product swiftly. These project teams came into being in first half of the 1970s, when in order to win out in a fierce calculator war in competition with Casio Computer Co., Ltd., the researchers and engineers from the calculator and liquid crystal technology divisions formed cross-organizational teams and developed the world's first LCD calculator within a year (see Figure 3.5).

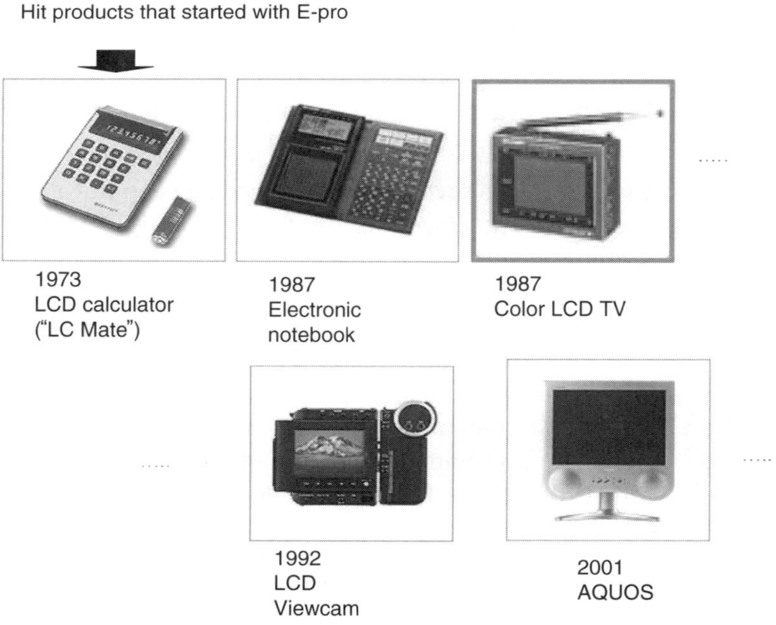

Hit products that started with E-pro

1973
LCD calculator
("LC Mate")

1987
Electronic
notebook

1987
Color LCD TV

1992
LCD
Viewcam

2001
AQUOS

Figure 3.5: Hit products from emergency projects.
Source: Data provided by Sharp.

The emergency project team was fully systematized in 1977. Responding to the theme, specialist engineers throughout the company (each project comprising of 10 to 13 or 14 people) were mobilized, and within a limited time period brought a product to its commercial phase. Sharp even today, implements this project system. The year 1979 saw the creation of a large number of hit products including the front loading VTR, the electronic notebook, the three-inch color liquid-crystal TV, the liquid-crystal Viewcam, the color-screen Zaurus PDA, and the Mebius computer (see Figure 3.5).

Sharp's current flagship hit, the liquid-crystal "Aquos" TV, got its start as a project to develop a large-scale, liquid-crystal TV. In 1998, Katsuhiko Machida, after assuming the post of CEO, concentrated management resources in liquid crystal, and in the fall of 1998, an elite group of engineers assembled from the TV and liquid crystal divisions. On this occasion, as with the camera-mounted mobile phones, various specialist engineers collaborated, cleared up a number of technology issues, and forged ahead to develop a liquid crystal TV that is related to the current version. The liquid crystal, TV and LSI engineers were completely focused on performance and quality. They persevered in making screen processing adjustments for screen contrast and rapid motion response, and for the visual aspects of good panel capability and a high-resolution screen.

In 2000, a "tatami project" was formed within the company. This project was initiated to produce a large-scale liquid-screen TV from mother glass that was the size of a large tatami mat used in traditional Japanese rooms. It later became possible to complete an integrated manufacturing plant that produced everything from the world's first liquid crystal to liquid-crystal TV.

Sharp's technology headquarters, centered on the technology and research & development divisions, comprises the platform technology laboratory, ecology technology development center, information electrical appliance development center, system development center and the overseas laboratory. The basic aim of the technology headquarters focused on pursuing a commercialized mindset and ingenuity. Both a short- and long-term strategy were planned, and the pursuit of ingenuity with regard to "only one technology" and "only one product," as well as success in creating business, were required.

The emergency projects are managed from this technology headquarters, where a technology general meeting is held every month and project teams are decided on. Usually around ten teams are active. Development application topics are deliberated on previously at a meeting of laboratory heads and considered for debate at the general technology meeting.

The project leaders are chosen from middle management, and have the authority to assemble people equipment and other necessary resources by crossing the divisional boundaries of the business and laboratory divisions. The project members are inevitably drawn from the planning division, and product planning that introduces and sells customer-focused marketing knowledge (customer focus) is also targeted. The division heads, as supervisors who propose development plans to general technology meetings, and selected project leaders must commit themselves to the development content and schedule determined at the technology general meeting. Moreover, the business divisions that account for a high share of emergency projects have a high reputation within the company for management, and this enhances competitive motivation among them. The butting and cannibalization for development among business divisions also disappears.

This emergency project system consists of a series of temporary projects that cross organizational and knowledge (specialist) boundaries. These emergency projects play an important role in training Sharp employees. When a project breaks up and returns to the business division once more, the new knowledge discipline in the emergency project becomes a driving force aimed at self-growth and taking on further challenges. The more capable the engineer, the more he or she is sought for emergency projects. Once one project is over, he or she is likely to be pulled in for the next one.

Graduates of these emergency projects, include the current head of Sharp's business division and the business general manager. Some employees, moreover, apply for emergency projects for new development repeatedly, and often become project members or leaders. CEO Katsuhiko Machida made the following comment about emergency projects:

> *"I used to suffer at the start of the emergency projects. There were organizational barriers to extracting good personnel, and the division head was not keen. Since that time, however, there has been a better understanding of the employees' emergency projects, and discussions among the business division have grown deeper. Engineers chosen for the emergency projects are all excellent, and many of them have become division heads or general managers. People are quick to understand the nature of*

emergency projects. The atmosphere is one where it is easy to break down organizational barriers and talk to people."

It follows that nearly all the Sharp employees have a high level of understanding about these projects, and this is supported by the company's corporate headquarters. A project management feature at Sharp, as a prime example, is that the accumulation of individual knowledge and expertise after the project is completed can be transferred to another project as tacit knowledge.

Moreover, employees learn through the projects, and a project learning spiral whereby knowledge and skills are enhanced through projects is embedded within the company. I am offering this Sharp project management as a case with a different viewpoint to that of an existing study, focused on the US and Europe, which suggests that project learning does not easily take root.

However, the development of the camera-mounted mobile phone described above was not an example of an emergency project. The IC business headquarters in charge of the camera module and the system business headquarters in charge of mobile phone business achieved their feat through the impetus of spontaneous informal dialog and collaboration. In other words each employee realized the development that shared and integrated knowledge and technologies from the routine activities of their business division by spontaneously crossing organizational and specialist knowledge boundaries. In Sharp, this kind of free cooperative system and teamwork among business divisions was embedded in the organizational culture. The emergency project was formed bottom-up through the proposals of middle managers, then top-down through authorization by the CEO or the general manager (of course, there are cases of emergency projects that are led top-down from the start).

The camera-mounted mobile phone development case can be thought of as a middle management, bottom-up project structure. The top role at this time was that of project support. Ideally, a climate is established where middle managers spontaneously implement informal projects crossing division boundaries. I would like to use the term "creative collaboration" for the kind of organizational behavior exhibited by the Sharp employees. The employees' creative collaboration promoted dialog between the organizational and knowledge (specialization) boundaries, and became a resource for the formation of ToBs.

This creative collaboration is a cooperative employee organizational behavior where all staff share the vision of "only one management," and are happy to help other divisions. Then they promote these new issues within ToBs through creative confrontation or abrasion (Leonard-Barton, 1995) and productive friction (Hagel III and Brown, 2005), or sometimes through political negotiating practice (Brown and Duguid, 2001).

In these ToBs, some actors form leadership teams among leaders from other divisions. So how did Sharp develop a climate conducive for ToBs and leadership teams?

I believe that in the background of the realization of "only one technology" and the "black box," there is the fusion of individuals. At Sharp, there is little resistance to engineers with different specialist technology knowledge gathering and working together. CEO Katsuhiko Machida says the following:

> *Sharp can be considered a company with "the power of harmony". I want to treat this importantly. "Harmony" indicates a fusion of technologies. We have skillfully integrated device products, and created the camera-mounted mobile phone and Sha-mail. Canon and Motorola only have communications technology. The camera-mounted mobile phone and Sha-mail grew out of a mix of communications technology, image technology and the Zaurus information processing technology. A chemical reaction yields the crystal. We make new products from the same principles. The question is how to bring about the chemical reaction. The distinctive power of harmony possessed by the Japanese is important. For example, the people who have been in charge of the latest semiconductor technology might be told to supervise the electrical home appliance products tomorrow. Usually, people would quit. At Sharp, we achieve harmony by accepting heterogeneous things. If you can easily get a chemical reaction, then you can build an environment that facilitates the creation of crystals. I will not accept corporate constraints on this quality. Corporate constraints cannot enable fusion. Technology grows more complex, and there are limits to what one person can think of alone. In the coming era, the concept of combining to create other products will become important.*

The power of this "harmony" that Machida observes seems to be more developed at Sharp than in other Japanese company. Gathering employees to pursue original technologies, jointly contributing individual knowledge, and developing a teamwork management style, while keeping the Japanese quality of harmony is one of Sharp's, key strengths.

"Harmony" as practiced by the Sharp management is the dual mindset of sincerity and originality, which have the following meanings. "Sincerity" is moral principle and devotion to one's work. "Harmony" is strength and solidarity in believing together. "Manners" is appreciating and respecting each other. "Originality" is progress effort and improvement. "Bravery" is the source of one's reason for living the willingnes approach a problem or difficulty. This DNA of sincerity and originality permeates and resonates with all employees as values (Kodama, 2001), promotes teamwork among different organizations, and gives rise to a "chemical reaction". The result is to return to "only one" technology, product and management.

3.6. Establishing Competitive Dominance with Networked ToBs

Sharp operates in an environment embracing market structures and technological innovations that are subject to rapid change. Companies that constantly need to come up with new strategies must have organizations that foster value-chain integration. I interpret Sharp's "spiral strategy" as the starting point of network strategy through ToBs. This strategy enhances the reciprocal elements of the product-to-product (device) spiral, development and production spiral, and people and organizations spiral, and creates synergistic effects. As mentioned below, the product-to-product (device) spiral, development and production spiral, and sales and production spiral can be realized through the formation of networked ToBs. The result is value-chain integration (see Figure 3.6). With the "research and development ToB," Sharp continuously created a new "black box" knowledge-accumulating core "only one" technology arising from technological dominance. With product development and manufacturing ToB, original, low-cost, high-quality products were created from improvements and increased efficiency of new design concepts and manufacturing processes.

The product planning ToB plans products based on new concepts through interactions with markets (customers). The sales ToB aims at quickly dominating the market for the created products and customer-oriented solutions through various sales channels, as well as global sales

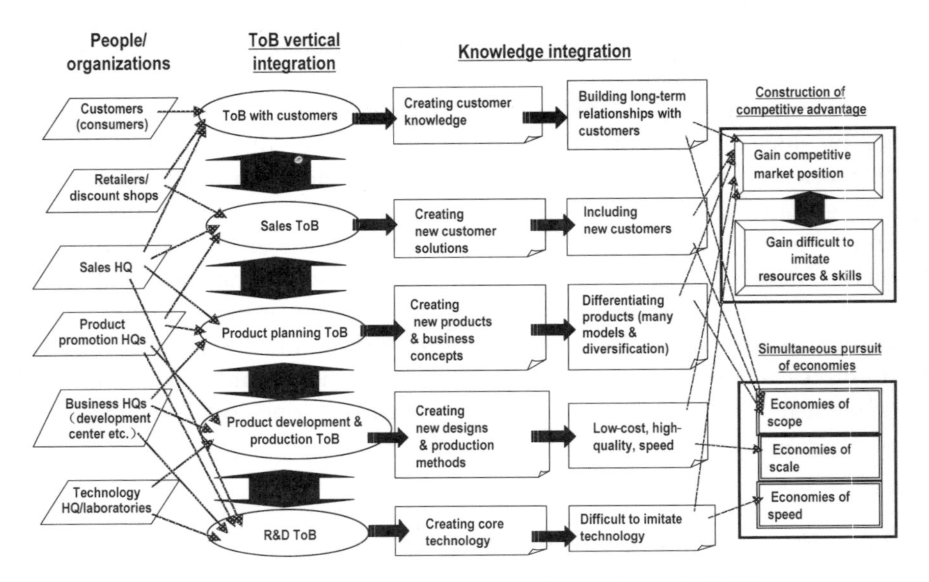

Figure 3.6: Value-chain integration from networked ToBs.

and advertising activities. The ToB with the customer receives feedback (opinions, hopes and complaints) from various sales routes (including the Internet) and customers, takes initiatives toward customer satisfaction and reflects new product planning. These ToBs do not exist independently, but each is linked organically. First, the networked ToB that links the research and development ToB and the product development and production ToB enables the creation of superior technology products under the "only one" principle that are difficult to imitate, and are based on new design concepts (simultaneously pursuing speed, quality, cost and other factors) that consider core technologies and the manufacturing process.

This is how the integrated production models of the liquid crystal TV (product division) and liquid crystal devices (device division), which transcended divisional and specialist borders, were realized. Image and liquid crystal experts worked together and practised daily improvement of the hands-on production process, swiftly dealt with issues, and linked up with engineers in the product planning and device divisions. They also prioritized cross-functional lateral links between laboratory, development centers at each business headquarters and manufacturing technology development promotion HQ (development and management of design and manufacturing processes). In this way, they contributed to the creation of new business models, while producing impressive results in terms of development efficiency and product performance. Also at the same time, the rationalizing of distribution and the product inspection process were linked to shorter production lead times. In the Mie prefecture, site of the Kameyama factory, around 40 liquid-crystal related companies have formed a production cluster. Sharp shares information and knowledge with other companies concerning development and production, and practices concurrent engineering.

The strong linkage between these ToBs helps optimize not just the ToB section, but also the technological strategy of the company. This further helps in reducing the lead time for product launch and improve quality, product innovation, cost leadership that contribute to economies of scale. It also becomes possible to achieve speed economies of product innovation simultaneously with product cost leadership, thus contributing to economies of scale.

For mobile phones, a product investment with numerous value chains becomes possible and also contributes to economies of scale. Camera-mounted mobile phones and large-scale liquid-crystal TVs are representatives of the "hands-on production" from networked ToBs. The interplay of products and devices arises from the creation of networks between research and development ToBs and product development and production ToBs. Sharp goes beyond user-oriented product development to concentrate on technology-oriented commercialization. Realistically, the customer can hardly describe the product he or she potentially desires in terms of formal knowledge. Accordingly, Sharp pursues management that effects social change. It emphasizes marketing at the research and development stage, and impresses the customer with new products based on innovative technology and devices.

Sharp emphasizes inter-engineer dialog, including the top management, to motivate its engineers. At Sharp, researchers, component developers and product planning engineers (including top management and sales supervisors) gather and hold meetings on research and development. During these meetings, sales, product planning, product development, and laboratory staff discuss at length their opinions on making a successful product. This kind of exchange among employees from different backgrounds and specializations is the source of the creation of new knowledge linking research and development ToBs, product development and production ToBs, product planning ToBs and sales ToBs.

The second point is that apart from creating a network of ToBs for product development and production, product planning, sales, and the customer, and strengthening sales and marketing prowess, the company must also grasp customer needs, and create differentiated new product concepts, along with the product diversity capability and speed to realise these products technologically.

Establishing the network contributes to economies of scale, enabling the acquisition of new customers and retaining the existing customers. At Sharp's domestic sales HQ's sales strategy force — "Attack Team of Market Promotion Division" (here, ATMPD) — various sales and customer branches are assembled to form of networks of sales ToB and customer ToB.

So expertise on how to sell Sharp's products (in Sharp's language, "developing stories that sell products") condensed through "only one" technology accumulates daily, and guides business at many sales branches. Moreover, the special sales force of the ATMPD itself takes on the role of building bridges between customers and sales branches. Furthermore, ATMPD develops sales and application technologies and incorporates scientific marketing techniques (academic marketing) to think of new product concepts. At present, it is linking development teams and involving them in new product development. Successful examples of ToB networks of product development and manufacturing, product and planning, and sales include an air cleaner and air conditioner loaded with antibacterial ions, and a fully-automated washing machine with an ion cleaner and odor-resistant coat.

In 1985, while Sharp was proposing and creating product concepts, it established a lifestyle software center division (currently a part of the Only One Planning and Product Promotion Headquarters). This organization collected and analyzed information by listening to lead users and exchanging opinions with representatives from other industries, executed planning promotion of the new product, and collaborated closely with each business headquarter, while dynamically promoting the development of new technologies. At the call center that integrates Sharp's product reliability headquarters, customer information (including complaints and hopes) relating to all Sharp products is gathered and promptly fed into a mechanism that sends the feedback to the product planning, product development, production, and quality control divisions. This results in ideas on improving existing products and planning new products.

The role of the integrated call center is to build bridges between product development and production, product planning, sales and customer ToBs. Further, in February 2006, Sharp's separate publicity, sales promotion and Internet divisions were clubbed together to establish a brand strategy promotion headquarters. From the standpoint of brand superiority, focusing on the customer, and overall optimization, this headquarters is taking on the role of collaborating with the product planning division and communicating Sharp's product concepts to the consumers. As mentioned above, Sharp's productivity and global sales ability, which demonstrates how product development power is linked to markets, and the power of hard-to-copy "only one" technology and cost leadership that supports it, has created a distinctive value chain that differs from those of its competitors. This has helped Sharp gain a competitive and distinctive market positioning (Porter,1985), and hard-to-copy resources and capacities (Barney, 1991).

Sharp has been successful in pursing and achieving the contradictions of economies of scale, scope, and speed as business drivers. Together with developing ICT (Information & Communication Technology), as transaction and interaction costs fall, the simultaneous pursuit of three different economies grows difficult, and well-informed people say that the concentration and selection strengthens a company's business domain specializations (Hegel and Singer, 1999). This holds good for implemenlation of strategies under conditions of certainity. On the other hand, the potential for creative and productive conflict and interaction, both within and among companies, to transcend existing core competences, acquire new competences, and create innovations is hidden. Accordingly, it is important to consider the interaction costs among and within companies not simply as an expense, but as a resource to foster innovation.

The ToBs comprise of employees with subjective viewpoints. In a changing environment, these employees create new meanings and pragmatic boundaries (Carlile, 2004; Kodama, 2006) related to vision and strategic objectives. It is important for project leaders and managers, whose stance is that of guiding subordinates, to change the heterogeneous contexts of a number of ToBs that the leaders or managers are committed to. The leaders or managers should appreciate and share, and then dynamically modify the context of the subjective ToB.

Project leaders, through dialog and creative collaboration, decide on either embracing the changing environment or form a completely new environment and thereby and generate and engender the creation of and links to ToB (Kodama, 2005). Then, in the networked ToB, based on trust among employees (Vangen *et al.*, 2003), deep knowledge and high embeddedness (Granovetter, 1985) is promoted, and new knowledge is constantly created as a result of close collaboration (high involvement) (DiMaggio and Powel, 1983). ToB dynamics — creating and linking ToBs — are necessary for employees to acquire new knowledge. This is the concept of Sharp's dynamic view of strategy through the creation of ToB networks (Kodama, 2006).

3.7. Conclusion

In the 21 century, where the construction of new business models through the integration of heterogeneous technologies and services is demanded (as in the case of Sharp), companies must synthesize the various boundaries existing within and outside the company from multiple perspectives, and continuously create new targeted knowledge.

Organizational capability that is at the core of innovation, is created from boundaries where professionals with various specializations from different organizations within and outside the company work together. The integration of the large number of boundaries within and outside the company, or in other words, the networked ToB, promotes knowledge integration and transformation, and enables a company to be competitive and consolidate its dominant market position.

4

Radical Innovation through Integrative Competencies of Project-Based Organizations: Case Study of Mitsubishi Electric

4.1. Introduction

This chapter proposes a basic framework in which the integration of various organizational and knowledge boundaries straddling different organizations within and outside a company can create new knowledge. Through an in-depth analysis of Mitsubishi Electric, this chapter considers the dynamism that integrates knowledge by promoting the absorption of external knowledge by horizontally-integrated teams of boundaries (ToBs) through strategic alliances among companies and the integration of knowledge by networking vertically-integrated ToBs within companies.

With recent developments in IT, there is an increasing need for merging different technologies, as well as developing products and services and building business models across different industries. Technological innovation, until now, has developed as a result of the deep pursuit of specialized knowledge. However, increasingly there are cases in which radical innovation is realized in the development new concepts for new products. Examples include development of new core components through technology integration where technologies of one field will merge with those in another fields, and the architecture of the product is transformed simultaneously.

In this chapter, I consider the product development process of Mitsubishi Electric, a traditional Japanese corporation, as it effected the integration of different technologies and the transformation of technology architecture in its aim to realize a new multimedia communication system.

4.2. Visual Communication

In the background of the development of broadband and great progress being made in video and audio encoding technology, the multimedia tool market that includes videoconferencing systems, videophones and web-conferencing systems (referred to in this volume as visual communication systems) has been taking off on a global scale. These visual communication systems are not only used in business to transmit video information, but also show promise in fields such as education, medicine and welfare, as well as a means for personal communication. From corporations to individuals, visual communication systems have become promising tools and have long been attracting attention in the domain of technology development.

With the rapid penetration of ISDN since 1995, the videoconferencing market in Japan has been growing and with the growth of broadband and IP over the past few years, there is a fall in the prices of visual communication systems. The past two or three years have witnessed the adoption of IP-based videoconferencing systems by users and the shift of existing ISDN-based systems to IP. Broadband and IP will continue to lower the costs of products and communications in future and these cost reductions will help in market expansion (Figure 4.1).

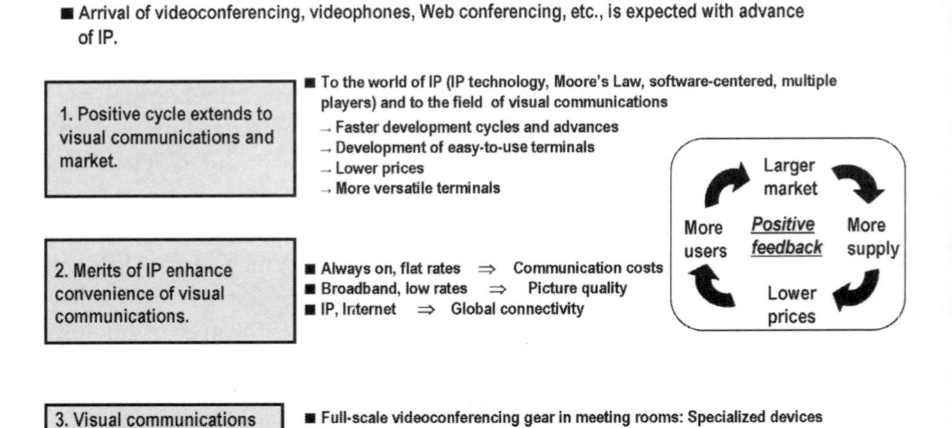

Figure 4.1: Growth in use of visual communications.

In this chapter, I review the history of product development in visual communication systems so far, and consider how advances in product architecture have greatly influenced the business strategies of individual businesses and have been decisive in determining key players in the world. I also introduce Mitsubishi Electric, a representative manufacturer of electrical devices in Japan, as a case study, in order to analyze and consider how the company has used visual communication systems to expand the Japanese market and introduce changes in product architecture.

4.3. Trends in Global Visual Communications

In the background of advancements in broadband and 3G mobile phones in Europe, France Telecom has already formed tie-ups with switch server gateway vendors such as Alcatel, Siemens, Lucent and Radvision (Israel), and with IP-based videophone companies such as Leadtek (Taiwan), to provide various broadband video services (including interconnectivity with 3G mobile phones) mainly within France (Figure 4.2). In Italy, a new fixed-line carrier called Fastweb, is offering triple-play service (video-on-demand, VoIP [Voice over IP], and high-speed Internet) that includes VoIP video communication service (Figure 4.3). And in Sweden, Bredbandsbolaget has been creating demand for their product — and is used by community housing and expanding corporate users. The product offers triple-play service that includes video VoIP.

It can be predicted that the separate fixed-line and mobile service markets that exist today will change into a single Fixed Mobile Convergence (FMC) market. (A portion of this service has already been launched in the UK.) It is also conceivable that technology development or service development concerning areas such as high-speed handover between 3G (and 4G) mobile and wireless LANs will advance. Fixed-line communications and mobile phones have had separate terminals and services. In the future, users might receive both mobile and fixed-line services for a single terminal, a single phone number and a single contract. Then, fixed-line communications and mobile communications will probably be merged as a single service. As mentioned earlier, the networked broadband (fixed-line and mobile communications) will trigger the market expansion for visual communication systems.

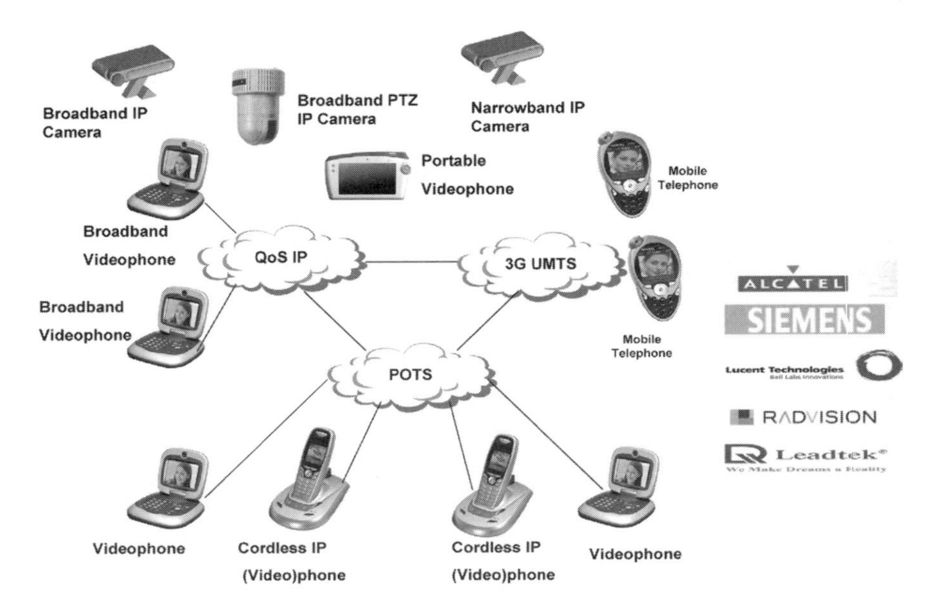

Figure 4.2: Broadband communications in France.
Source: Leadtek

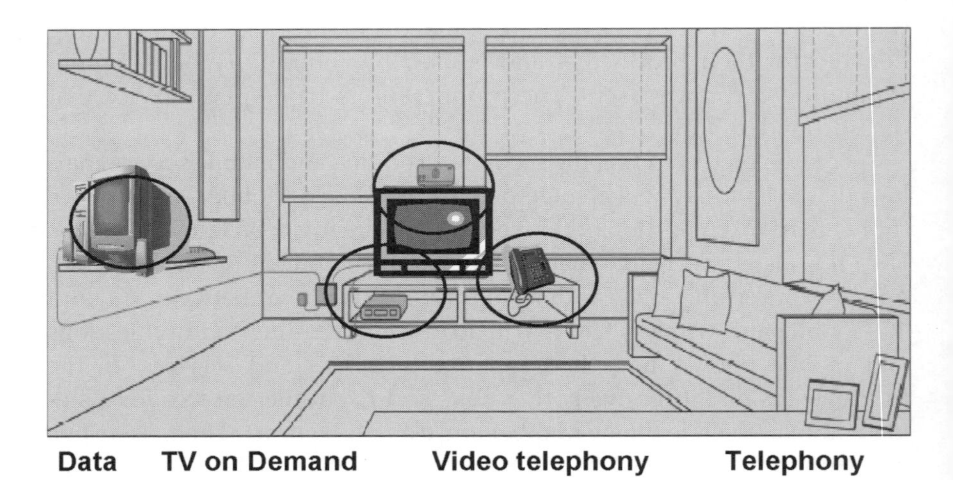

Figure 4.3: Integrated IP service using Italy's fastWeb.
Source: RADVISION

4.4. Changes in the Product Architecture and Market for Visual Communication Systems

For manufacturers of visual communication systems in the beginning of the 1990s, the central technological theme for visual communication systems utilizing leased lines or ISDN was high-quality video and audio coding and compression based on switching circuit technology. In developing this system, reliability and stability were constant requirements, and developers had to concentrate on compression of high-quality multimedia data and transmission of through a narrow transmission band. It was necessary to develop dedicated LSIs as technical hardware to realize this high-quality video and audio encoding and compression (Step 1 in Figure 4.4). Engineers thus aimed to boost the processing power (calculations/second) of dedicated LSIs, reduce power consumption, and improve performance in the architecture of the manufacturer's main proprietary hardware. Dedicated LSIs in the 1980s used hardware-based architecture in which the various function blocks realizing video and audio encoding were designed with dedicated logic wiring.

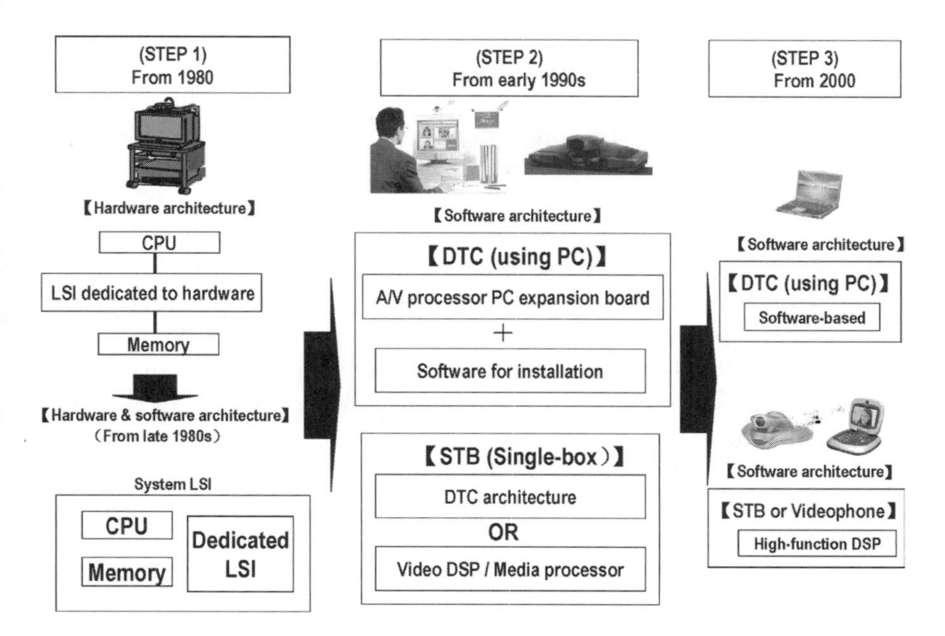

Figure 4.4: Advances in visual communication system architecture.

From the late 1980s through the first half of the 1990s, a hybrid type (the so-called system LSIs) that merged the method of using multiple processors to realize each function block and the method of configuration involving multiple dedicated hardware blocks was used. Since the hardware body of dedicated LSIs evolved into system LSIs with built-in CPUs, the element of software was added as part of the architecture.

The method of realizing dedicated LSI varies from manufacturer to manufacturer, and engineers at each company polish core technologies to realize a visual communication system. However, the price of visual communication systems was high — at several millions of yen — and the market for these systems consisted of mainly the corporate users. Besides the high cost of the systems, communication charges were based on volume which presented a major hurdle to users who preferred the system. During this time, PictureTel of the US had around 40% of the market share and Sony of Japan had around 20%.

Compared to this, Mitsubishi Electric known for its dedicated LSIs for video processing had around 40% market share in the Japanese market. Mitsubishi Electric's road map of video communication system products is shown in Figure 4.5. The company developed its own dedicated LSIs for the MELFACE 300, 700, 810 and 880 series, and sold them as large dedicated visual communication systems, thus expanding its presence in the Japanese market. The videoconferencing systems at the Japanese Ministry of Internal Affairs and Communications are made by Mitsubishi Electric.

Soon visual communication systems became affordable (Step 2 in Figure 4.4). Products with new architectures that did not use dedicated LSIs entered the market. These products were manufactured mostly by American companies. A representative example is the DTC (Desk Top Conference) with videoconferencing functions running on Windows 3.1 PC, which. PictureTel introduced as a commercial product in 1992. After that, Intel released ProShare, a DTC product with a price tag of less than 300,000 yen. In 1995, NTT of Japan released Phoenix, a DTC product for less than 200,000 yen. The DTC market expanded locally and globally Apart from large corporations, this market comprised of small and medium-sized corporations and individuals.

This DTC enables not only the exchange of video and audio data, but also helps share data on a PC (using the T.120 international standard that allowed Whiteboard, Word, Excel and other application software to communicate with each other). Dedicated boards with general-purpose

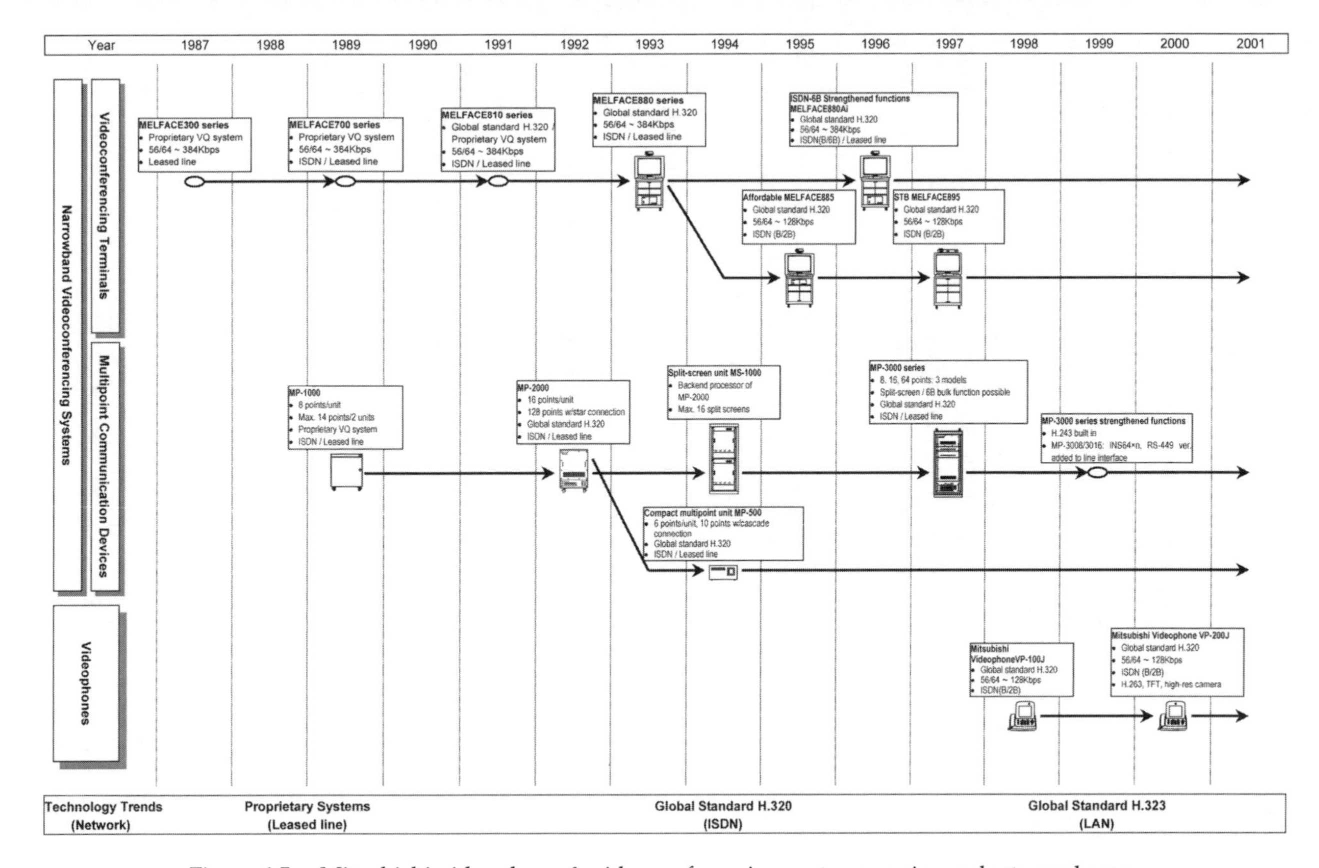

Figure 4.5: Mitsubishi videophone & videoconferencing systems: main products road map.

processors such as DSPs (digital signal processors) could be inserted into the expansion slots of PCs. The transmission of video and audio data occurred over the PCI bus of the PC, which also allowed high-speed data transmissions.

In Step 2, American manufacturers realized affordable visual communication systems by developing PC expansion boards with low-cost, general-purpose processors and software drivers capable of running in the Windows 95 environment, and did not utilize the dedicated LSIs in Step 1. They also used GUIs (graphical user interfaces) to build a system configuration that allowed users to easily set parameters for the PC expansion boards and control the system. This expansion PC board with bundled software was based on an architecture that could be used with PCs made by any manufacturer. This was known as epoch-making technology.

PictureTel used this sort of PC architecture to develop and release to the market a single-unit dedicated visual communication system that did not use a PC. This system was a set-top box (STB) product that was even more affordable than dedicated devices utilizing existing dedicated LSIs.

The DTC and STB also represented the realization of modular innovation utilizing software-based architecture. Modularization establishes individual interfaces with little mutual dependence among configuration elements.[1] Compared with the visual communication system where an integral architecture based on dedicated LSIs in which configuration elements in the hardware body at Step 1 were strongly dependent on each other, DTC and STB were realized with software operating on general-purpose processors (such as CPUs and DSPs) as modules. In DTC, a data was sharing function was then added as a software module. Since DTC and STB are software-based architectures, support was very easy, as products could be updated to new versions without changing the hardware.

---

[1] Modular architecture possesses the merits of diversity and strategic flexibility in product version upgrade and lineup variation (Sanchez, 1995, 1996, 2000; Worren *et al.*, 2002). However, from the manufacturer's perspective, it is more important to add value to the independently-developed modules. In black-box module development, it is necessary for the company to embed proprietary technological know-how through an integral architecture. For instance, Japanese manufacturers' expertise in system LSI, various analog devices, precision instrument components, TI's DSP and Intel's MPU all possess such value in their modules. As was discussed in Chapter 6, the key is in developing the black-box modules used in digital consumer products such as DVD recorders and digital cameras (Kodama, 2007).

In this way, product architecture changed from being hardware-centered to a software-based modular architecture utilizing general-purpose processors. If we focus on the video and audio signal processing functions or the communication processing functions of videoconferencing systems, there have been no major changes (regarding links between configuration elements) in the architecture in Step 1 and Step 2. However, since the core concept of the configuration elements making the architecture possible has undergone a major change, it can be said that DTC and STB are also modular innovations (Henderson and Clark, 1990). PictureTel and Sony were able to quickly dominate the global market by successfully downsizing expensive dedicated systems through affordable DTCs and STBs.

On the other hand, companies such as Mitsubishi Electric and NEC which were developing visual communication systems released products that supported new architectures. (As shown in Figure 4.5, Mitsubishi Electric's products were the affordable Melface STB, and the VP-100J and VP-200J videoconferencing systems.) From 1995, the Japanese market was dominated by the US-based companies, PictureTel and Polycom. (Later, Polycom acquired PictureTel and now enjoys the No. 1 position in the global market with 40% market share.)

One of the factors that contributed to the failure of Japanese manufacturers was their delay in their technological response to new modular innovations. In 1995, ISDN was enjoying rapid growth in Japan, and Japanese manufacturers were focusing mainly on how to transmit high-quality video over the narrow band that was ISDN. Japanese manufacturers, therefore, concentrated their resources on developing dedicated LSIs that was their strongpoint (or system LSIs with software elements), and developed highly-functional visual communication systems. Viewed from the market perspective, visual communication systems have not yet penetrated the market in Japan as they have in Europe or American markets and only large corporations have been adopting them. The face that high video quality was more important than price seems to have encouraged Japanese manufacturers to focus on technology. Japanese corporate users' preference for high video quality has kept Japanese manufacturers focused on technological solutions.

On the other hand, the adoption of IT at corporations in Europe and America has progressed faster than it has in Japan, and the penetration of visual communication systems has also been increasing each year in America and Europe. In such a market environment in Europe and

America, corporations have been demanding affordable visual communication systems, and they have also been increasingly requesting application-sharing or data-sharing, which utilizes not only video and audio, but also the PCs. User needs at corporations in Europe and America focused on sharing audio and data; video quality was not their foremost requirement. To lower prices of visual communication systems, American videoconferencing vendors reviewed the picture compression requirements of processing capabilities, and adopted new architecture that focused on general-use parts, modularization and software processing. At the same time, they aimed at cutting production costs by outsourcing the assembly of boards and other hardware products.

It is important to note that except Sony, Japanese manufacturers did not dominate the global market. In the corporate adoption of videoconferencing systems, elements that are particularly emphasized in sales also became part of the decision-making videoconferencing system process in which the manufacturer decides on adoption of its products by overseas subsidiaries or sales/manufacturing partners. Accordingly, the advantage of American vendors such as PictureTel or Polycom, which have been enjoying strong sales overseas, was high. On the other hand, Sony whose visual communication systems had penetrated the global market from the beginning, fell slightly behind American manufacturers in supporting the new architecture, and now has the No. 2 position behind Polycom in terms of Japanese market share. Sony has 13% of the global market and is No. 3 behind Polycom and Tandberg of Finland.

We have touched upon Step 3 of Figure 4.4. The destructive technology of IP (Christensen, 1997) and the higher performance of CPUs (Central Processing Units) in PCs have led to further lowering costs of visual communication systems compared to the conventional videoconferencing system. Real-time encoding of not only audio, but also moving video is enabled by improvements in CPU performance following Moore's Law, and videoconferencing became possible with CPUs already existing in PCs, instead of dedicated processors, A/V processing software and commercially-available cameras (for instance, Skype, familiar to most readers, uses this sort of technology).

At present, global vendors are developing and selling products that use this software-based architecture, and competition in the market is building up. Compared with processor-type products in Step 2, software-based products are restricted by the disadvantage of lower-quality video and audio, and by the fact that PCs have to be used. Software-based products are also subject to price competition, and manufacturers cannot make large profits without pursuing scale or range of economy. High-performance, low-priced DSPs are also penetrating the market, in addition to low-priced STB-type or videophone-type videoconferencing systems that utilize DSPs. All these products use broadband IP networks.

During the transformation from Step 1 to Step 3, the cost of visual communication systems experienced a huge drop over the past 10 years. Figure 4.6 shows the average prices of the products of manufacturers over the years. These products are single-box dedicated types (room types), videophone types and DTC types, which utilize PCs. I can, therefore, say that changes in core technology and technology architecture have accelerated product downsizing and lower prices, while at the same time stimulating the competitive advantages of products.

Furthermore, multipoint connection units (MCUs; the MP-2000 series, 3000 series and other MCUs in Figure 4.4) where multiple video conferencing systems, Mitsubishi Electric's stronghold, are connected to enable multipoint conferences are gradually replacing software architecture products that utilize high-performance servers or PCs and their prices have fallen. This low-priced, software-based MCU is being used more frequently by corporate users within their own company, while corporate

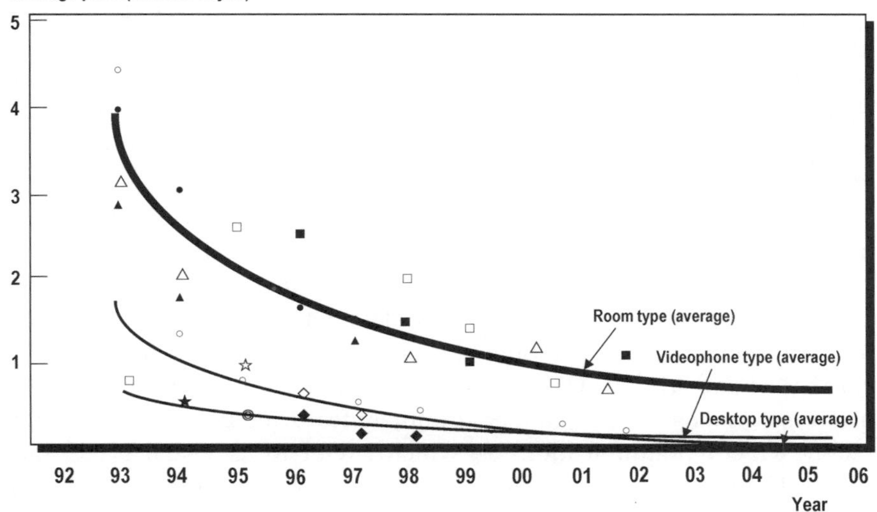

Figure 4.6: Price busting of visual communication systems.

users focusing on the reliability and high quality of IP networks are actively outsourcing multipoint connections to ASPs (Application Service Providers) (Kodama, 1999b).

As seen above, major advances in core technologies such as semiconductors and broadband have introduced changes to core components and technological architecture, and have determined the competitive advantage of products (Henderson and Clark, 1994). With the exception of Sony and NEC, most of Japan's large manufacturers, including Mitsubishi Electric, Hitachi, Matsushita, Fujitsu, Toshiba, Oki Electric and Sharp could not respond rapidly to these changes in technology and withdrew from developing and marketing their own products. At present, Hitachi, Fujitsu and Oki Electric are working on the development and marketing of DTC and MCU products with software architecture that utilizes PCs as shown in Step 3. Diverting management resources to the development of software architecture-based products is, at this point in time, a judicious choice, and a major challenge is to respond to price competition and competition with other market players. (Skype is not a product that can be interconnected with the products of any manufacturer.) Since software is free, Skype cannot be ignored by the vendors.

Despite the fact that Polycom and Sony are currently proud of their market share with single-box dedicated devices, the influence of such products based on software architecture cannot be overlooked. In future, products utilizing more advanced processors and software-centered architecture will maintain product competitiveness in this age of broadband. Compared to conventional products based on switching circuits or products such as dedicated boards that have some hardware costs, these software-based products have become advantageous, that in terms of cost and performance.

Technologies that will attract attention in the future are wireless technologies such as 3G, 4G, Wireless-LAN and WiMax. At present, broadband in mobile communications does not have any advantages in terms of cost or performance, but as more wireless networks adopt broadband, terminals will increasingly offer greater performance and lower costs, closing the gap with visual communication systems in fixed-line communications. And as a convergent environment featuring both fixed-line and mobile video communications — which I refer to as Visual Fixed and Mobile Convergence (Visual FMC) — is built (Kodama 2002a, 2002b), it is also possible that a new architecture and a new product business model based on this architecture will emerge (Figure 4.7).

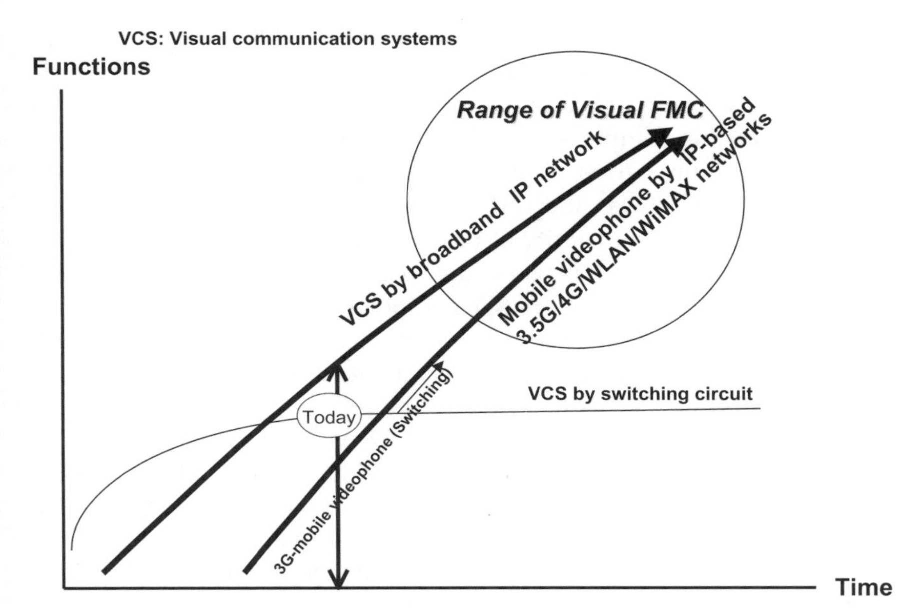

Figure 4.7: Technological innovation in VCS from advances in IP and semiconductors.

As seen above, Mitsubishi Electric implemented a new strategy amidst a dramatically-changing environment. Instead of withdrawing from visual communication systems for fixed-line communications, the company focused its management resources on 3G mobile phones and aimed to formulate and realize a new technological architecture on their own. The next section discusses this in detail.

4.5. New Challenges for Mitsubishi Electric

4.5.1. *New videophone development*

As previously mentioned, Mitsubishi Electric was involved in dynamic picture image compression encoding technology from early stages. The development of compression encoding technology began in the first half of the 1980s, and by the second half, the first commercial product using the technology was developed — a television conferencing system for businesses. The screen had a pixel density of 352 × 288, which was lower than the resolution of a standard television at 720 × 480. Even so, this was the most advanced, large-scale system for its time. The Mitsubishi Electric Information & Communication Laboratory was the first in the world to develop encoding compression technology for dynamic picture images. Commercialization started with television conferencing and Mitsubishi Electric's technology was adopted as an element for transmission in television broadcasts by a majority of broadcast stations. Its application further expanded to DVD players and recorders. A low-cost LSI was implemented for commercial public equipment that met the demand for high-screen quality. The commercial know-how acquired through work with dynamic picture image compression encoding is currently used in consumer applications.

In June 2000, the Telecommunications Division of Mitsubishi Electric began actively marketing a videoconferencing system compatible with the fixed telecommunication network for the third-generation mobile phone service scheduled to start in spring 2001. Videoconferencing systems over a fixed network were already used worldwide by businesses to improve management efficiency (remote conference systems and other decision-making support) and as IT tools in education, medical treatment and welfare fields (Kodama, 1999b). If a TV phone is re-invented in the size of a mobile phone, then business video conferencing would be easier than ever. Businesses can function efficiently, regardless of locations and time.

The Telecommunications Division marketing and development team had ample opportunities for informal dialog with Japan's largest telecommunications carrier, NTT, regarding a development project being implemented at NTT's Multimedia Division. They also implemented analyses mainly of corporate user marketing surveys and unrealized customer needs (including customer usage patterns and actual functionality requirements). The implementation of this new videoconferencing system not only improved system sales at Mitsubishi Electric, but also made it possible for NTT to increase its communication traffic for image communication between fixed and mobile transmission. Between the development project members at NTT and the Telecommunications Division members of Mitsubishi Electric, it was recognized that the results of the marketing research of users who implemented videoconferencing systems made it possible to forecast the potential needs of users of the new video conferencing systems that were capable of connecting to 3G mobile TV phones on a fixed network. In developing the new video conferencing system, new value was created between the two teams, and an informal ToB (ToB-1) was formed (see Figure 4.8). The ToB-1 then agreed to develop

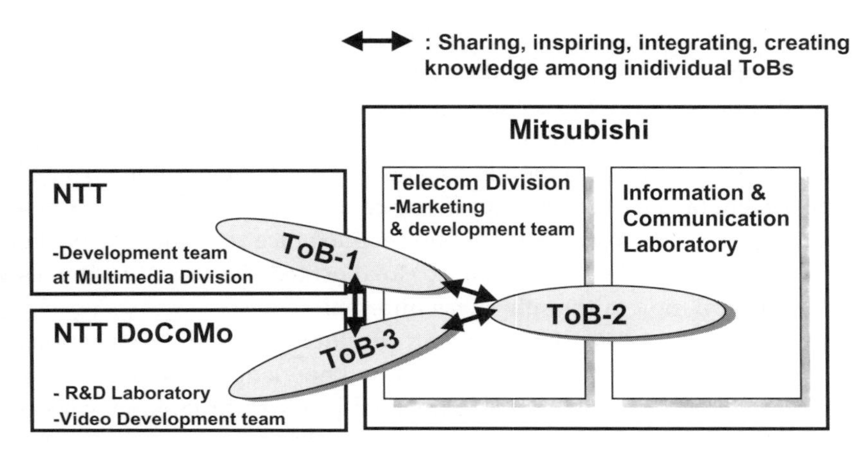

Figure 4.8: Teams of Boundaries at Mitsubishi and NTT.

the specifications for the new product to be developed in order to create a product that could be connected with conventional existing TV conferencing systems, as well as 3G mobile TV phones.

For the development of a new videoconferencing system simultaneously capable of handling existing TV conferencing system and the 3G mobile TV phone (in other words, a product having dual mode functionality), a major hurdle was developing a new system LSI (large-scale integrated circuit) that could handle multimedia. During this time, it proved difficult to use the popular modular architecture of an all-purpose processor in the product for this new development. The marketing and development team of the Telecommunications Division formed an informal ToB (ToB-2) with the Information and Communication Laboratory in the company, which was responsible for R&D, and the technical evaluation of the LSI system had begun (see Figure 4.8). Because the fixed transmission image and voice codec, and the 3G mobile TV phone image and voice codec were based on different international standards, it was necessary to build both codecs into a single LSI for the new system architecture for the TV phone development. This meant a system LSI had to be newly developed with a complex integral architecture having the functions of a dual codec.

Another informal ToB (ToB-3) was formed between the NTT DoCoMo image service development project and Mitsubishi Electric R&D Laboratory in order to merge the new image and voice compression core technologies, and begin a technical evaluation on the connectivity of the 3G mobile TV phone and the new video conferencing system transmission interface details with a fixed network (see Figure 4.7). For DoCoMo, the ability to connect to Mitsubishi's 3G mobile TV phone with the new video conferencing system on a fixed network offered a new demand for image transmission traffic of obvious merit beyond mobile voice transmission or the mobile Internet. It followed that DoCoMo allocated significant resources to this technical topic, although it was informal.

Toward new product development, product technical specifications were determined based on user needs. New knowledge produced in the ToBs during study of issues such as detailed product design and system LSI architecture was merged and integrated through the sharing and mutual inspiration from within and among the ToB-1, ToB-2, ToB-3 boundaries, leading to the creation of knowledge of the networked teams (see Figure 4.8). After one year, the core technology of the new product was finally completed, achieving an even more compact product in December 2001. The core technology was for the system LSI, the world's first system LSI that combined the function of both the fixed-network videoconferencing system and the 3G TV mobile phone (see Figure 4.9).

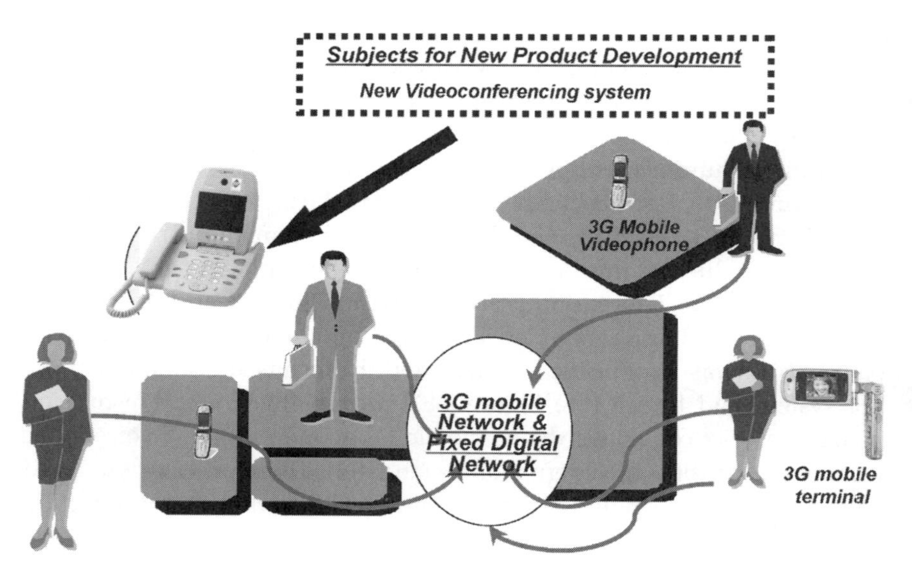

Figure 4.9: New videophone developed by Mitsubishi.

4.5.2. *Development of a new multipoint connection unit (MCU)*

After the 3G mobile service became popular, the next challenge for Mitsubishi Electric was that only few users would use the TV mobile phone, and a majority of users would want to use TV conferencing or video chat. So Mitsubishi. At this time, NTT DoCoMo's image service development project was considering the same image service, and the core members in both companies initiated an informal study group.[2]

As the dialog progressed, members of the Development Center and Sales Division of Mitsubishi Electric and the DoCoMo project members arrived at a common vision and conceptualization to realize a video chat platform that would be a virtual meeting mobile videophone — "anywhere, anytime, with anyone." The members from both companies had previously been involved in, and were experienced in areas such as marketing, product development and sales for the fixed line network used for videophones and videoconferencing systems. However, they were not familiar with business development for video conferencing using mobile videophones. Nevertheless, they were all certain that a mobile multimedia culture using image communication would form and believed it necessary to take on this challenging concept, especially since there was nothing like it in the market at the time.

The previous business model for Mitsubishi Electric's visual communication system was selling sold-out products and OEM supply to communication carriers. But this time, the development of a new product compatible with a 3G mobile phone was proposed as a system solution for communication carrier DoCoMo. Now, the jointly-developed system solution developed by both companies would be supplied by DoCoMo to a number of end-users for videoconferencing and for consumer oriented video chat services. In other words, B2B2C (Business-to-Business-to-Consumer) would be the focus of the business model. If the service took off, there was the possibility to build a win-win relationship between DoCoMo and Mitsubishi Electric.

Mitsubishi Electric had to consider how to come up with the system architecture based upon the service architecture (service concept and business model) presented by DoCoMo. For its system architecture,

[2] The communications carrier, DoCoMo, focuses its internal resources on R&D and service development (mainly, business model proposal, service and product architecture development) and does not have a manufacturing department. As such, DoCoMo realizes its planned system (hardware and software) of business models and service/product architectures through joint development with internal and external manufacturers.

Mitsubishi Electric had accumulated technology and know-how for some parts, but needed to consider bridging technology integration and a new architecture for a number of technical areas (technologies such as image handling, digital transmission, mobile transmission, computer, LSI, software and database, for example). Although Mitsubishi Electric had accumulated and was utilizing image handling technology for fixed communication networks, they proceeded to begin studies without using any of their existent technology, starting from a blank slate.

The directors of Mitsubishi Electric's Telecom and Sales Divisions and Information & Communication Laboratory respectively were central to the effort; with support from the president, officers of the related divisions headed the large-scale project, requiring a variety of technical elements for the development of the system, which involved many divisions, research laboratories and plants, along with various experts.

There were a number of negative opinions within DoCoMo about the development of the platform. "It is still unclear whether a peer-to-peer image communication market via mobile videophones will develop and, furthermore, will many people have a need to teleconference using such a small LCD screen?" was one such opinion. "Is this a service that should be developed at this time even if the risk of development burden is covered?" was another. There were not only concerns within DoCoMo, but there was also technical knowledge lacking in some development areas, and there was an element of uncertainty over the question of whether there were any eager manufacturers that would be willing to take on risky hi-tech development with DoCoMo.

However, in order to realize the concept of the DoCoMo project team members, intensive explanations were made to achieve consensus within the related divisions of DoCoMo, and at the same time, a number of corporate customers (those already using videoconferencing via fixed line networks) were approached to actively collect information on the potential needs for videoconferencing via mobile videophone. Further, a repeated number of private meetings were held for to joint development of technology with domestic and overseas manufacturers, and opinions were exchanged on technical development problems and possible solutions. As a result of the above efforts, it was possible to attain a certain degree of understanding, as well as empathy and resonance from within DoCoMo, along with business customers and the large electrical equipment manufacturer Mitsubishi Electric, in the form of a vision and value-based view of "The Future Realization of Mobile Multimedia."

ToB-a was formed with the object of sharing the business context and knowledge with the DoCoMo service development project thorough dialog with the Development Center of the Sales and Telecommunications Divisions and the Information and Communication Laboratory at Mitsubishi Electric. Approval was granted within DoCoMo for the new product and service, and in February 2001, DoCoMo agreed to form a strategic partnership with Mitsubishi, which was strong in the core multimedia technology of videoconferencing. The partnership's purpose was the joint development of a mobile videoconferencing multipoint system. For DoCoMo, the objective of the strategic partnership with Mitsubishi was to initiate the Japanese mobile videoconferencing market and at the same time, launch the new wireless videoconferencing service to promote 3G mobile market. For ToB-a, the value judgment was the "realization of mobile multimedia", and between the players, this had a shared meaning of creating, while at the same time "developing the necessary platform for a new image service", and an agreement was built for the understanding of new knowledge between the players (see Figure 4.10). ToB-a was not composed of just middle managers and staff members of the Telecommunication

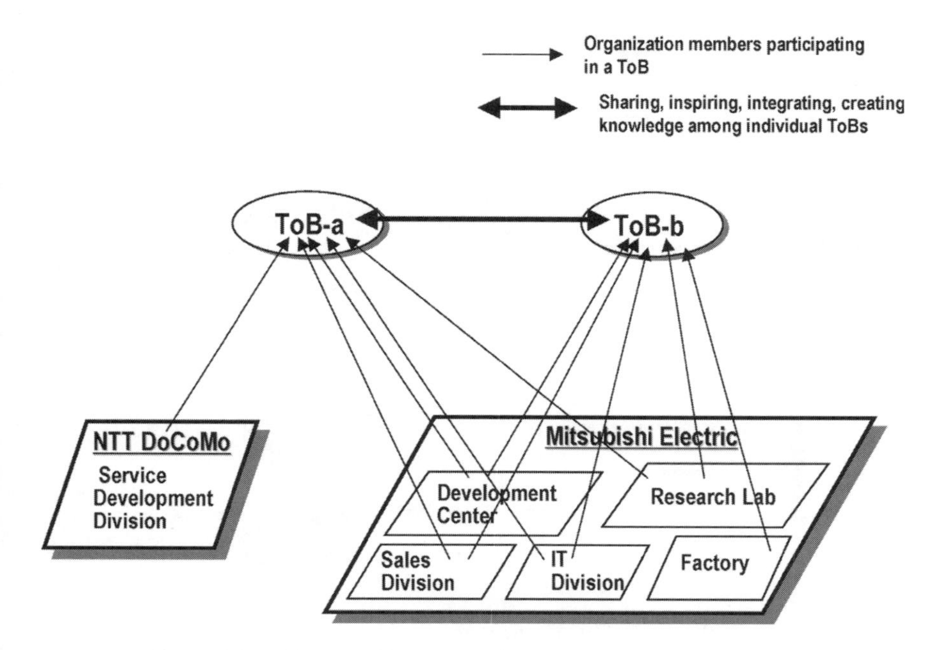

Figure 4.10: Horizontally-integrated ToB (DoCoMo — Mitsubishi).

and Sales Divisions of Mitsubishi Electric; in addition, the middle management and staff members of the IT Division and research labs participated in the planning stage and discussed the service architecture proposed by DoCoMo. (Figure 4.11 shows a part of the service architecture.) Service architecture means the fundamental, specific concepts for actually delivering the service to the end-user. The newly proposed service architecture allows a number of people-to-video conference or use a mobile video phone, and the end user operating phase requires a communication reservation phase and a multipoint communication phase.

In order to conduct multipoint communication, first the multipoint communication platform (MCU: Multipoint Connection Unit) connects to the server through the i-mode (DoCoMo mobile internet service) and sets items such as the connection time, connection partner and display mode. Based upon the specified content, the MCU senses when the system is available, reserves the resources and completes the communication reservation. After the communication reservation is completed, the MCU transmits to each communication member the time, date, member and the telephone number of the connection partner via a reservation e-mail.

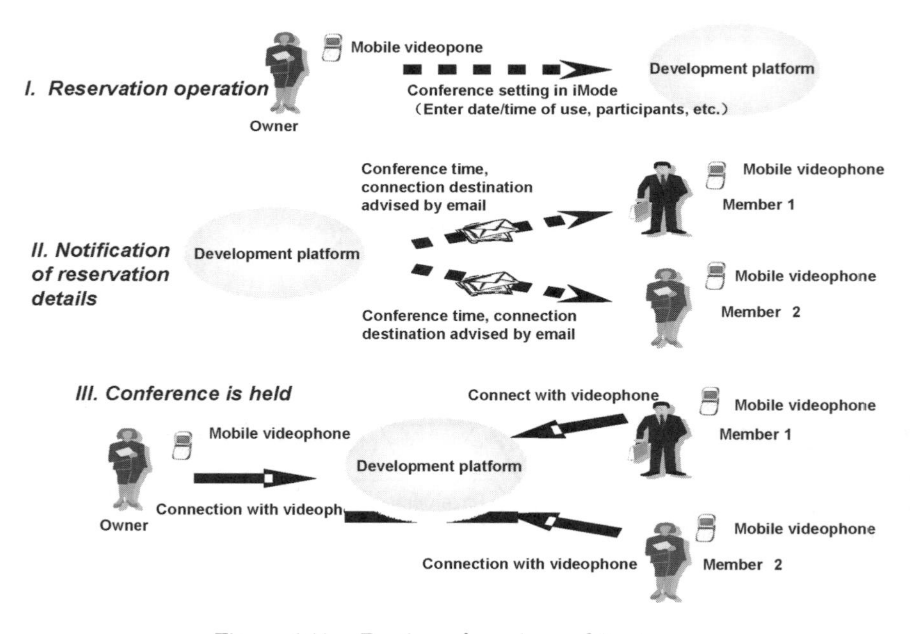

Figure 4.11: Portion of service architecture.
Source: Prepared by author referring to pamphlets and media materials from DoCoMo.

When accessing the server to make a communication reservation, a fixed distinct number from the member information and mobile phone number registered with the server is used to identify the user and used to protect security.

For multipoint communication, the communication member and time must have been previously registered in the MCU, and the service architecture supports each member connecting at the specified time via the MCU of the mobile videophone (a later addition is a function for the TV conferencing host to quickly and automatically call other members). Multipoint communication via a mobile videophone should be performed during the reservation time in the MCU of the mobile videophone (the phone number is announced through a reservation email). Images can appear on 40 percent of the screen (see Figure 4.14), and as a single screen is possible, the speaker's image is transmitted to the mobile videophone. When a member whose picture is not shown on the display speaks, the image can be changed to display the person speaking. The development platform should allow 60 mobile videophones to be connected at the same time. For example if three people are communicating, 20 conferences can be conducted at the same time. It is also possible for a maximum of eight people to connected during a single conference.

Figure 4.12 shows a general depiction of the system architecture that implements this service architecture. As shown in the figure, this system architecture is configured with the MCU and the servers. The MCU sends/receives cellular videophone, video and voice stream, and combines image and voice. The servers govern the control of the MCU and user interfaces, such as call reservations. The server group mainly mans the "reception function," "control function" and "MCU management function". The "reception function" implements the exchange of requests and responses via HTTP communications as the receiver of user interfaces for call reservations using i-mode. It also implements e-mail notification, such as reservation e-mails. In collaboration with the reception function, the "control function" implements resource management, such as search function for system availability based on users' requests, the accumulation and management of the user database and reservation information, and the user authentication of WWW access. The "MCU management function" controls instructions for the MCU, such as starting the service. It also receives varied information from the MCU, and updates the resource information in collaboration with the control function.

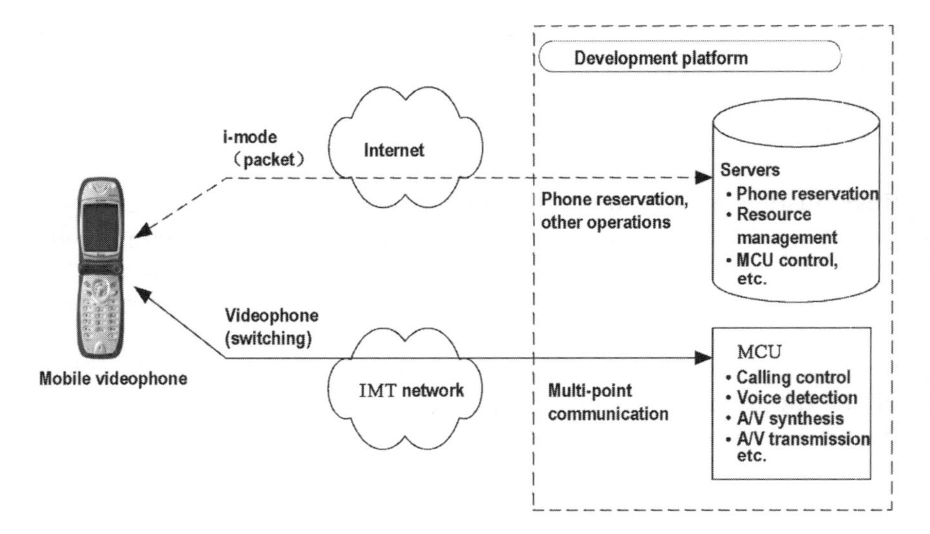

Figure 4.12: Portion of system architecture.
Source: Prepared by author referring to media materials and publicly-available technical materials from DoCoMo.

The MCU processes calls, voice and video from the cellular videophone, and enables multipoint telephone calls. Self-voice/-video from the cellular videophone connected to the MCU is sent to the MCU by image processing communication protocols for mobile communications similar to normal fixed communication videoconferencing systems. The MCU recognizes the speaker based on voice information, and combines three voices in the prefetch plus method (the voice that is altered earlier is given priority to be added to the data that will be transferred) to send it to each cellular videophone.

There has been much discourse between concerned parties regarding the content relevant to the basic service architecture and system architecture mentioned above. The architecture was created by implementing radically, new services and systems that did not exist before. The engineers at DoCoMo and Mitsubishi resolved problems by learning from their own mistakes. This led to the revision of the MCU's architecture for existing fixed communications, and new developments for the various components that configured the architecture, which is equivalent to the "radical innovation" referred by Henderson and Clark (1990). At the same time, managers of both companies consulted on issues regarding business models and user interfaces.

The first important viewpoint is that engineers grasp basic categories of required tasks for developments, based on their embedded knowledge; for example, which part of existing technology should be utilized for the development of this new system; which existing technologies should be reformed and which part required new development. This author refers to it as "knowledge difference" (Kodama, 2006). The second viewpoint is that the engineers require architectural competence (Henderson and Clark, 1994) to generate architectural knowledge (Henderson and Clark, 1990), such as new service architectures or system architectures. Henderson and Clark (1990) referred the innovation based on architectural knowledge as "architectural innovation." This innovation reviews the linkage of constituent parts, such as existing components, and develops new, competitive functions (or a wide improvement in functions). This means that to combine existing components and integrate them, and to link them with other integrated components to develop a new product, the linkage method needs to be changed from that used by existing components.

These architectural innovations are engineering innovations that are frequently applied to IT equipment, precision machine tools and digital consumer-electronics through the development of fine processing technology of semiconductors, micro electronics, mechatronics, software technology, etc. However, this author thinks that the important innovation for the future is not the change in the components' linkage method, but the radical innovation that widely changes the component itself. A radical innovation that widely changes the component itself (including the integration of existing components), changes the linkage method of the components, integrates the component that has new technological linkage components, and is configured with technology integration that transverses various technological fields and new architectures.

Based on most of the current research centered around Europe and America, (Leonard-Barton, 1995; Tashman and Romanelli, 1985; Henderson and Clark, 1990; Christensen, 1997; Tushman and Anderson, 1986; Tushman and O'Reilly III, 1997; Rosenbloom, 2000; O'Reilly III and O'Reilly III, 2004), it is suggested that for significant architectural innovation (including radical innovation) accompanying product development, the organizational control used currently should be replaced with new structures. This can also be observed in the case of Mitsubishi Electric where fixed-line visual communication system developers were teamed up with personnel from other areas of expertise and a new project organization was established. The absorption of external knowledge (introduction of external resources) was conducted via a ToB (ToB-a) collaboration with DoCoMo (See Figure 4.10).

Although this kind of sharing and inspiring of linkage and knowledge between internal and external organizations are conducted via ToB-a as depicted in Figure 4.10, in this case study, the personnel who play critical roles with respect to organizational behavior are the project leaders and the project managers of DoCoMo, and the directors and managers of organizations related to Mitsubishi Electric. These people do not act solely as bridges in information processing, like gate keepers (Allen and Cohen, 1969; Allen, 1977), they also consider overall perspectives such as business, technology and management, before committing on pragmatic issues and targets. In other words, boundary spanners (Allen and Cohen, 1969; Tushman, 1977; Ancona and Caldwell, 1992) are the actors in this case study who exhibit holistic commitment in development and management issues.

The ToB-a of this collaborative development, as depicted in Figure 4.10, realizes the horizontal integration of knowledge between DoCoMo and Mitsubishi. This ToB-a is considered as the strategic alliance between the communication carrier and the manufacturers, which, from the business model and technological viewpoints, horizontally integrates various knowledge and is equivalent to organizational and knowledge boundaries, which give rise to knowledge creation. On the other hand, DoCoMo and Mitsubishi Electric, through the establishment of ToB-a, actively absorb external knowledge and build up their absorptive capability (Cohen and Levinthal, 1983). While exhibiting awareness to the competency trap and core rigidity, they had set their aims to create new knowledge that crosses organizational boundaries, regardless of existent concepts. (Leonard-Barton, 1992, 1995). As such, DoCoMo and Mitsubishi integrated new knowledge created from ToB through the horizontal integration network of ToB, thereby establishing external integration capability in both companies.

In Mitsubishi, through the strategic alliance with DoCoMo, the development system was enhanced and ToB-b involving various related departments was newly established (Figure 4.10). This ToB-b was implemented with a layered structure as depicted in Figure 4.13.

In particular, for a large scale product development that required an integration of different technologies such as video technology, audio technology, mobile communication technology, semiconductor technology,

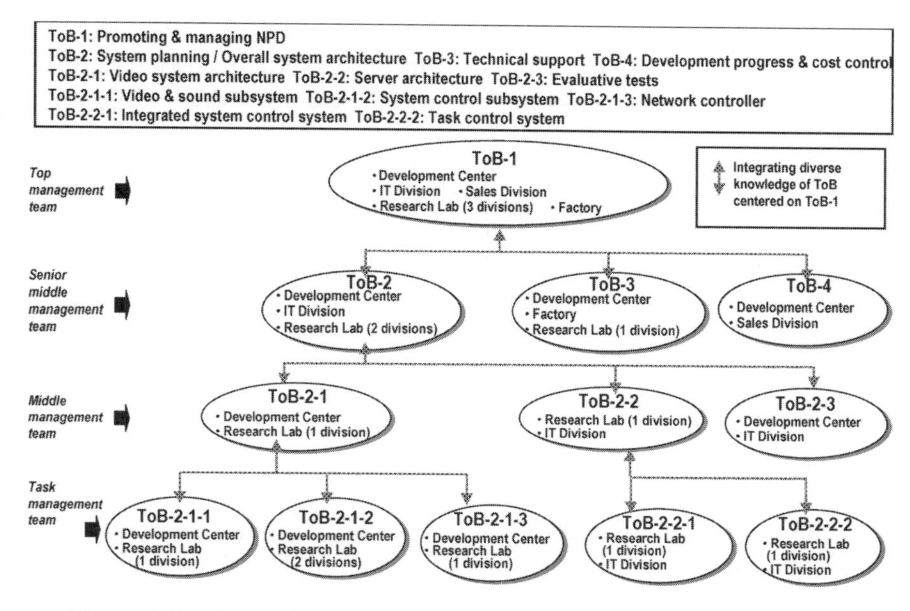

Figure 4.13: Vertically-integrated ToB (Mitsubishi) — simplified version.

software technology, computer technology and human interface technology, experts were assembled from the research and development centers, software engineering centers and manufacturing plants of three divisions to form cross-functional task teams as shown in the structured model in Figure 4.13.

Figure 4.13 shows the functional details (the job scope and knowledge of each expert?of the ToB-b in Figure 4.10 and its structure (components for defining subsystems for forming the overall system, etc.). ToB was constructed at each management level (top management level, senior-middle management level, middle management level, task management level) and these ToBs were vertically integrated across the management levels to form a network. In short, various knowledge boundaries (inter-field knowledge boundaries) in Mitsubishi were integrated through this process.

ToB-1 (Figure 4.13) shows the ToB formed from the Mitsubishi-related department head (top management level) leader team that holds all responsibilities to the planning and the execution of new product development. ToB-2 shows the senior-middle management team that is responsible for reviewing the system architecture to realize new product development. ToB-3 shows the senior-middle management team that focuses on implementing total technical support. ToB-4 is the senior-middle management team that is responsible for development progress monitoring and cost management for new product development. ToB-2-1 shows the middle management team responsible for the review of the video system architecture, which is the core of new product development and ToB-2-2 shows the middle management team responsible for the server architecture review.

In reality, the ToB-2 structure in Figure 4.13 is more complex. This is because the top level ToB-2, which is involved in the system architecture review, depends on product functions and product structures (integral or module, or mixed components), and the overall system is further modularized into several subsystems (ToB-2-1, ToB-2-2, ToB-2-3 are further expanded in detail in the lower levels) (e.g. Simon, 1996; Clark, 1985; Baldwin and Clark, 2000). As such, in the development of each subsystem, individual ToCs were formed as cross-functional teams that consisted of technical experts with different backgrounds and skills (e.g. video processing engineer, audio processing engineer, semiconductor design engineer, semiconductor software engineer, communication interface engineer, computer engineer, software engineer, human interface engineer, etc.). Furthermore, along with the expansion of multiple level structures of the overall system to various subsystems, ToB resembles the hierarchy shown in Figure 4.13. This complex structure can be observed from the middle managers and chief engineers who participate in numerous ToBs simultaneously, integrating inter-subsystem interfaces (between each module) and ensuring the compliance of the overall system architecture. Daily work includes extracting problem areas and issues from official and non-official meetings and devising suitable solutions.

Many ToBs were formed similarly in Mitsubishi, and through a network derived from the vertical integration of these ToBs, new knowledge was acquired and integrated, which strengthened the company's internal integration capability. This internal integration capability was supported by the person-in-charge for each ToB. However, the "Leadership Team" of ToB-1 held the most important responsibility for making critical decisions based on simultaneously managing different business areas and solving technical issues such as integration, production management, test evaluation and general development management.

The system development in Mitsubishi was realized through the building up of external integration capability and internal integration

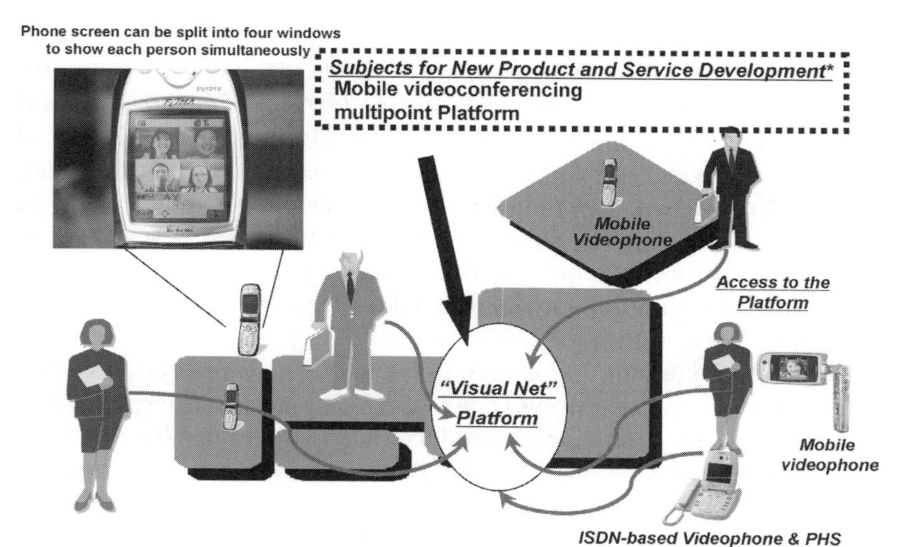

Figure 4.14: New product and service development targets.

capability. The former was established via the horizontal integration network of ToB (ToB-a) (Figure 4.10), while the latter was established via the vertical integration network of ToB (ToB-b) (Figure 4.13). DoCoMo also launched a multipoint mobile videoconferencing commercial service called "M-Stage Visual Net" in the beginning of October, 2002 (see Figure 4.14).

4.6. New Framework Resulting from the In-depth Case Study

In this in-depth case study, a unique organizational behavior of the deployment of organizational boundaries internally and externally for promoting new product and service development was observed. The deployed ToB exhibited two unique features.

The first is the inter-company horizontal integration of ToB. As this horizontal integration of ToB aims to provide products and services answering to market needs and demands, it promotes the external integration of knowledge in inter-company organizational boundaries. This is called the external integration capability. The horizontally-integrated ToB has enabled the flexible and efficient flow of external knowledge and this external integration capability has firmly established in Mitsubishi. In this case study, a link (bridge) between the DoCoMo project and Mitsubishi departments, which promotes the collaborative development activities, exists as the ToB-a, as shown in Figure 4.10. This ToB-a mainly comprises DoCoMo and Mitsubishi Electric middle managers and task managers (top management and senior-middle managers may be included, if critical issues and decisions are involved). These people are leaders who hold a defined level of authority in their areas of responsibilities. In other words, ToB-a represents the Leadership Team (LT) that supports the sharing of the dynamic business context and core knowledge in their respective organizations. As a pragmatic boundary, the LT can be involved in creating new knowledge required for new product and service development.

The second point is the intra-company establishment of a vertically-integrated ToB at inter-management levels. This vertically-integrated ToB integrates the required core knowledge distributed in the organization after new business models and technology development in the specific new product and service development was realized. This promotes internal integration of knowledge in the organizational boundaries between management levels within the organization. This is called the internal integration capability. As shown in Figure 4.13, through the internal integration capability, Mitsubishi established the integration of core knowledge (e.g. service architecture, product architecture, component technology, etc.) in each ToB via the vertically-networked ToB.

In this case study on new product and service development of mobile phone applications based on a new business model, complex technological integration and a new architecture, there was a need to conduct an architectural review of the current products. In the ToB-b of Mitsubishi (Figure 4.10), actors exceeding organization boundaries in each department which exhibit both horizontal relationships at each management level and hierarchical vertical relationships in the organization, are depicted in the network shown in Figure 4.13.

This kind of vertically-integrated networked ToB is also monitored and reported by Toyota Motors in its TQM promotion activities and new product development (Amasaka, 2004). For instance, the flexible and organic networking of intra-company ToB in response to changes in component (subsystems and modules) requirements arises from changes in the system architecture of new product development. During this time, actors in each ToB play important roles in the module development. Subsequently, the components (modules) developed by each ToB will integrate with ToBs of other components (modules), forming a ToB network system. The middle managers, senior engineers and chief engineers who participate in multiple ToBs, act as bridges between ToBs, sharing context and knowledge and ensuring the compliance of each module. This networking of ToBs contributes to the overall system architecture design and optimization.

Henderson and Clark (1990) have pointed out that, though the internal structure of the development organization reflects the technological structure, organizations protect themselves through the current organizational structure during the shift of fundamental technology (as in this case study, a change in product architecture). For Mitsubishi Electric, it was also a huge challenge in achieving targets based on the originally restrictive organizational structure. However, Mitsubishi Electric employed a flexible approach of forming an organic vertically-integrated networked ToB within the corporation and successfully achieved new product developments that responded to customer needs and technological changes.

On the other hand, from the field research on vertically-integrated networked ToBs, it is observed that there exists a team at the core of the networked ToB which plays a central role. From the network theory perspective, this can be considered as hubs and nodes, which exhibit centrality (Barabashi, 2002; Watts, 2003; Kodama, 2006). This is the "Leadership Team (LT)" that comprises a top management team managing various positions and tasks (various technologies, business processes, cross cultural issues, etc.) and holding the final decision-making authority. LT's existence is proved in Mitsubishi Electric. The leaders in LT participate in multiple ToBs in the company and are responsible for the integration of core knowledge.

The combination of the external and the internal integration capability serves as the integrative competence (Kodama, 2003), which is the driving force for the organization in creating new markets responding to dynamic changes. In this study, Mitsubishi was able to acquire the capability to develop new products and services by building two different ToBs simultaneously (see Figure 4.15). For an organization to continuously respond to environmental (market) changes, to create new environments (markets) or to maintain its competitiveness, it is always vital to focus on building its integrative competencies, which reflects its ability to flexibly integrate internal knowledge and external knowledge resources.

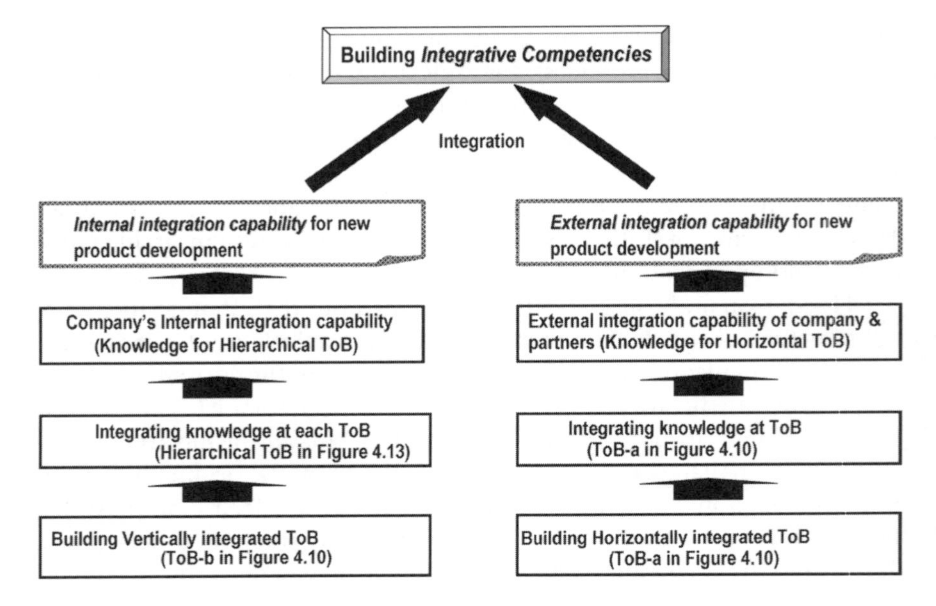

Figure 4.15: Integrative competencies through internal and external integration capabilities.

In responding to market changes, through the swift activities based on ToB deployment internally and externally, the organization promotes the concept of building business models and the developing new systems to support its aim of new product and service development.

However, how should the (LT) integrate these numerous ToBs that are embedded with in different business contexts and core knowledge? I think that the key in promoting knowledge integration lies in the LT leaders' dialectical thought and action. Dialectical thought was also reported in the institutional theory and strategic alliance literature (Creed, 2002; Das and Teng, 2000; Rond and Bouchikhi, 2004; Benson, 1977).

Nisbett (2003) suggested that the Asians "view the world through wide-angle lens" and the Westerners have "tunnel visions". He hypothesized that Westerners possess an "analytical mindset," in contrast to Asians who exhibit a "holistic mindset" or dialectical thought. In this study, although all the actors are of Japanese roots, they attempted to converse and analyze dialectically in technology, business model, job scope and cross cultural issues within pragmatic boundaries. The issues in this study involve complex business models, complex technological integration and product architecture. The holistic thinking of the actors may be an effective solution in resolving the friction and conflict, arise from various organizational cultures in multiple organizations.

However, I do not suggest that dialectical thought is flawless and does not emphasize that the "Asian thinking of dialectical management must be practiced by leaders and managers". I suggest that holistic thinking and analytical thinking should be employed based on the business situation. For example, the application of an "analytic mindset" can be applied for short-term targets and a "holistic mindset" for long-term targets. This topic, which affects the day-to-day work of a business person, requires further exploration.

5

Business Model Innovation through Boundary Management: Case Study of PlayStation by Sony

5.1. Innovation by Means of Corporate Ventures

This chapter deals with knowledge integration and technological innovation with respect to a framework leading to the successful management of projects as corporate ventures in a large company. The game business centered on PlayStation by Sony is taken up as a case study. From the in-depth case study, we present a new insight relating to an "enabler" to expedite new business models and technical innovation with respect to corporate ventures in a large company.

In cross-functional teams that transect the organization, as well as scattered organizational boundaries inside and outside the corporation, there exist between actors knowledge boundaries that arise from (Carlile, 2002, 2004) domain-specific differences such as diverse values and specialties, and unique thought worlds (Dougherty, 1992) that the actors possess. The existence of these knowledge boundaries can become knowledge integration enablers and, at the same time, constraints (Leonard–Barton, 1995; Hagel III and Brown, 2005). Generally, while forming a business model, the actors transect different industries and, by forming organizational boundaries, many knowledge boundaries are perceived and recognized.

I believe that elucidating the mechanism of knowledge integration that transects organizational boundaries (that are the knowledge boundaries between actors) inside and outside the corporation, which are associated with the complexity of business models as in the game business, would present beneficial implications for many practitioners from academic and practical viewpoints. The realization of a complicated business model involving product development and distribution systems means that the actors commit to many knowledge and organizational boundaries, and bridge several knowledge boundaries with different contexts and knowledge to achieve knowledge integration. The idea and action of networking organizational boundaries by project leaders and team leaders lead to the realization of new services and business models.

The first viewpoint of this case study is that in the knowledge boundaries between the project team, the existing organization and extramural partners, the factors of productive friction and creative abrasion between actors will expedite collaboration between the actors for building the new business model. The second viewpoint is that by means of "creative collaboration", the organization's actors such as team leaders will implement the formation of a project network of scattered knowledge boundaries inside and outside the corporation. Then the existence of networked knowledge boundaries that transect inside and outside the corporation will enable specialized knowledge to be integrated, and technological innovation (incremental innovation, architectural innovation and radical innovation) to be achieved as new products are developed.

5.2. A Case Study of Sony

PlayStation is a very popular household game device. In December 1994, Sony Computer Entertainment (SCE) released PlayStation, loaded with a leading-edge games system LSI using innovative architecture for processing epoch-making three-dimensional computer graphics images. In three years, Nintendo Sony overtook and this changed the business model of the games industry. Sony's strategy for dominating the games device market is not only successful product development, but also a close interconnection between innovative marketing strategy and technical strategy. A new business concept was discovered through trial and error and hard work by innovative actors across different industrial and organizational boundaries and knowledge boundaries in diverse specialized fields, and this was successfully implemented.

This chapter discusses in detail Sony's games market strategy and investigates how they destroyed the existing business model and constructed a new value chain in the household games market. It will also analyze and, examine the PlayStation product development that triggered Sony's games business success, from technology and innovation viewpoints.

5.2.1. *The beginning of a new enterprise*

In January 1990, Sony was a vendor providing semiconductor chips (such as games device sound source ICs) for Nintendo was that a market leader in household games market, and in charge of manufacturing development tools for software makers. Nintendo was promoting the development of Super Famicon, a superior model of its hit product, Famicon. Because Nintendo was not a semiconductor manufacturer, the development of the semiconductor chips that were its core components had to be outsourced to Sony. During this time Nintendo that had commissioned this development that, conceded to Sony the right to market the peripheral devices that Sony had developed to activate the Super Famicon processor. Then Sony developed a games device integrated with a CD-ROM and Nintendo agreed to the development of a CD-ROM adaptor that could be connected to Super Famicon units mounted with this newly-developed semiconductor chip. These products were games devices that not only had semiconductor read-only memory (ROM), but could also use compact disc ROM (CD-ROM).

During this time, Sony was thinking of incorporating the CD-ROM used by some personal computers into one device. CDs were developed by Sony and Philips and were used in portable music players. Consequently, Sony and Nintendo were jointly developing a device that combined this CD player and Super Famicon. (However, Sony intended to develop an integrated model, instead of the separated model being considered by Nintendo.) If the appeal of the Nintendo games devices in use in many ordinary families were to be utilized, the recognition of CD-ROMs would be increased immediately. They thought this would give impetus to starting a new market utilizing the CD-ROM. Moreover, Sony was thinking that mass production would increase Sony's cost competitiveness and technical strength, and that business related to projects with CD-ROM components would boom.

However, in June 1991, while it promoted joint development with Sony, Nintendo made a deal with Philips to develop a CD-ROM player. Nintendo's sudden treachery prompted Sony to break off its relations with Nintendo. The reasons for this are that Nintendo that was in a dominant position at that time in the games market was well-aware of Sony's technical strength, and feared that Sony would suppress the technical platform for games devices. They also considered that Sony would exert a great influence on their future business. (They feared Sony would become a competitor.) Norio Ohga, then CEO of Sony, was outraged at Nintendo's treacherous behavior. Various adjustment works were carried out between Sony and Nintendo concerning their tie-up, but in the end, the contract negotiations were broken off in May 1992.

At a management conference in May 1992, Sony decided that the games business would be investigated afresh as an independent Sony line. Ken Kutaragi (now SCE president) who was responsible for joint development with Nintendo found that his previous beliefs and ideas came into conflict with Ohga at the management conference. Kutaragi had faith in the development of next-generation games devices that had been derived from his strong technical background. Ohga himself had felt that computers were the only area where Sony had not been successful and he wished to develop products that used of Sony's computer technology. However, the tie-up with Nintendo had broken down. Ohga who had signed the contract, was very angry that he had been put to shame.

Kutaragi spoke to Ohga at the management conference. "Are you going to keep quiet about what Nintenedo has done to us? When Sony develops its own new games machine (with a one-million-gate LSI), we should use it to get into the games business. Make a decision!" he demanded. Ohga replied emotionally, "If that's what you say, let's see whether it's true (to realize a games machine with one-million-gate LSI)." He thumped the table with his fist and said, "Do it!"

Triggered by Ohga's anger, the PlayStation project began. During this time, in the prolonged recession that followed the bursting of the bubble, Sony's business downturn was inevitable. New products such as MiniDisk and HiVision that were expected to trigger the dull audio-visual devices, made no major contribution to sales, and the overseas market was also stagnant. Ohga himself was full of ideas for the new games business project successful not only as a games device, but as a 3D graphics computer and Sony's audio-visual business (including television and Walkman). Kutaragi also, having been told by Ohga to "do it", obtained powerful support and became the key figure in the major growth of Sony's household games business.

Sony quickly began the games business development project as an independent line. However, at that time, many people within the Sony Corporation were opposed to the games business. The culture was completely different from that of the audio and visual businesses. Many questioned whether Sony should venture into the games business which consisted of merely toys. Even a major Japanese corporation such as Sony was no exception, and because of his uncommon ability in technology and foresight, Kutaragi's assertions and opinions were beset by discord and friction from various departments within the company and Kutaragi himself was unable to behave in accordance with his ideas. Keeping in view Kutaragi's situation, Ohga came to a decision.

Ohga believed that if he left Kutaragi in this situation, others would surely destroy him. In a snap decision, Ohga borrowed a part of the office of a subsidiary company, Sony Music Entertainment (SME), to provide an environment for Kutaragi's development team to carry out its development work. There was dissatisfaction within Sony regarding this decision, but Ohga ignored this and went ahead with it.

Sony researched a variety of business forms when this new games business project was started. To implement a games business at Sony itself would be regarded as heresy, so that was not an option. Therefore, Tamotsu Iba, an employee of Sony who was at the management conference at that time, planned a joint venture with the Sony Group of companies keeping in view that the games business is both a hardware and a software business. The group targeted was SME, a record company that was already listed and partly working on some games software. The Sony Group formally entered the household games devices market in October 1993 with the establishment of SCE, a business company specializing in games, with Sony and SME providing half of the funding for the project. There was a great benefit to be derived from a joint venture with the group because the new company could efficiently use the resources of the parent company (human, material and financial). In other words, it was able to effectively access the support of big business from the parent company Sony and SME, and venture business compared to a, the new business could which just began run faster. In Japan, this form of joint venture business supported by large businesses is often used by big corporations and most of them have been successful (Kodama, 1999).

5.2.2. *Strategy for a new business model*

The newly established SCE gathered a variety of human resources, including Kutaragi's PlayStation development team and core members of Sony Laboratory. For the necessary unification of SCE's business strategy came

Tokunaka (first president of SCE), a Sony management strategy staff member and other business management and financial management staff. From SME as the games software marketing strategy and sales team came Shigeo Maruyama (now SME president and a director of SCE) who was responsible for Epic Sony Business Division, and his subordinate from the New Media Division (development and marketing of personal computer and Famicon games software), Yuji Takahashi, (later SCE director and general manager) and his team. In addition to these conspicuous professionals, came Akira Sato (now a SME director) from CBS and Sony Records with marketing and sales expertise.

As a late entrant (Nintendo and Sega Enterprises dominated the market) Sony's ideas of new business revolved around doing what they could do and what they must do. Therefore, their work began with a thorough study of Nintendo's current business model. Centered around Nintendo, they listened to the practical voices of many players and customers including many software makers, wholesalers, retailers and users, thus finding out about a variety of problems and sources of dissatisfaction. Then, with these raw data as a base, they focussed on overtaking Nintendo.

The business model of the games world with Nintendo at the top was very complicated. There were several steps before the games software reached the hands of the user involving an "original intention meeting" in which a primary wholesaler makes a lump-sum purchase of the software from a software maker, or the wholesalers and retailers. Since software with little user appeal remains in inventory, merchants fear dead stock (since it cannot be returned) and deal in quantities that can be sold quickly. If the software is popular and certain to be sold, they will wait for the increase in price. There were also cases in the used software market where software could be sold at prices above the list price.

Behind this distinctive vendor behavior lay the use of mask ROM media (cartridge-type semiconductor memory) by the software. Even with extra demand for software, the use of semiconductor memory extended production lead time to as much as two months. This often resulted in dead stock from the arrival of mask ROM two months after the hit had passed. Meanwhile high production costs raised the retail price of the software to an average 10,000 yen. Moreover, the inability of the software maker to guage demand for the product (whether or not it would be a hit) and the wholesaler's uncertainity regarding the purchase volume resulted in over-production by the software maker and over-procurement by the wholesaler. This in turn led to disposal to another wholesaler or a cash-wholesaler, or selling together with popular software as a package deal, and left both vendor and user with a vicious circle. A vicious circle like this led to shortages of stock if the software maker was able to sell, or redundant inventory if it could not. The games business was therefore a high-risk, high-return business (Figure 5.1).

Thus the wholesalers who have to order software before it has been completed have a strong tendency to restrict their purchases to items that are similar to products that are sure to be hits, or sequels to hit products, or those that use famous copyrights. Also, since the goods may not be returned, the software makers want to make high-volume sales to wholesalers, and the content of the software tends to be continuously simplistic. Therefore, the business model made it difficult to produce a new and unique software. Moreover, the software makers paid Nintendo for the mask ROM and high royalties, and added to these expenses were development costs and distribution margins, as well as risk fees (a risk fee relating to demand variation, peculiar to mask ROM-compatible game software) so that the price to the end-user was eventually very high (about 10 thousand yen). Only large companies manufactured software for Nintendo. Medium-to-small software makers with skilled creators, but, little or no administrative

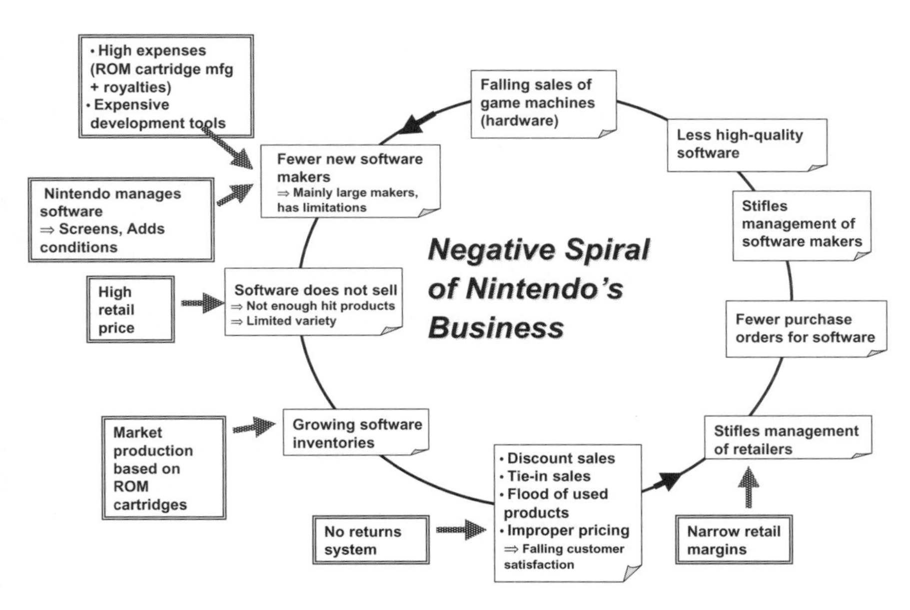

Figure 5.1: Problems in Nintendo's business model.

strength with found it very difficult to get started because of the costs involved in developing software for Nintendo. Thus, in this business model, Nintendo operated a complete software and distribution system, and controlled, the game business value chain.

How to make an ideal business model that has the user at its top and provides all players with reasonable benefits, while making the user happy? For SCE, it was important to avoid the dissatisfaction of software makers, retailers and users a fact that arose have been obtained from their factual analysis of Nintendo's game business. Achieving this meant building the value chain of a new business model by cooperating with software makers and retailers in a win–win situation.

At SCE, the discussion between the core members began for making strategic decisions on the games business. The important viewpoints that were expressed there were about a platform that would support the games software makers and creating a win–win relationship among all players including end-users and retailers. The first step was to develop a technical strategy to provide a platform (format, etc.) for an attractive games device that could motivate software creators. The second step was to develop a software strategy to show whether there is a business structure (for instance, license and royalties etc.) in which the software makers' managerial ranks could develop and provide software. The third step was to develop a distribution strategy to enable the construction of a distribution system that gave all players a win–win situation (Figure 5.2).

Kutaragi's development team conceived the basic architecture of a LSI system with the world's leading three-dimensional computer graphics. At that time, the design of the specific logic circuits for this LSI and the layout design and construction were developed jointly with the US LSI Logic Company that was the world's foremost company with the ability to achieve this level of LSI. This was a device to rival the functions of the US Silicon Graphics Company's computer graphics work stations (priced at more than 10 million yen each) that was to be mounted in an ordinary household games device. An order for one million units from SCE provided economies of scale thus resulting or in an affordable price. Kutaragi also predicted beforehand the trend towards lower prices and increased functionality of components such as the semiconductor memory, and he planned from the outset to develop the LSI architecture to enable the number of components to be reduced in stages. These measures achieved production improvements that enabled the hardware to be mass-produced, and subsequently resulted in lowering the price of the PlayStation.

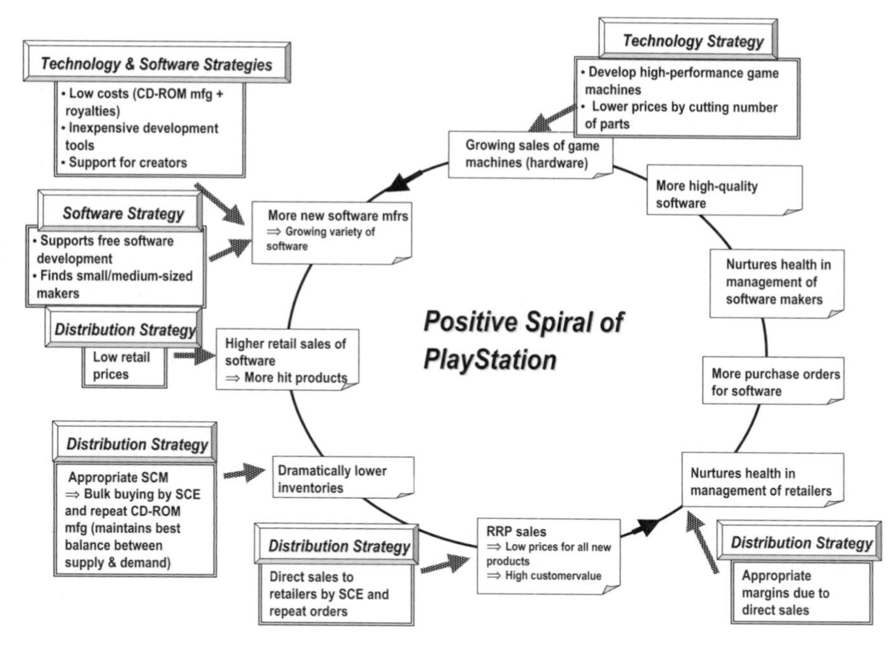

Figure 5.2: PlayStation's business cycle.

The second technical strategy item involved the use of CD-ROM optical discs as media for the games device, instead of the mask ROM that had been in use until now in the Famicon. The CD-ROM was most suitable for handling the high volumes of data for the pictures, sound and moving images in three-dimensional games. Access time and poor operability were the weaknesses of the CD-ROM, and Kutaragi's team achieved a new form of usage for drawing in real time by reading all of the CD data into the games device at once and using an image creation and compilation engine that had been developed. The third technical strategy item was the provision of software support tools for games software creators. This was the provision of all sorts of libraries for the online support of creators and their software works. Kutaragi's team then created an easy-to-use environment for the software creators.

The second item, software strategy, appeals to the software makers' management. One is strongly linked to the technical strategy that used the CD-ROM. The members of the Business Division teams of Maruyama and Takahashi proposed new royalties for software makers based on the strategy of using this CD-ROM, and together with Kutaragi's team, proceeded to promote the involvement of the software makers. Compared with the previous mask ROM, the CD-ROM is not only most suitable for containing larger volumes of multimedia data, but also has the advantage of low production cost. In other words, for the software makers, their production costs could be cut to one-third if they used the CD-ROM. Moreover, software OEM production fees and the way of thinking about royalties brought about a drastic transformation of the existing Nintendo rules.

As a result, the CD-ROM manufacturing expense paid to SCE by the software makers was set at 900 yen, including commission production and royalty fees. By comparison, the fee for the Nintendo mask ROM system is 3000 yen. This represents a considerable cost reduction for a software maker. Furthermore, with the CD-ROM additional production, it is possible and there is no need for the 500-yen risk avoidance fee due to read errors that occur with the mask ROM. The CD-ROM allows additional production in three days, and it is possible to construct an appropriate software supply chain obviating the need for dead stock storage costs. To realize this supply chain, SCE arranged a factory equipped with the latest facilities such as the enormous delivery center of SME's subsidiary JARED (record delivery) Shizuoka delivery center and the newest CD-ROM press line. These business tricks by SCE dramatically reduced the hurdles for software makers participating in PlayStation and made the business side more attractive for the managers of software makers.

The third item is a distribution system that is win–win situation for all players. Here, SCE has implemented a distribution policy that is revolutionary in the games business. Sato's sales promotion team, utilizing its accumulated experience and knowledge, brought the record business model across to the games business. The music business is basically one with a small volume production of many items and they had accumulated know-how regarding coping with user needs related to demand. The music CD business model involves gathering complete sets of many titles and making selective purchases of works from the sets in accordance with user preferences. The supply chain involves prompt supply as soon as a work becomes a hit. Because there is no need to stock CDs, as repeat supplies can be readily arranged, the appropriate distribution system supports direct purchasing by SCE and direct selling.

The purpose of this system is for software that can be sold to be immediately repeated such that production and inventory are balanced and problems with the former mask ROM such as package deal selling, wholesaling and pressuring retailers simply do not occur. In other words, this is unified marketing by SCE. It establishes a system of specialization in which sales are promoted by the makers of the software and SCE does the actual selling. Since SCE knows accurately and in real-time the number of games devices shipped and the amounts of software shipped and supplemented, SCE can not only build the appropriate supply chain, but can also exercise unitary control over marketing data and feed back predictions of future demand and data on the development of new software to the software makers.

This direct purchasing system also aids in increasing the participation of software makers in PlayStation — in other words, participation in planning by small-to-medium software makers with limited funds. This system is also a device for cultivating potential and skillful software creators, and for having good products produced by software makers who do not have the capacity to make software sales. Nintendo exercises unitary control over software from content through production and quality. Many at Nintendo felt that few interesting software products could make the games market; however they also felt that bad software could destroy the market. SCE, on the other hand, stressed the potential capabilities of software makers, and thought that software should be developed by creators with freedom of expression. Consequently, SCE had its door wide open to people who wished to make games software. SCE found excellent creators and worked hard to discover excellent talent for the next generation from amongst software products filled with variety. This comes from the idea that the mountain becomes higher, if its base is expanded.

During this time, it was difficult to have the concept of this direct purchasing system accepted even within SCE. Here are some of the incandescent arguments that were raised: "SCE provides hardware. Why do we have to act like wholesalers?", "Can it make more profit? Can we manage it with few members?" and "Will there be economies of scale?" However, from his experience and knowledge of the record business, Sato maintained that this system could drastically change the games business distribution system.

The software makers also disapproved these ideas. It was a simple question of why they were not allowed to use their own sales routes to sell the software that they had developed. On the other hand, the software makers were gradually persuaded to agree with the great benefits such as maintaining a reasonable stockpile and shared marketing data. (This direct purchasing system was later operated flexibly through separate negotiations with software makers.)

As a result of a mutually-potentiating effect of the technical the software, and the distribution strategies outlined above, license contracts were made in August 1994 before PlayStation was released for sale, with more then 200 companies, including Namco, Konami and Square. At the same time, contracts were made with 50 corporations and 3000 bulk stores and retail stores. Also, a sales network was steadily built up including SME — major toy wholesaler and a major record wholesaler — and wholesalers for electrical shops in the nationwide Sony Group. PlayStation was then introduced to the world in December 1994. On the opening day, 150,000 units were sold. At present the PlayStation Series (PlayStation, PlayStation2, PSX and PlayStation Portable) is spread throughout the world. This is the result of the synergy of the three strategies mentioned above. PlayStation is an excellent platform that calls in many software makers and is an attractive environment for creators, but this increases the motivation of the creators who create many software works. The results was a sudden increase in the number of software works and games devices shipped as hardware, further resulting in an increase in the number of PlayStation users are increased. In other words, it generates positive feedback due to network externalities (Shapiro and Varian, 1998) (Figure 5.3). This kind of games business, centered on PlayStation, is similar to the mobile telephone service that can be connected to the Internet. NTT DoCoMo i-mode service, that provided the world's first mobile Internet service using mobile telephones increased the content of mobile telephones, more subscribers, and also increased the number of mobile telephones shipped (e.g. Kodama, 2002).

5.2.3. *Integration of different areas of knowledge by project network formation*

These PlayStation business models consist of the integration of knowledge of hardware such as games devices, knowledge of software such as games software, intellectual property such as copyrights and royalties, as well as knowledge related to marketing and management including distribution and sales channels. While SCE was being established, Kutaragi and Tokuyama from the Sony and staff members Maruyama, Sato and Takahashi from the SME together with their teams, were searching for

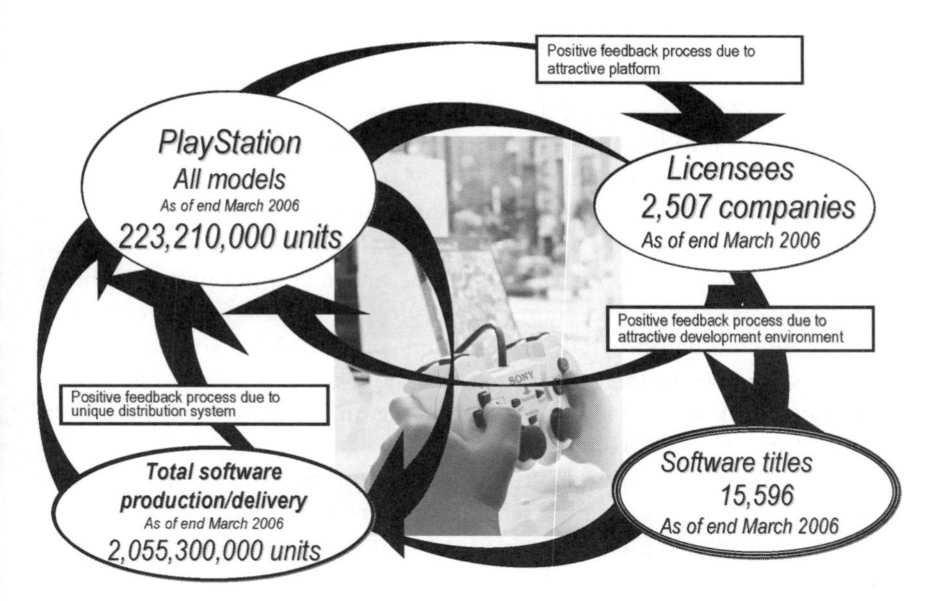

Figure 5.3: PlayStation's positive feedback.
Source: Prepared by author based on publicly-available SCE materials.

a new games business model through trial and error, while mutually opposing and being in friction with each other. Sony employees had the knowledge of consumer electronics computer technology and business models. On the other hand, SME, originally a record company, looked after the development and marketing of games software for Nintendo. Together with Epic Sony employees who had experience in games business, formed a single organization called SCE. Not all of the members at that time were aware of details such as the commercial customs of the games world headed by Nintendo. However, they studied the existing persistent business structure, and discovered these problems and issues. Then, as SCE, they proceeded to form new business strategies that would creatively destroy the existing business model. What supported the actions of these SCE actors?

Maruyama, who was in charge of games at SME's Epic Sony, was very interested in games software and was keen to write his own epoch-making game at some time, but did not have the hardware to achieve this. On the other hand, Sony's Kutaragi focussed on developing a games device that would achieve three-dimensional computer graphics. Kutaragi had the technical ability, but was not able to write the software. Ohga, then president of Sony, had discovered Kutaragi's talent earlier, and before establishing SCE, he ensured that Kutaragi and Maruyama worked in the same office. Therefore, the games business concept was a topic of common interest to both Kutaragi and Maruyama's, respective teams. Tokunaka, a business management professional, and Sato, a record business professional, together with their teams, also shared the same interest. Each of them argued about various ideas, and a context with a definite coherence was formed and shared. Querying the reason for the existence of this new context on behalf of SCE, they produced the strong will and strength of purpose as actors for realizing the establishment of this precise strategic objective: "To radically reform the games business with our own hands!" (Bruch and Ghoshal, 2004).

Individually, they demonstrated leadership, but specific individuals were not there to persuade the team. Nor were they there to coerce team members. The starting point for leadership behavior in SCE was collaborative leadership (Chrislip and Larson, 1994; Bryson and Crosby, 1992) in which they acknowledged each other's abilities, made up for their partners' abilities, had their own abilities compensated for by their partners and mutually collaborated (devoting themselves especially to *kuroko*). This created the leadership teams (LT) in Figure 5.4. Kutaragi said: In the end, everything we did was a success for PlayStation. People make business. We do our best because we do it with best friends. We take it so everyone will think that that is true. We were lucky it went well. When something has been achieved, it's best when this is thought to be the result of one's own ideas (Asakura, 1998).

In project management, what succeeds is a common strategic objective among members and the project leaders facilitating resources to achieve those objectives. This results in an environment that enables project members to act harmoniously and autonomously. One of the factors for the success of the PlayStation business is that this "setting the stage for power" is big. For example, this "setting the stage for power" is also the connection between Kutaragi's development team and the creators of software. The creators of software were provided with software development tools and online support as and when needed. The purpose was to support their creative actions and further motivate them. SCE joined with creators throughout the world to provide end-users with new values called computer entertainment, and these became a great motive power of PlayStation.

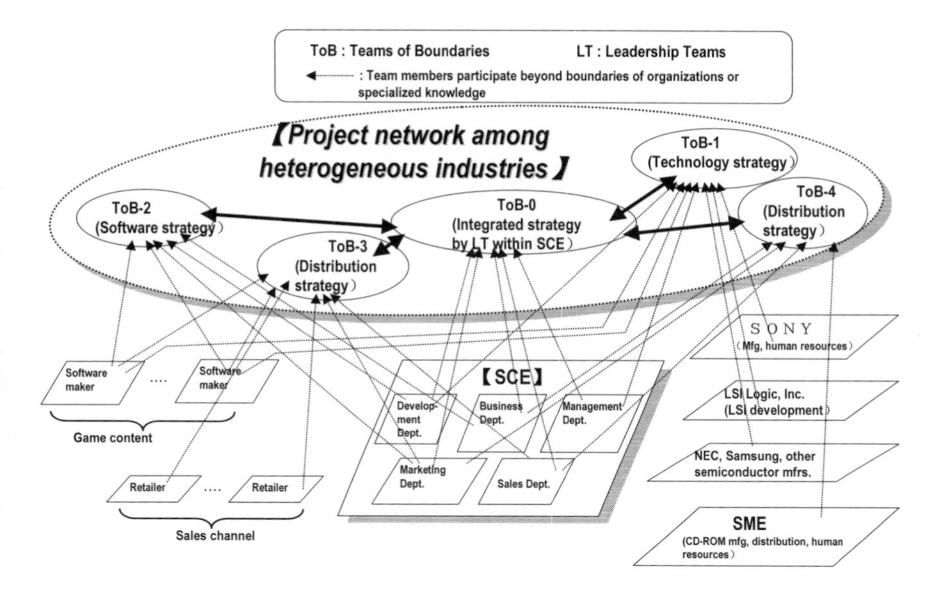

Figure 5.4: Project networks for nurturing PlayStation business.

Formation of ToB and LT and networking

Innovation stems from conflicts between heterogeneous fields of technology (Leonard–Barton, 1994). Surely, this PlayStation business concept was also born from conflict between actors with diverse backgrounds within SCE. Kutaragi's superior technical power, the creative and imaginative conceptualization of Maruyama and Takahashi, Sato's marketing knowhow in the record business and the holistic business planning faculty of Tokunaga, at the top of SCE — new knowledge was formulated by the skillful blending and integration of the knowledge possessed by individuals within SCE. Various repetitive conflicts and frictions among individuals gave rise to new knowledge in the form of definite strategic objectives.

However, a characteristic point is that in the case of SCE, facing the building of the strategy "win–win relationships for all players including users" gave rise to creative discussion and the "creative collaboration" discussed in Chapter 3. The result of the discussion was definitely not a compromise, but building a dialectically strategic objective, while repeating various denials, and it is to be noted is that they acted towards achieving this (Kodama, 2004). In Figure 5.3, strategic objectives that anyone could understand and accept dialectically would be formed in the leadership teams (LT) within SCE. Accordingly, resonance (Kodama, 2001) and confidence (Vangen and Huxham, 2003) in mutual values became the base and the motive power for achieving the strategic objectives.

Collaboration with various players was important for implementation of a technical strategy. For the development of PlayStation, a games machine with leading-edge technology, tight cooperative connections were made with semiconductor makers such as LSI Logic, Samsung Electronics and NEC. Sony's Kisarazu factory was fully used for assembling the sets. PlayStation's features were not confined to the functional aspects of the product. Sony's designers were seeking the design of a unique and original games device (including a controller). The design aspect was very important as a good design is sure to be a hit with the consumers. (The mobile telephone is a typical example of this.) However, a complicated design that was difficult for mass production would mean that product supply does not meet demand and opportunities to secure users would be lost. Therefore, Sony's designers investigated the proposition of "what kind of design could be mass produced?" The designers gathered at the plant and met the engineers responsible for production and metal mold-making to obtain a definitive solution to the proposition of compatibility between product design and improved productivity. As a result, the PlayStation body and controller became an extremely novel design that made PlayStation a hit product. Furthermore, among the software makers, the prototype games machines and several development tools functioned as boundary objects (Star, 1989; Cramton, 2001), and the sharing of knowledge between Kutaragi's development team and the creators gave rise to knowledge inspiration that led to the manufacturing of a better product.

In implementing these technical strategies, strategic alliances were formed with a number of enterprises. SCE and other companies shared their knowledge strongly, and facing the strategic technical objectives accelerated the creation of new knowledge. New objectives were set during repeated business meetings with other companies and these confirmed the levels of affirmation and attainment. Many ToBs were formed as space-time intervals of the strong sharing and creation of knowledge among these companies (ToB-1 in Figure 5.4).

Software strategy involved appealing to many software makers for their participation in the PlayStation format. Before PlayStation prototypes became available, hardly any software makers became participants (doubting the feasibility of games devices for household use having three-dimensional computer graphics functions), but SCE leadership teams (LTs) continued with persistent explanations. Then, following an explanatory demonstration meeting with a PlayStation prototype (where software makers became aware of its feasibility), the SCE leader team began to actively involve themselves the software makers. Having discovered common values in the cost structure of games software that made the maximum use of the benefits of PlayStation performance with the CD-ROM, the software makers were enthusiastic to create new software products. SCE built many networks with software makers and these networks formed many ToBs as space-time intervals of the strong sharing and creation of knowledge (ToB-2 in Figure 5.4).

Furthermore, the distribution strategy involved SCE calling on many software makers and retailers and explaining persistently to make them understand the new distribution system with its bundled buying system and prices. Many software makers were opposed to the bundled buying system. However, they gradually understood that SCE was thinking of "materializing" the most suitable supply chain management". This distribution system was the first of its kind in the games industry. At first software makers familiar with Nintendo's existing commercial customs found it difficult to understand. However, not for their own company, but also for users who had bought software, the ability to propose prices (the ability to procure new software inexpensively and promptly) made them change their way of thinking. As for the technical and software strategies, the distribution strategy involved forming strong networks with many software makers and retailers. These networks formed many ToBs as space-time intervals of the strong sharing and creation of knowledge (ToB-3 and 4 in Figure 5.3).

These ToBs that were dissimilar in context and knowledge and a cross different businesses, became strongly linked to LTs within SCE. The linkage of ToBs allows different contexts and knowledge to be shared dynamically among various organizations and solutions actors, and for new problems and issues are implemented. This network of LTs and ToBs is neither physical nor tangible. However, the actors who are actually performing deliberately form these invisible networks. PlayStation's business driving force was certainly implemented by the project network as LT and ToB networks found inside and outside the company, and they constructed a new value chain in the games business. This project network was dispersed within each ToB and integrated knowledge that was implemented by the three strategies.

5.2.4. *Relativity of ToB networks and formal organizations*

In a ToB, various data and contexts are shared among actors at the boundaries of dissimilar organizations and knowledge. Specific tactics and an action plan for implementing this strategic objective or a new strategic objective will be discussed from the viewpoint of individual actors. Then a specific action plan is developed as a vision, which takes the form of a tree with the strategic objective at the apex. The leaders identify specific roles and foster the required behavior within their teams and the formal organization. Many discussions about strategy, tactics, action plans, and content, negotiations on the specific details of "by whom, what, by when, to whom and how" take place within a ToB. Therefore, for the actors, it is not just an abstract all-embracing critical strategy, but the "Strategy as Practice" that is important (e.g. Pettigrew, 2003; Whittington, 2004). Within the ToB, the actors decide important issues through constructive dialog and "creative collaboration". Then, the issues dealt are decided upon by the actors in the formal organizations.

With regard to "how and by whom will it be done" the actors must work towards forming a new ToB as they are dynamically intensifying the collaboration of the actors inside and outside the company and those within the existing ToB. Of particular importance while forming a new ToB is the need to transmit the context and knowledge of other ToBs with which one is associated to the prospective members of the new ToB. Transmission alone is not enough. New meaning must be created based on the context to be communicated (Nonaka and Takeuchi, 1994). Then it is important that specific pragmatic issues are tackled (or executed by partners) in collaboration with new actors on the basis of this new meaning. Because of the dynamic changes to context, ToBs are formed. This produces new contexts and meanings and new ToBs are formed. The formation of a new ToB produces new issues and action plans (or changes the action plan already being executed) and the actors implement the action plan that must be executed by the team that is their formal organization.

Furthermore, the actors appropriately confirm the extent to which the action plan has been attained within the ToB and discover more problems and issues. Then, they reinforce the execution of a problem-solving action plan in more formal organizations and form a new ToB. Then the actors participate in several ToBs and arrange for context and knowledge to be shared among ToBs. It is necessary for middle management in particular to be committed to many ToBs. This is connected to knowledge integration by means of ToB networking. The unseen human networking in the background that builds inter-company networks and organization networks signifies this ToB network. At different times and in different locations (physically in the office or in cyberspace on the net), actors share the context with ToBs and networked ToBs, and generate new meanings on the basis of which strategies and action plans are made, and these are transferred to specific action through the formal organization.

5.2.5. *PlayStation technological innovation*

Among the factors that led to the success of the PlayStation business model, technical strategy was the most important one. Kutaragi, the leader who implemented the technical strategy, studied details and future trends associated with technology, and research and development everyday. In 1985, 10 years before the realization of the high-performance LSI that was mounted in the first PlayStation sold in 1994, he had predicted the advancement of LSI process technology and he foresaw the possibility of realizing new games machines. As reference data for Kutaragi's technical predictions, there is a rule of experience proposed in 1965 by Gordon Moore, president of Intel Corporation of the US, concerning the advances in computer operating capacity that is supported by the evolution of semiconductor miniaturization technology — "the rule of experience that the capacity for CPU operations will probably be doubled every 18 months". He predicted that "gate scale and capability will be doubled in eighteen months and quadrupled in three years" and this trend still holds true for the semiconductor industry.

Using Moore's Law as a reference and taking into account the accelerating evolution of semiconductor processing, in 1994 Kutaragi read that the feasible LSI thread width in mass production was 0.5 micron (in fact, a 0.5 micron million-gate system LSI was realized in 1993–94: Figure 5.5). Kutaragi then set out on the development of a 0.5 micron million-gate system LSI. Subsequently, the development of a LSI (called the Cell) mounted in PlayStation2 and later in PlayStation3 was based on this technological revolution.

The technical innovation that would become the core of PlayStation was not only a system LSI. It was an accumulation of several technical

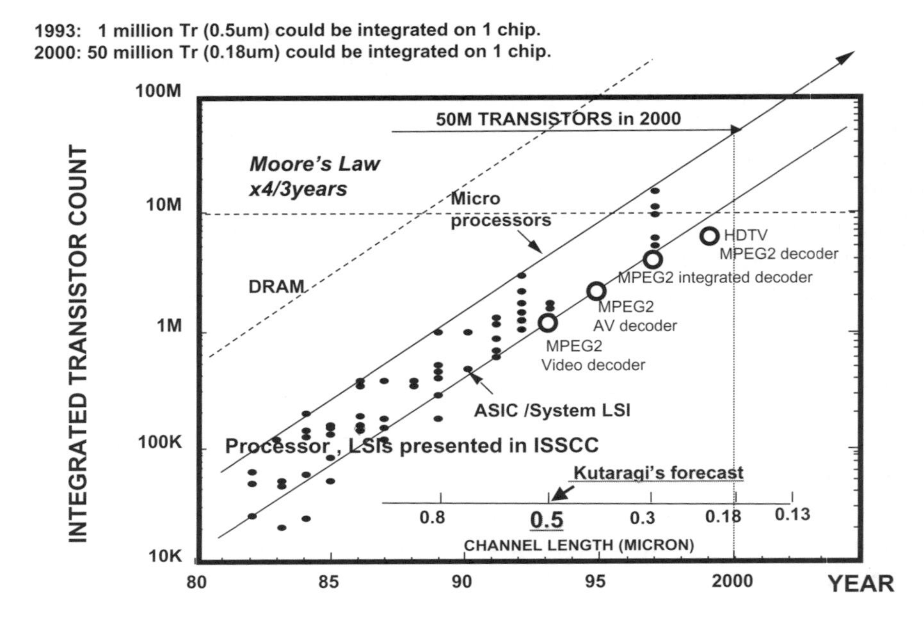

Figure 5.5: Integration of transistors over time.
Source: Prepared by author based on ISSCC data.

innovations, but here, we will take up PlayStation (PSX), a dual wavelength laser compatible optical pickup and DVD recorder, which is a case of relevant architectural innovation (Henderson and Clark, 1990), the case of the development of a system LSI (Cell) for PlayStation3, which is a radical innovation, and consider the process of how the project networks inside and outside the company tackled the new technical developments.

5.2.5.1. *Development of dual wavelength laser compatible optical pickup: realization of architectural innovation*

The development of PlayStation2, the successor to PlayStation that was released in March 2000, began in early part of 1998. One of the themes discussed at that time was the development of an optical pickup unit. It had not yet been commercialized anywhere and a team was needed for the development of a unit that could cope with CD-ROM and DVD-ROM. The first model, PlayStation, handled CD-ROM for games, as well as music CD, but for PlayStation2, the development team intended to mount a DVD-ROM to store games software and images, and provide the functions of a DVD player. The device that would become the key to materializing these functions was an optical pickup that could read data recorded on CD-ROM and DVD-ROM discs.

In 1998, an optical pickup was already available as a Sony product that was compatible with both CD-ROM and DVD-ROM. This had been developed for a Sony portable DVD player. However, that product had two laser diodes (LDs) that were required to read the separate types of data on CD-ROM and DVD-ROM. The oscillation wavelengths of each laser are 780 nm for CD-ROM and 650 nm for DVD-ROM. On the CD-ROM side, the LD and optical components (microprisms) had been miniaturized and united as a laser coupler. On the other hand, the DVD-ROM side is not a laser coupler, but consists of separate discrete components: LD, photo detector (PD) and optical components (grating, beam splitter, detection lens, etc.) From the SCE development project leader's viewpoint, it was clear that Sony optical pickups could cause yield rate problems for the mass-produced PlayStation by adding too many components. This was in addition to the optical pickups' demerits such as lowering price, enhancing performance and reducing weight (Figure 5.6).

Could an optical unit with a simple structure and fewer components be developed? When only 18 months were left for the PlayStation2 to be released, project leader, Kazuo Miura, requested directors of Sony's optical devices operations and semiconductor laser operations departments highly to provide talented people to form a team that would study the development of this new optical pickup. In July 1998, nine selected LD

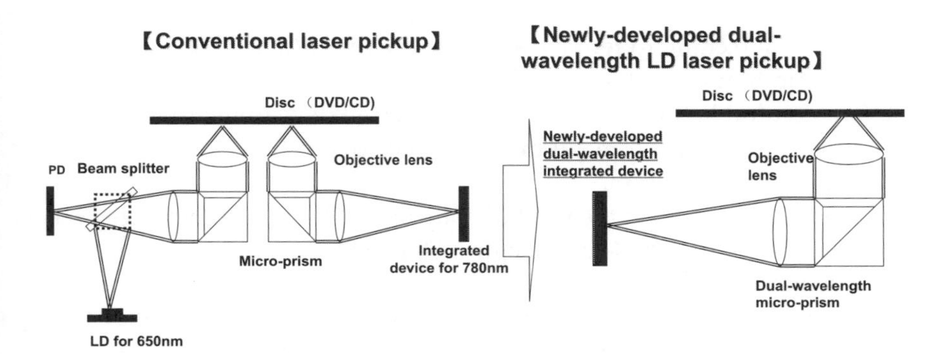

Figure 5.6: Development of dual-wavelength LD laser pickup.
Source: Prepared by author based on publicly-available Sony materials.

developers, optical system developers and circuit design engineers gathered together to form a development project on behalf of the Sony Group. Kutaragi, who was responsible for SCE developments, told the project members "instead of using two laser couplers, make it a single unit (including the optics system)". As shown in Figure 5.6, making two laser couplers into a single unit including the optics system was extremely difficult for the engineers. Moreover, it would be extremely difficult to undertake mass production in 18 months. Making the laser couplers into a single unit would not only reduce the number of components, but would also reduce the cost and improve productivity. For an engineer, this was clearly an important technical issue to be tackled.

Kutaragi always set a high target. He presented a challenging theme not only for himself, but also for his subordinate engineers, and they obliged. This denoted Sony's spirit of unity. The task was to make one unit of the laser couplers. The development project members discussed this each week and discovered that the two types of LD would be made into one. In other words, it was a matter of whether they could develop one LD to oscillate at two wavelengths (780 nm for CD-ROM and 650 nm for DVD-ROM), and a dual-wavelength laser (a dual-wavelength LD). This was a breakthrough discovery as a dual wavelength laser was unheard of in the business games industry, not to mention its commercialization.

During this time, an experienced semiconductor laser developer named Kazuhiko Emoto came up with the idea of devising a semiconductor thin-film crystal growth process to become the LD base. The 780 nm and 650 nm LD would use the same gallium arsenide (GaAs) substrate. First, grow a thin film for 780 nm on the GaAs substrate. Second, use chemical etching to remove a part of the thin film for 780 nm. Third, grow a thin film for 650 nm (Figure 5.7). Keishu Narui, a member of staff of Sony Central Laboratory who had substantial development experience in crystal growth using metal organic vapor deposition (MOCVD), was asked to develop the film.

Nobuyuki Idei, then the CEO of Sony (after Ohga), also promoted the development of this dual-wavelength LD. PlayStation, became a strategic Sony commodity, representing a positive investment of Sony's resources and technological strength in the development of games machines that possessed new core technology. Realizing the development of the dual-wavelength laser enables it to be marketed directly as a discrete item. Narui, who was later shifted from the laboratory to the Atsugi Semiconductor Laser

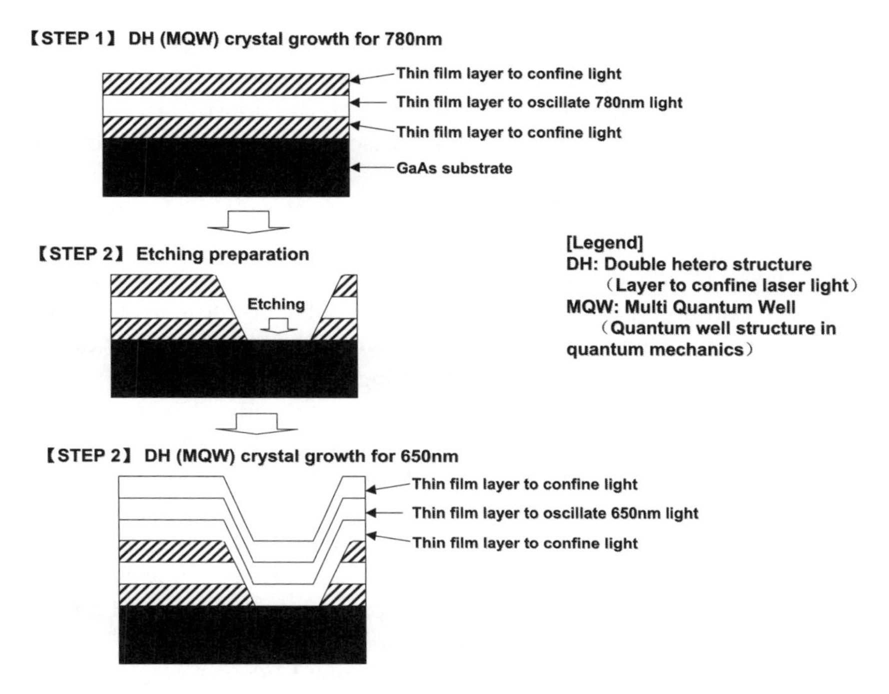

Figure 5.7: Process of dual-wavelength LD crystal growth.
Source: Prepared by author based on publicly-available Sony materials.

Operations Department, and Masafumi Kamei, in charge of LD production, tackled this new crystal growth process and LD production. At the same time, handled the manufacturing of dual-wavelength LD on the grown thin film and gathered data on the output characteristics (current and light output characteristics). At the same time, other development team members went ahead with the development and trial manufacture of the components needed for the dual-wavelength LD laser coupler including the substrate needed for mounting the dual-wavelength LD, dual-wavelength LD compatible prisms and photo detectors (PD).

In the beginning, grown crystal dual-wavelength LD prototypes had a short lifespan for light output and lacked the endurance for practical use, but optimum conditions were discovered at the laboratory level by changing the parameters (substrate temperature, etching time, etc.) with various crystal growth times. This solved the problem. Then a laser coupler for mounting the dual-wavelength LD was completed at the prototype level. The next problem was mass production. The development project proceeded in parallel with the prototype development. The semiconductor plant at Sony Shiraishi Semiconductor, a Sony Group company, was equipped with facilities for the mass production of laser couplers mounted with dual-wavelength LD and discussions were carried on with respect to the technical issues.

The mass production began at the semiconductor plant. However, there were unanticipated problems. One MOCVD apparatus was used at the laboratory level. The development team had been successful in discovering the optimum conditions for the crystal growth to resolve the lifespan of the dual-wavelength LD using that apparatus. However, several MOCVD devices (made by the same manufacturer and having the same input parameters as the one in the laboratory) had to be used at the semiconductor plant for mass production, and it was found that there was a wide variation in the characteristics of many of the dual-wavelength LD cut from the GaAs thin film growth semiconductor wafers. To resolve this problem, a development member of the semiconductor Operations Department at Atsugi was stationed permanently at Sony Shiraishi Semiconductor. Then, one by one, the optimum conditions for each MOCVD apparatus was discovered and the yield rate of dual-wavelength LD was improved.

At length, the dual-wavelength LD-mounted laser couplers shipped from Sony Shiraishi Semiconductor were combined with other components at Sony Hamamatsu plant and the process was completed at a mechanical deck. However, there was a problem. When the current applied to the DVD LD (part of the dual-wavelength LD) was increased, the light output disappeared. This is called the "kink phenomenon" (nonlinearity in the LD light output operating current). There was also a problem with improving the mounting precision of the dual-wavelength LD and the object lens, etc. In order to resolve these problems, the construction of the dual-wavelength LD was reviewed by improving component mounting surfaces, and a dozen or more parameters such as crystal growth temperatures and etching times. Then optimum parameters were discovered that eliminated the kink phenomenon and somehow the commercial manufacture of dual-wavelength LD-mounted laser couplers was successful at the mass production level (Figure 5.6). In March 2000, the first batch of 1.5 million PlayStation2 units, meant to initiate sales, were delivered successfully. The dual-wavelength LD-mounted laser coupler that is one of the core technologies of PlayStation2 was the first in the world to be commercialized, and it was realized by a project network that involved technicians from various organizations.

The development of this dual-wavelength LD-mounted laser coupler, an improvement of existing technology, represents the integration of two types of LD by means of a new crystal growth process. A major feature is that the structure is simple, and the optical system components are integrated by means of a sophisticated mounting technology. Although there is no major change in the functions of the individual components that make up the system called the laser coupler, the organization and connection of the individual components resulting from integration by means of semiconductor processing technology and mounting technology represent major changes compared with the internal structure of previous laser couplers. This is equivalent to changing the system architecture. This can thought of as being equal to architectural innovation (Henderson and Clark, 1990), but this dual-wavelength LD-mounted laser coupler is not simply the integration of components and an altered combination of components. Technical know-how is not just the integration of components by mounting technology. Engineers' tacit knowledge also plays an important role in the design and manufacturing process of dual-wavelength LD. The dual-wavelength LD is not a simple module combination of two LD with different wavelengths. The technical know-how that is difficult for other companies to imitate is condensed in the method of growing a thin film of crystals on a semiconductor wafer and the process of the LD manufacture (Figure 5.7). In other words, the integration of individual LD (modules) in this case is an interface between closed modules that are peculiar to Sony. The various technical parameters on semiconductor processing are a black box that has been condensed as know-how. Having experienced the accumulation of know-how by technical improvements over many years to the technology for compound semiconductor crystal growth and the technology for the high-density mounting of optical components, called incremental innovation, rearranging the system structure and new integration technology and made architectural innovation possible (Figure 5.9).

5.2.5.2. *Towards architectural innovation and radical innovation of LSI*

Incremental innovation through miniaturization of manufacturing processes and smaller chip size

The chip that is the core of PlayStation2, which was launched in March 2000, contains two LSI developed jointly by SCE, Sony and Toshiba. One LSI is the game machine's main processor, "Emotion Engine (EE)" and the other is a graphics LSI, "Graphics Synthesizer (GS)". During the first sales in March 2000, the LSI design began with the 0.25 micron rule (about 10 million transistors). This was the highest semiconductor processing technology during that time. Later, LSI layout designs were revised to match the advance of the miniaturization technology (0.18 micron: 13.5 million transistors). As a result, the two individual LSI chips were smaller in area and power consumption was also reduced, which resulted in a lower production costs of the games machine (Figure 5.8). An additional incremental technical improvement by the development project, matched to the advance of semiconductor process technology, was an incremental innovation that improved productivity and, at the same time, reduced the cost of the product.

By January 2003, Sony had sold more than 50 million units of PlayStation2. This is about four times the sales of all PlayStation units. EE and GS series had been miniaturized, but even so, the component costs for LSI such as EE and GS, power circuits, radiation mechanisms and all kinds of noise reduction, accounted for a large proportion of the overall manufacturing cost of games machines. Accordingly, new targets

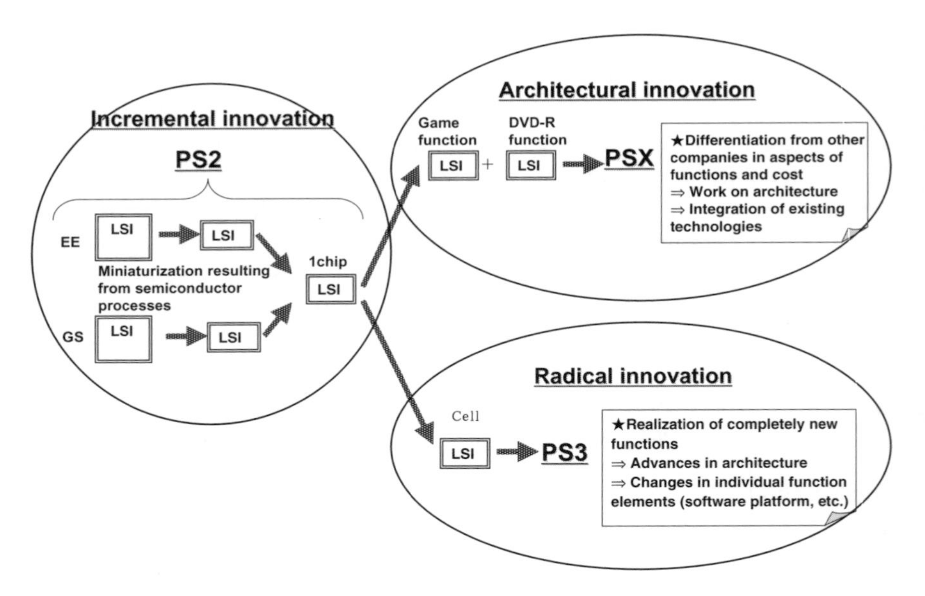

Figure 5.8: Changes in innovation (PlayStation LSI).

were set for the SCE, Sony and Toshiba development project. The development objective was not only greater reduction in manufacturing cost and improved productivity, but also the greatest challenge to semiconductor processing technology, a shift from 0.18 micron processing technology to 90 nm in one jump. Then they aimed at cost reduction and improved productivity by combining two LSI in a single chip. This was a big hurdle based on the long relationship of the mutual trust that had been fostered in the development of the EE and GS, the SCE, Sony and Toshiba project team pooled their technical know-how and held vehement discussions.

However, a timeperiod of seven months was allocated for the development schedule for the single chip combination. The engineers made the best use of intellectual assets such as previous design and inspection materials. It was important to note that the single chip combination was the process of verification — the operation of the separate EE and GS and the single chip form (EE and GS in one chip). The engineers considered new circuits for verifying the operation and an interface circuit (clock) to synchronize the operating frequencies of the two LSI. Toshiba's plasma nitriding technology (to increase the transistor reliability by introducing nitrogen between silicon dioxide (SiO2) electrodes) and new photo lithography were used to enable 90-nm miniaturized semiconductor processing. The single chip combination was achieved by means of incremental semiconductor electronic engineering innovations such as these. Subsequently, Oita T S Semiconductor (OTSS), a joint venture of SCE and Toshiba, began to manufacture this new single chip, which enabled cheaper mass production of PlayStation2.

Architectural innovation by integration and replacement of knowledge assets

Kutaragi has predicted that computer entertainment systems such as games machines, as well as digital consumer electronics (including DVD players, digital TV, digital cameras) and networking applications (including PDA and videophones) would become very popular. As a first step towards the development of a LSI that could cope in common with a variety of products for consumer electronics and networking, Kutaragi's SCE development project aimed at making effective practical use of the technical assets of PlayStation2 to develop a games machine (called PSX) that has the functions of a DVD recorder, a digital consumer electronics product.

In 2003, he hurriedly gathered all 200 of SCE and Sony's engineers and formed a great development project. The basic guidelines of the development were to make the greatest possible practical use of technical materials as knowledge assets held up to now by the Sony Group in order to quickly market games machines with DVD recorder functions. Sony already had the elemental technology for terrestrial TV tuners and DVD recorders.

The conceptual design for the basic construction of PSX comprises the electronic circuit block that is the core of PS2 and an electronic circuit block that realizes DVD recorder functions and a hard-disk drive with adjustment interfaces between each function block. The PSX concept is to utilize the Sony Group's existing technical assets, to adjust every kind of element with individual technical interfaces and to integrate dissimilar technical elements. In other words, although there are no sweeping changes such as separate function blocks, associated with technical architectural changes, the assembly of separate technical elements is different, keeping in view the architectural innovation mentioned in Henderson and Clark (1990) (Figure 5.8). When PSX was released, its price was JPY79,800. During this time engineers of other companies had problems understanding how it was possible to set such a low price (less than half) for a device with DVD recorder functions. The difference between this and other companies' products was not only due, to the shorter product development lead time and broad cost reduction but also the architectural innovation that enabled SCE to transplant the excellent graphical user interface (GUI) as a games machine into digital consumer electronics. In a technical development of this kind, for the adjustment and integration of technical interface sections, not only is it necessary to divert existing hardware and software assets to include a function in a function block, but also make new ones. However, this architectural innovation is not a sudden process. The ability to realize new architecture by integrating dissimilar technical elements depends on the accumulation of know-how in various technical fields through incremental innovation related to many years of technology (Figure 5.9). In this case, PSX was materialized by the incremental accumulation of elemental technologies (LSI design technology, semiconductor processing technology, software technology) in several product fields, and new ideas on product concepts and technological architecture levels.

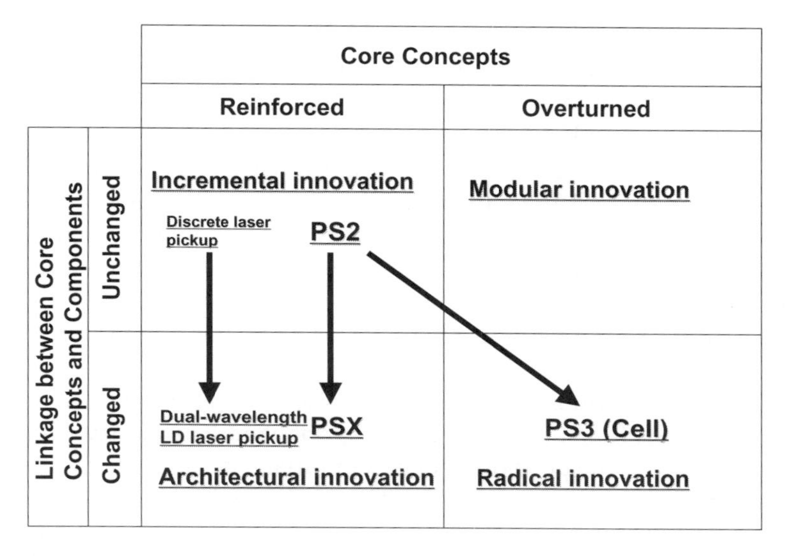

Figure 5.9: Dynamics of innovation shifts: LSI and laser pickups in PlayStation.
Source: Prepared by author based on Henderson and Clark (1990).

The challenge of shifting from incremental innovation to radical innovation

In parallel with the development of PSX, Kutaragi was pondering over the concept of a next-generation microprocessor, PlayStation3, as the successor to PS2. His idea was to go beyond the world of games machines and develop a product based on new concepts in the era of ubiquitous 21st century broadband. Specifically, this would involve not only entertainment tools, which are games machines, but the development of a general-purpose microprocessor for so-called digital consumer electronics (including digital TV, DVD-R, digital video recorders, high-performance digital cameras), networking devices (such as home servers and high-performance commercial servers), as well as terminal devices such as PDAs.

At present, each digital consumer electronics product, including the current mobile telephones, has a separate LSI, and each company competes to give its LSI greater functionality at a lower cost. Consequently, development costs increase and it is a challenge to decrease these costs. The mobile telephone business, in particular, suffers from drastic market changes and technical reforms, and large amounts of money are needed for the development of the LSI that is mounted in mobile telephones. Recently there have been examples of strategic alliances and joint venture companies between the makers of mobile telephones for the development of LSI for mobile telephones (five companies — NEC, NEC Electronics, Matsushita Electric Industrial, Panasonic Mobile Communications and Texas Instruments — recently announced the establishment of Adcore-Tech, a new joint venture company to conduct the development, design and technology licensing of a communications platform in July 2006) and communications carriers (NTT and DoCoMo, for instance) and semiconductor makers (Texas Instruments in the US and RNESAS in Japan).

Global competition for the development of electronic calculators began in the 1970s. At first, a separate specialized IC was developed for each product, but the development cost gradually became a heavy burden for each maker and they turned to the development of microprocessors that were capable of upgrading the functions with a software program. In the world of personal computers, Intel and AMD were the actual default standards.

Therefore, just as the microprocessors that had been developed for electronic calculators had created new applications for PC and all kinds of integration machines (such as machine tools, for instance), from among the furious market changes and technical reforms, it was also possible to produce a new platform for the field of digital consumer electronics. Videoconferencing systems and videophones are also among the technical trends discussed in Chapter 4. In future, digital consumer electronics including mobile telephones will shift from dedicated chips to general-purpose chips. In other words, it is highly probable that high-performance microprocessors and high-value-added software will invade the market. Compared to the development of products until now, the development of semiconductors was very difficult to follow, but for the last several years, the miniaturization of semiconductors has accelerated and the demand for these products has been increasing.

Therefore, taking trend into consideration, and thinking of new architecture for the development of the next-generation microprocessor and its realization, Kutaragi made strategic alliances with the world's best partners. Then, as a step towards the development of the next-generation LSI for PlayStation3, he joined hands with Sony and Toshiba who have been partners until now that specializes in and IBM microprocessor development and is the world's leading semiconductor processing technology.

While deciding on the initial product concept, the project network consisting of SCE, Sony, Toshiba and IBM, decided on a target of 1 TeraFLOPS (10^{12} floating operations per second) for the performance of the newly-developed microprocessor. At this time, PlayStation2's EE achieved what was considered an astounding 6.2 gigaFLOPS, but the new generation processor would surpass this figure by a factor of 160. For the project members, this meant that new architecture must be planned in order to realize this figure. The most important requirement was to have a multi-core structure that could combines several CPU cores. With this architecture, several microprocessors connected to a network and acting in harmony would be able to reach a high operations performance. As a result of various discussions among the project members, including Kutaragi, the architecture that was finally decided on was IBM's ultra-fine technology, "Power4", as the main CPU core and eight RISC processors combined in a network bus. They called this microprocessor architecture the "Cell".

Although this new architecture is similar to EE that has been the PlayStation2 microprocessor until now, the fundamental difference is that the flexible system architecture allows the Power4 and the eight RISC processors to act separately and independently, or work together through the network bus. For instance, several software applications can be processed simultaneously on these several microprocessors. In other words, the development of most consumer electronics products is inefficient in many cases, because the maker had to develop a special LSI whenever a new function was needed. Encoding and composing multimedia contents, which has been mainly done up to now with hardware, can now be done with software by using this Cell. In other words the Cell further advances the architecture of PlayStation2 until now and is a way of broadly diverting the realization of individual functions from hardware to software (Figure 5.8). By utilizing a software platform on this Cell, the maker is now able to realize various functions to meet the needs of the market. In other words, multimedia data (images, sounds, data), functions can be realized by mounting this Cell. In this way, the development of the Cell has changed the architecture of the LSI in existing products, and at the same time, has also changed the individual functions (hardware and software) that the product realizes. This can be interpreted as a dynamic shift from incremental innovation to radical innovation (Figure 5.9).

The dynamics of the Cell development project system

Considering this new development project from the point of view of the organizations, the fact that SCE reviewed this radical innovation project is important. In other words, until the development of PlayStation2 and PSX, the Sony Group was not able to escape from a path-dependent frame with existing technology as its base, although the integration of extra-mural (Toshiba) knowledge had been realized. Many existing studies until now (Leonard-Barton, 1995; Tushman and Romanelli, 1985; Henderson and Clark, 1990; Christensen, 1997; Tushman and Anderson, 1986; Tushman and O'Reilly III, 1997; Rosenbloom, 2000; O'Reilly III and O'Reilly III, 2004) point out that organization systems for product development and new business that accompany radical innovation must be implemented not by existing organizations, but a new organizational system. However, in the advanced field of semiconductor engineering, the engineers who have been engaged until now in developing games machines should not be replaced. This is because in the technical field of LSI technology, various technical fields including system design, electronic circuit engineering, semiconductor design, computer engineering, software technology and semiconductor processing technology, the ability to extend knowledge, skill and know-how to diverse contexts are essential for an engineer. Project leaders and senior development managers, in particular, need to be conversant in several of the above-mentioned specialized fields. Furthermore, for many engineers, their experience and knowledge derived from their participation in the development of PlayStation2 have enabled them to feel various contexts on their skin.

In the case of the development of the Cell, Kutaragi judged that IBM employees who possessed advanced technical skills in the above-mentioned technical fields. Then he formed a project network with IBM professionals in various specialized fields (Figure 5.10). The Cell is a good integration of Japanese and American wisdom. Needless to add, there were various frictions among the project members. For example, the IBM engineers proposed that they wanted to integrate the processors that realize distributed processing, which is Cell architecture, entirely into the IBM Power4. The Japanese engineers strongly opposed this proposal. The project members argued among themselves for better solutions. Finally, they agreed to adopt a middle path between Japan and the US. The IBM plan to integrate everything into Power4 and the Japanese plan to integrate into the general-purpose CPU were combined and this

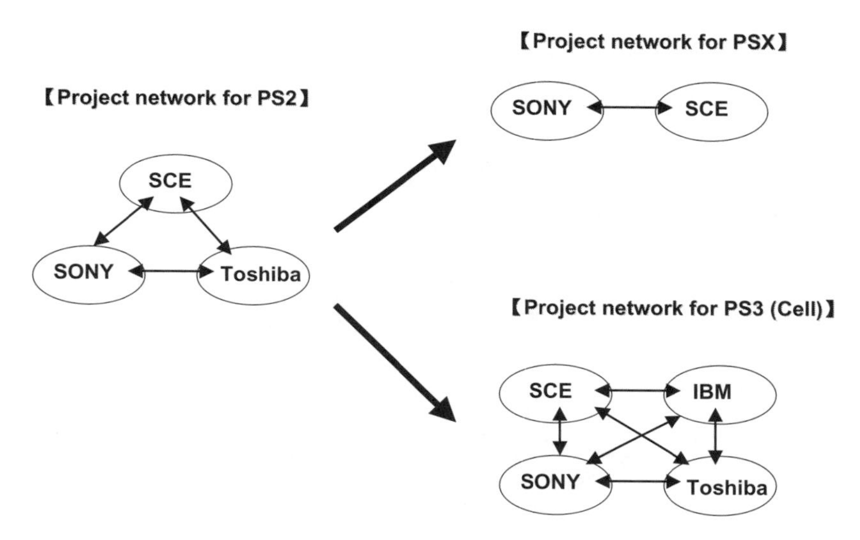

Figure 5.10: Changes in project networks of LSI development.

resulted in the current architecture (one Power4 and eight CPUs). The PlayStation2 EE concept had also been taken into account while making the decision.

Until basic architecture of the Cell was confirmed, the Japanese and Americans worked on the project separately and held meetings once a month. In the beginning of 2001, when the Cell architecture was confirmed, the project members gathered at the IBM semiconductor design division in Austin, Texas, to implement the LSI design process including the detailed design of the LSI, simulation, verification, etc. Several new members from Sony and Toshiba volunteered to help the members of Cell project. Engineers from IBM also joined them. For a professional skilled in the field of semiconductor design, this was an unparalleled chance of realizing a dream of developing the world's greatest LSI. If resonance of value (Kodama, 2001) was the common technical objective, the engineers would have no need for superfluous theory. Of course, there was a heated discussion, but because the main objective was to materialize the Cell, this too gave rise to constructive and creative dialogs, as well as the "creative collaboration" explained in Chapter 3.

The task of the LSI development project extended over many alternatives. As shown in Figure 5.11, several teams were formed under the SCE

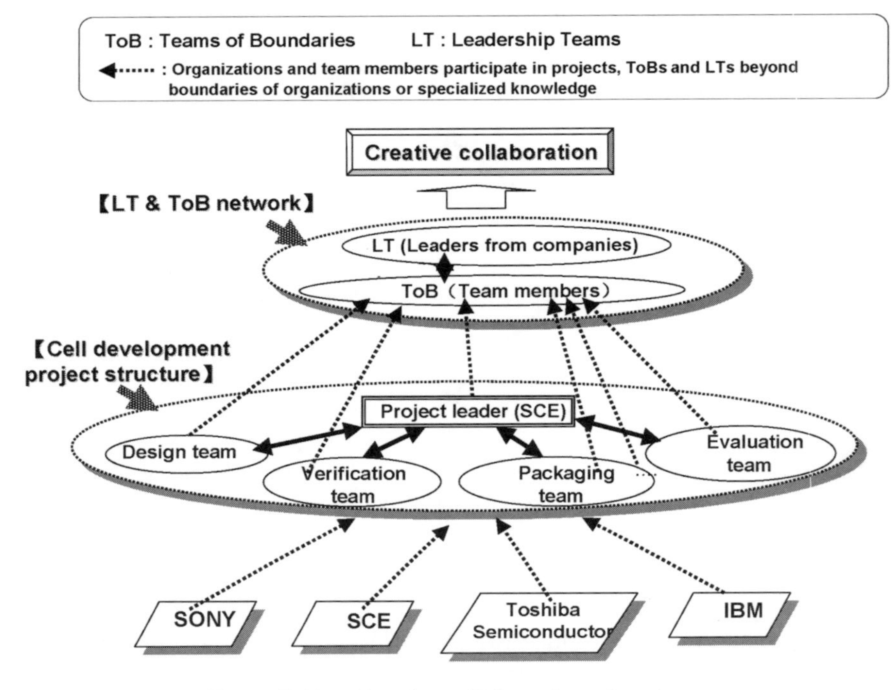

Figure 5.11: Creative collaboration of projects.

project leader to design the theoretical circuit of the Cell, verify whether the design was in accordance with the specifications, check the theoretical circuit layout design and to verify all kinds of actions and evaluate the prototype chip. Apart from these teams, many experienced professionals were hired. For instance, a project manager was in charge of project progress control, a general technical leader, as well as others supported the project.

A large-scale project such as the Cell requires technical skills of individuals in specialized fields and cooperation among teams. What is more important is the collaboration among the members of the various teams and teamwork among the leaders of each company. When the LSI architecture and basic technology were confirmed the task allotted to each team had to be carried out reliably in accordance with the pre-arranged development flow. The tasks of each team overlapped on the time axis as they advanced, but the interfaces between the tasks of each team had to be clearly-defined, and plenty of adjustment and cooperation was needed whenever a development task was passed to the next team. Then, whenever a project team was faced with an urgent issue (such as specification change or a technical problem), that issue had to be resolved flexibly and reliably through cooperation with each team.

Consequently, the project members not only had to drive the tasks they had been allotted under the formal project system, but as shown in Figure 5.11, it was also important to form ToBs to facilitate inter-team cooperation beyond the formal project system and to form LTs to facilitate teamwork among the leaders of each team. These ToBs and LTs were an invisible system, but their formation was timed in accordance with conditions and context, and gave rise to "creative collaboration" among leaders and members. Then the project members resolved any problems or issues, which had occurred, and the entire project team was able to create even greater knowledge.

The Cell development process resulted in a variety of problems and new issues. They included the problem of power consumption that resulted from Cell construction; the issue of realizing a high-speed interface between components; the method of connecting the CPU core and signal processors; a new proposed idea from Kutaragi to arrange for processor redundancy; and a proposal from IBM for a partial change to the specification for the CPU core when the design had been nearly completed. In the complicated LSI development process, the thoughts and actions of project members inevitably created unexpected conditions. Thus in a dynamically, changing context, the project members formed ToBs and LTs, and discovered measures for resolution through trial and error by "creative collaboration".

To use a sports analogy, LSI development project was surely a form of soccer. In aiming at the goal, the players not only used their individual skills and fulfilled their roles in the positions they had been given, but also cooperated skillfully with players in other positions. However, in accordance with the circumstances, players went beyond the role of their own position to temporarily improvise and play by ear, fulfilling a separate role in collaboration with other players.

Training project leaders and team leaders

The project leader and team leaders shouldered the responsibility for system LSI development. The number of outstanding leaders determined the company's system LSI projects, and product competitiveness. Due to advances in semiconductor miniaturization technology, LSIs in 2000 had already passed the 50-million transistor level, and in 2005, based on 0.1 micron technology, about 200 million elements had been reached. This means that technically, all the necessary functions for digital consumer electronics products, including games machines, can be concentrated on a single silicon chip. In other words, microprocessor, memory, analog circuits and logic circuits can be combined. At the same time, higher speeds and lower power consumption would be promoted. Moreover, the improved performance of microprocessors such as the Cell would further improve the action and scope of add-on software.

Consequently, various issues such as development costs and the complexity of designing for higher performance and verification of faster performance, the expanded scope of a project such as the LSI design make the existence of high-quality project leaders and team leaders indispensable for overseeing the development process. Projects such as this require experienced project leaders who are knowledgeable about system algorithms, silicon technology, hardware and software, upstream and downstream designs, electronic design automation (EDA) tools and analog circuit design. The role of project leaders is not simply to control the progress of the project, but being experienced in various technologies, they should be able to guide and train team leaders, and execute the precise technical management of the project.

Besides being talented people who can create new ideas and concepts, they must be well-versed in individual skills and have an overall understanding of other technical fields.

6

Boundaries Synchronization: Case Study of Matsushita Electric and Canon

6.1. Project Strategies Flexible to Changes

This section examines the strategies for projects in an industry that faces extreme changes in the market and by competition. High-tech industries aiming at mass markets such as IT and digital appliances have to focus on technological innovations that are driven by the changing needs of customers, as well as market organizational reforms. Those who fail to pursue an economy of scale, range and speed are unlikely to survive in this industry. This section examines and discusses business strategies for digital household appliances. Digital household appliance strategies of Matsushita Electric and Canon are studied. I attempt to provide a new viewpoint on the two companies' new product development processes. In the project networks formed by Matsushita Electric and Canon, the project does not focus on product development; rather, a number of actors work through close interactions among the departments including sales, product planning, development design, manufacturing technology and production. The manufacturing of digital household appliances such as DVD recorders and digital cameras is subject to extreme environmental changes like market changes and technological innovation. Matsushita Electric and Canon have been able to acquire healthy market share only by continuously delivering new products to the market at the right time. Both companies continue to use the global "vertical launch" strategy as a time-pacing strategy. This section describes the concept of boundaries synchronization in project networks, which enables this time-pacing strategy to operate.

6.2. Innovation by Matsushita Electric

6.2.1. *Departure from the past: abolishment and rebuilding of systems in addition to breakthroughs*

Matsushita Electric, with 270 thousand employees and ¥7 trillion in turnovers, has led the post-war Japanese economy. After recording a loss of ¥43.1 million, the largest in its history, in the fiscal year 2001, 1,300 employees left Matsushita Electric voluntarily on an early retirement plan, indicating that the lifetime employment system was no longer a Japanese workplace fundamental practice. The business model of "Mass Production and Mass Selling," built by its founder, Konosuke Matsushita, does not hold good today. The myth that Matsushita will never collapse no longer exists. "The 21st century is all about speed" said Matsushita Electric's president, Kunio Nakamura (now chairman).

Over the past 20 years, Matsushita has not had a single hit product that contributed to their profits. Although sales rose from 1970, sales profit declined steadily from 1980, eventually leading to debt. Matsushita could not initiate drastic reforms until it had fallen into debt. Looking back at the situation of the company then, Nakamura mentions, "people were arrogant, self-satisfied and always held meetings. They didn't like conflict. More than half of them expressed their satisfaction with the present system at that time. They were bound by the past. If we change the system, conflict occurs. As the top management of the company, we are responsible for all changes."

This atmosphere in Matsushita prevented it from producing a hit product. The longtime success of the Mass Production and Mass Selling business model pressurized and prevented the employees from committing themselves to producing a new hit product. "People from the business department who were involved in invention were not looking at their customers. Their focus was somewhere distant from their customers" (Nakamura).

The business model of the 20th century, "Mass Production and Mass Selling," was created by Matsushita's founder, Konosuke Matsushita, based on the business department system. Matsushita continued to open new business departments that were in charge of newly released products (there were 127 business departments at its peak, for example, TV, video, refrigerator, iron, etc.). The business departments became the driving force for the company's growth as they competed against each other to improve their sales. Individual business departments were independent with their own capacity for sales, manufacturing and R&D. Products were developed and manufactured by these business departments, and sold by retailers belonging to Matsushita Group's nationwide network (27 thousand at its peak). The company lost touch with its customers with their business model, "the company sells as many products as they make." Matsushita lost customers to giant retailers that entered the market in 1980. There was a rapid decline in group retail companies, with a significant portion of them eventually going out of business. Matsushita Electric began to lose sales profit, as well. Thus, the Mass Production and Mass Selling business model quickly become invalid in the new era.

No one in the company challenged the business department system because it had been created by the founder. Since the company was in crisis, the system had to be abolished and rebuilt (Nakamura). Since his appointment as president of Matsushita Electric in June 2000, Nakamura has dismantled the business department system and has been committed to reforms with the theme of "Abolishment and Rebuilding" and "Leap 21." In January 2004, Matsushita Electric announced its "Great Leap 21 Plan," a mid-term management plan for the coming three years starting in the fiscal year 2004. This plan set targets of ¥8.2 trillion in consolidated sales and return on investment (ROI) of better than 5% for the fiscal year 2006. Furthermore, 1,300 employees left Matsushita Electric voluntarily with the early retirement plan, indicating that the lifetime employment system was no longer a Japanese workplace fundamental.

Matsushita Electric enjoyed a sudden V-shaped recovery in business results after instituting drastic organizational reforms. The dismantling of the business department system, one of the pillars of these reforms, allowed the company to select and concentrate on management resources and business domains. The purpose of introducing the domain system was to develop products that would meet changing customer needs and integrate the company's resources in response to technological changes. An example of this is the integration of video images, music and PC media as shown in Figure 6.1. As most of the products dealt with at the time of the business department system were analog technologies, the products were simply stand-alone video or audio devices. To use digitalized technologies, individual products now needed to be connected to the network. This obviously to organizational reform.

Take the Audio Visual department as an example. As data, including video image data and audio data, are used in various devices (digital TVs,

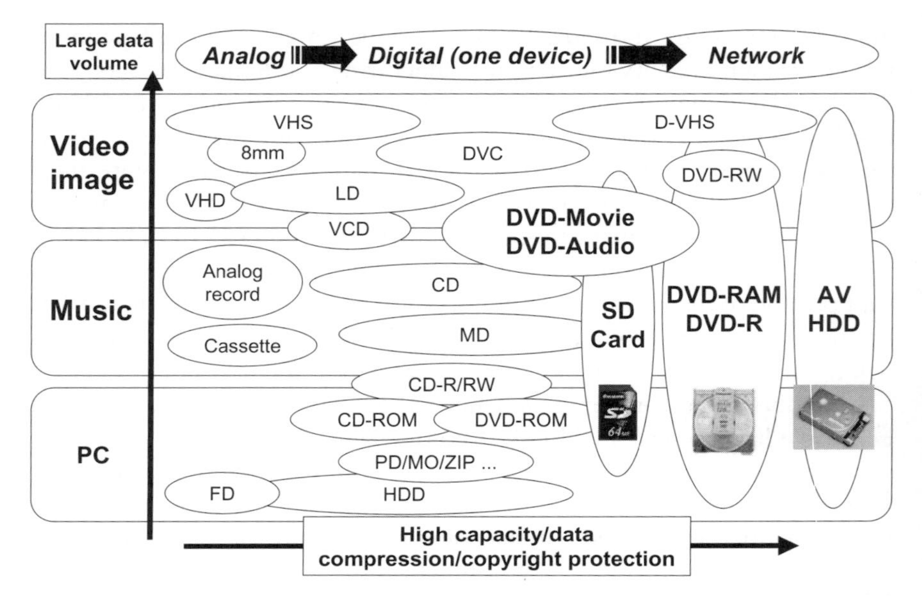

Figure 6.1: Integration of video images, music and PC Media.
Source: Constructed by the author based on the author's interview with Matsushita Electric.

digital videos, digital cameras, mobile data terminals) via DVD or SD cards, the separate technologies used for video, audio, and PCs need to be integrated. Therefore, given that these devices require a common platform, developing a particular product at an independent business department level was made extremely inefficient in terms of resources, as well as the overlapping of developments. Furthermore, development teams from all business departments needed to be integrated into the audio visual technology center (see Figure 6.2).

In addition, the business departments, specially designed for specific products (video, digital A/V network, electric musical instrument), needed to be restructured according to customer usage (home and personal purposes, A/V product media and device types). Figure 6.2 shows the reformed structure of Panasonic AVC (PAVC), in charge of project planning, product planning, development, and the production of digital household appliances (DVD recorders, digital cameras, digital TVs). PAVC was responsible for the planning, development and production of audiovisual products including overseas models, particularly digital household appliances.

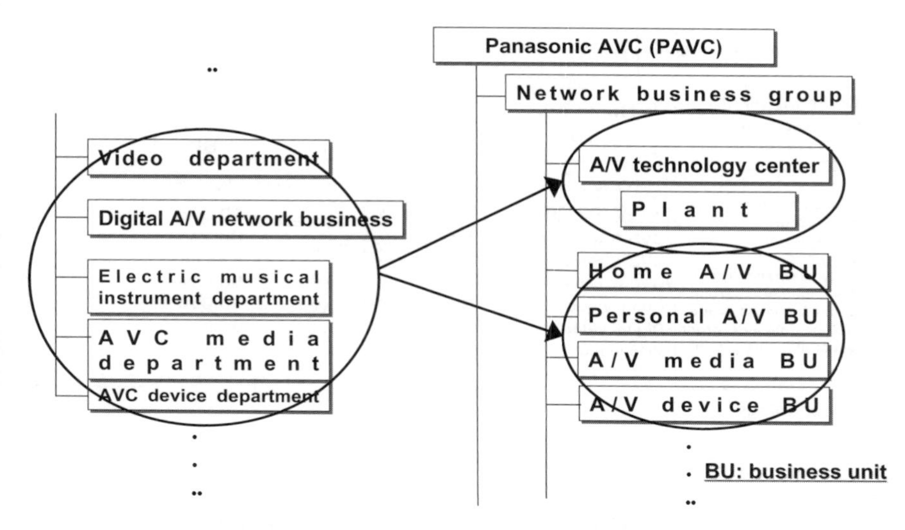

Figure 6.2: Structural reform — business domain and its role in development.
Source: Constructed by the author based on the author's interview with Matsushita Electric.

Another important organizational reform for Matsushita Electric was its marketing and sales capacities in Japan. There was a widespread view among employees that the sales department was responsible for any unsold products. In addition, no one in the marketing and sales departments was held accountable. The role of the marketing division (PM Division) was to change this viewpoint and attempt to discover customer needs.

The PM Division, as an organization, combined the different marketing and sales capacities of the old business departments, and planned, sold, and advertised the products according to customer needs. Monitoring the market, this PM Division, not the business departments, made decisions related to marketing and sales matters including products and pricing. The PM Division is responsible for inventory and actively involved in product planning, while PAVC was in charge of development and production. Matsushita saw this as a drastic organizational reform.

Thus, with the division between the business departments abolished, the sales departments, no longer belonging to any business department, can express their honest opinions (e.g. the product will not sell well, they want this function, they want a certain number of the product ready for delivery). Nakamura employed young, capable and talented people in the

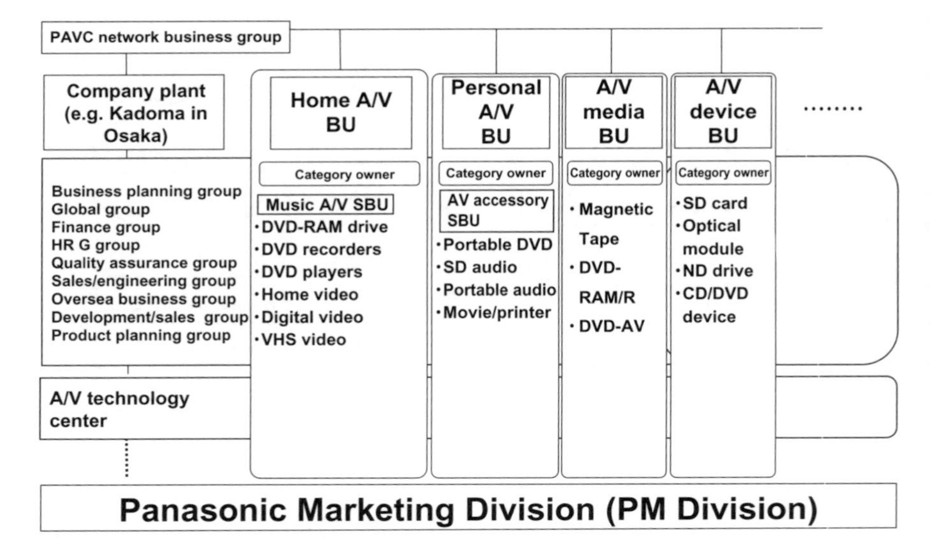

Figure 6.3: Structural reform (partial) — review of marketing/sales, development and production processes.

Source: Constructed by the author based on the author's interview with Matsushita Electric.

PM Division and began to build an organizational infrastructure to produce hit products. Figure 6.3 shows the organizational structure of the PM Division and PAVC. The role of the PM Division in product planning is not to explore the possible technological function of a product, but to suggest to PAVC the requirements for product function from the users' perspective. In response to this, the product planning manager of the home A/V business unit (BU) in the Network Business Group of PAVC, in cooperation with the A/V Technology Center development team within the Group, analyzes from a technical perspective and develops product design data (required system configuration, function block, schematic level) from the function requirement requested by the PM Division.

The PM Division amalgamated development and production into a strategic product planning and business unit to create an organic organizational operation structure that freshly questioned the existence of any value in making things from the users' point of view. This reform led the way to the so-called "V products" that were digital appliances such as DVD recorders, digital TVs and digital cameras. President Nakamura's strong faith in the revival of Japan's manufacturing industry was reflected in the organizational reforms at Matsushita. "The manufacturing industry has been declining in recent years and this had to be addressed. It is important to concentrate on technology and transform the company into a distinguished manufacturer. During the '90s, Matsushita Electric had individual departments including R&D. During the period of mass production, it was fine for us to imitate other companies, but now with the growth of digital technology, we need to quickly develop our own distinctive products. The most important part of this strategy is to do what other companies are not doing. To achieve this, we need to concentrate on black-box type technology development, and then I believe Japan will once again become a manufacturing nation." (Nakamura)

The "V products" that lead Matsushita's "Great Leap 21" have three features: Black box technology, environmental considerations (energy-saving, recycling) and universal design. Supporting the marketing, development and production of "V products" have been the positive activities of middle management and young employees who have a vision, something that was not seen by the old business department system. One of the features of the organizational reform is that the pyramid organization of the old business department system was changed from a peak 13-layer structure to a four-layer structure, creating a flat, web-type organization. New posts such as Business Unit Manager and Team Leader were also established, providing an environment in which ambitious young employees ("chiefs" or "managers" who are also union members) could play major roles. This "Nakamura Reform" gave birth to an organic organizational system — an integration of business departments in which middle managers and young employees could participate and be responsible for business projects.

6.2.2. *DVD recorder innovations*

6.2.2.1. *Myth of "vertical launch" coming into reality: PM division*

In his management policy announcement for the fiscal year 2002, President Nakamura's aim was to use "V products" to either capture or maintain top market share and realize a V-shaped recovery in profits. The DVD recorder, positioned as a representative V product, records and plays back digital video images, thus replacing the video tape recorder

(VCR). With the expansion of the market for DVD recorders, Matsushita is aiming to make DVD-RAM a *defacto* worldwide standard.

The PM Division, split from the various sales departments, is a group that aspires to generate new product strategies aimed at creating post-VHS businesses. As a product supervision division, the PM Division is responsible for the planning, marketing and sales of a product, as well as buying back all products. This represents a significant departure from the days of the old business department system at Matsushita Electric. In those days of mass production and the business department system, when it was easy to sell any product, this confidence game between sales and technology was fine. However, in this age of digital technology, where product life cycles are short, this is no longer valid. In the PM Division, personnel responsible for products are committed to the entire process of a new product from planning to sales. The core element of sales & marketing is "human resources". Eversince the PM Division was formed, division manager, Shunzo Ushimaru, by communicating with a number of employees, has been trying to spread a common value for reforms and promote unity in the division. The introduction of a flat, web-type organization enabled 600 employees in the PM Division to work efficiently and flexibly for the "vertical launch" of "V products" and closely with customers.

The following pages describe the structure of PM Division. The Product Planning Group is responsible for marketing of A/V products. The Home A/V Team is divided based on each product category. Ishihara is responsible for DVD recorder marketing and product planning. Alongside the Product Planning Group is the Communication Group, in charge of public relations (PR), advertising, sales promotions, websites and other areas. Osaka is responsible for the PR Team in charge of DVD recorder PR and advertising. There is also the Sales Planning Group that governs sales companies and outlets and manages sales of all products. Before the PM Division was established, the business departments pursued their operations independently, and an overall synergy at Matsushita was stifled. After the PM Division was formed, the flattening of the organizational structure enabled quick sharing of information and decision-making.

"When we were on the business department system, from the beginning, we concentrated on a single product such as videos in product planning and the same with sales, development and production. Each business department had its own sales promotions and advertising organization.

What changed radically here was that the broad concept for digital network-based Panasonic brand products, increasing information sharing and organic collaboration with sales promotions and advertising organization, has provided the best overall picture of a product. In addition, once the organizational structure was largely flattened, managers and their technical teams became closer and communicated more effectively with each other. As a result, things worked faster. Since sales persons from the business departments were suddenly transferred to the PM Division, there were different styles of doing jobs. So we had to look for the best way to work as a division and eventually set a single style. With the organization flattened, it became clear regarding who was in charge of products, making it better from a management point of view. We regularly exchange views with related departments, and as a result, we can plan products from a market point of view." (Fumiyasu Ishihara, home A/V team)

"We used to have some difficulties in providing information, but now consensuses are reached quickly and so are decisions. In the PM Division, product managers have authority. In relation to DVD recorder sales promotions, Ishihara and I report to the top after agreeing on an issue. Assigning a key person to products enables decisions on important issues among the few people involved." (Osaka, communication group sales promotion team)

The PM Division implemented a completely different sales strategy for DVD recorders, which was named "vertical launch". It refers to selling large quantities of new product at the time of release and capturing high market share within a month. When sales of that particular product begins to decline large quantities of the next new product are sold. This means that the market share continues to grow as this process is repeated. The essence of this sales strategy is speed. See Figure 6.4.

In the past, Matsushita maintained its top position in the Japanese market share, thanks to "No. 2 Player Selling Practice", using its outstanding production and selling capacities for video recorders. Yet, the development of digital technologies shortened the product development period and life cycle and delayed price reduction, making it impossible for Matsushita to use its strengths, mass production and selling power among group retailers. In other words, the old business model did not hold good for digital household appliances.

The PM Division Manager, Ushimaru, states that "reverse marketing" is needed to realize "vertical launch". "Reverse marketing" involves the

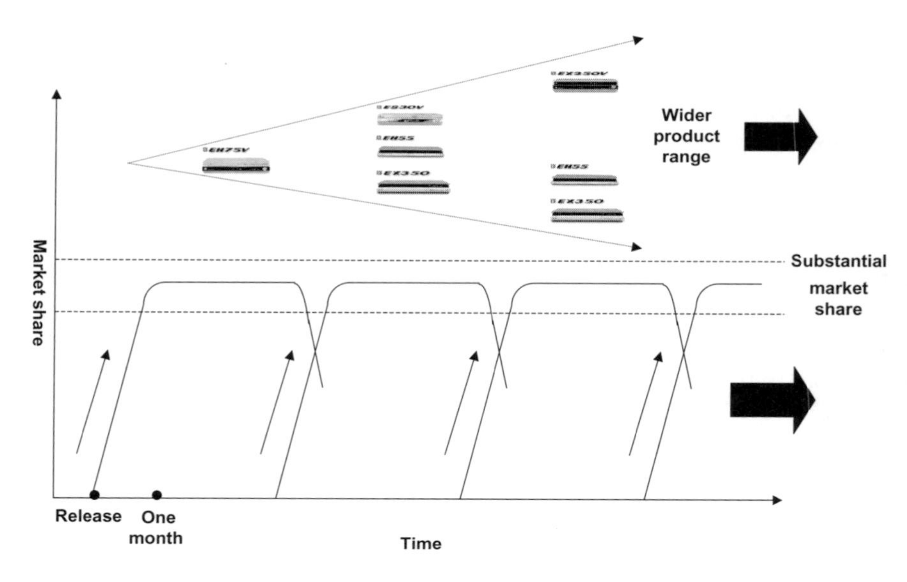

Figure 6.4: "Vertical launch" strategy for DVD recorders.

earlier setting of product sales start dates, and detailed work plan creation for relevant team members based on calculating in reverse from these dates. Thus, at Matsushita Electric, once the roadmaps (long-term, mid-term, short-term) for digital household appliance sales and development were completed, the members of the relevant departments made full adjustment and reached a consensus. The PM Division, PAVC and Matsushita Semiconductor, through the formation of ToB Network (mentioned later), worked simultaneously towards "vertical launch". Based on a time-pacing strategy (Gersick, 1994; Eisenherdt, 1998; Kodama, 2003), this "vertical launch strategy" focuses on the work process, moving backwards from the future point (when the goal is set) to present. This process has several stages and a detailed task(s) is set for each of these stages. Time frames are also set for completing the task. In the inter-organizational ToB boundaries that are related to this time-pacing strategy, synchronization, or "strategy as action" is a key concept. This is discussed in another section.

In 1999, the then Video Department, having succeeded in developing a DVD recorder from the research center, began preparing for a product launch. However, Matsushita's first DVD recorder, "E-10," was overtaken by a product that competitors product had a reinforced user interface and captured 80% of the market share, because of the price (then ¥250,000) and its technology-oriented product function (speedy data transfer and PC connection). Consequently, Matsushita conducted a fundamental review of its product concept during the organizational reform in the A/V Department as shown in Figure 6.3. Under the leadership of the then PAVC President, Fumio Ohtsubo (currently the president of Matsushita Electric and Nakamura's successor), the Home A/V Business Unit, Development Center, Kadoma Plant, and PM Division together launched the "Waku-waku Project."

Ohtsubo instructed the project members to move up the product plan by one year. After comprehensive marketing research and customer activity research was conducted by the PM Division, the development process of system LSIs and the production of core parts of the DVD recorder was hastened. The second newest product, "E-20," priced at ¥135,000, was released in July 2001. In March 2002, "E-30," priced at ¥93,000, was released below the ¥100,000 mark. Then, "E-50" priced initially at ¥60,000, was released in March 2003. With "vertical launch", Matsushita established both Japanese and overseas DVD recorder market in just three years and quickly emerged as a market leader. Behind the success of this "vertical launch" lies an organic collaboration in business processes like marketing, sales promotions and advertising, sales, development and production through project networks.

A major feature of the organic collaboration within this project team was that it came as a result of dense, multi-layered ToBs that were formed among a variety of groups (see Figure 6.5). For example, an organic, multi-layered, cross-functional ToB of various sections (the Product Planning Group, Communication Group, Sales Planning Group, etc.), spanning marketing, product planning, sales and advertising, was formed within the PM Division, and various strategies and tactics were narrowed down toward the "vertical launch". ToBs were also actively formed with group companies Matsushita LEC, Matsushita CE, and other sales and distribution companies, which shared with the PM Division detailed volume information about customers, discounts and specialty shops. In relation to the collaboration with marketing, as well as development and production in new DVD recorder product planning, a close ToB was formed with PAVC, which was responsible for device development and production, and Matsushita Design. The divisions of PAVC and Matsushita Semiconductor had formed a dense collaboration ToB

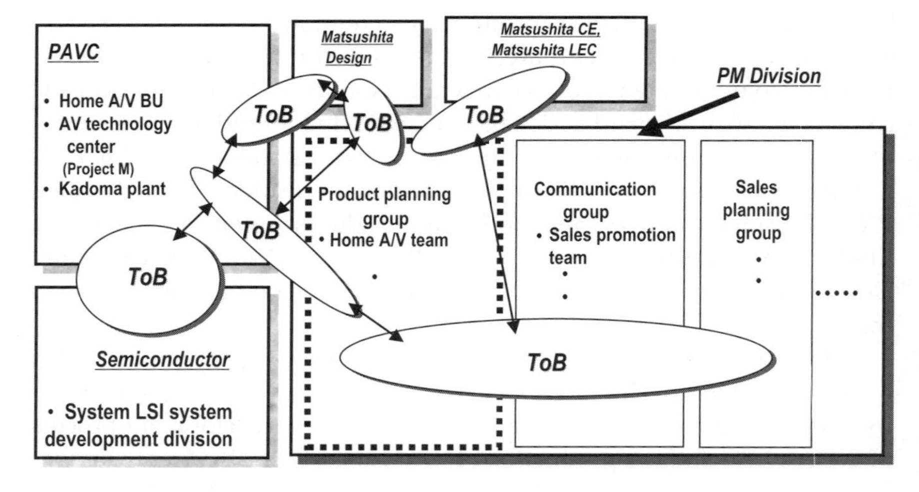

Figure 6.5: Formation of inter-organizational ToB.

towards developing system LSIs, one of the black-boxed technologies of DVD recorders.

The formation of an often fierce discussion ToB has frequently brought about a new dynamic context, especially in product planning, development and production processes involving PAVC and the PM Division.

> *"Since we monitor the market closely, we receive a constant stream of information from customers. In our efforts to plan new DVD recorders, we monitor changes in the market and engage in various interactions with the PAVC Product Planning and Development teams. The PM Division gives advice on what needs to be done to make a product that will sell well. Though it is important to study trends at other companies, as well as listen to feedback from customers and the market, it is also important to incorporate our own ideas into the products. Since the PM Division is responsible for taking the delivery of the product and selling it, it cannot expect PAVC to buy back products that were difficult to sell. The PM Division's expanded* right to speak *has increased its responsibilities. We never compromise with the content of a product plan. There are times when a product's specifications or design changes just before it goes to market. Technical issues that remain difficult at the end are solved, but the solution often imposes conditions." (Ishihara, Home A/V Team)*

"Until now, sales people simply sold whatever the business department made, and anything it couldn't sell was returned to the business division. The tug of war between sales and technology always ended up with both sides blaming each other. After the PM Division and the buy-back system was set up, if a product didn't sell, the PM Division had to take responsibility for it, and this have enabled the PM Division to inform PAVC that they wouldn't buy a product if it does not meet their requirements. PAVC understands the request and do their best to make such a product, so the discussions are now positive, and constructive. In the past, sales mainly followed a product-out concept in which they simply sold whatever was made. I can feel the huge change that has occurred in the quality and speed of interactions between the PM Division and PAVC after the organizational structure was revamped. PAVC is making stringent requests concerning both technology and price. The two sides are also providing feedback to each other concerning distribution as early as in the product planning stage, so the work now progresses very smoothly. As a result, relationships of trust can be built among the various groups." (Osaka, Communication Group PR Team).

On the other hand, the key players in Matsushita's successful development of DVD recorders with better function and price are PAVC and Matsushita Semiconductor, both newly formed as a result of organizational reforms: the former is solely responsible for DVD recorder development and production, and the latter the development of system LSIs, one of the black-boxed technologies of DVD recorders.

6.2.2.2. *Reform in manufacturing and the challenge in black-boxing: PAVC and Matsushita Semiconductor*

The product specifications for DVD recorders requested by the PM Division including target price were very demanding. To meet every requirement suggested by the PM Division, Tokikazu Matsumoto of PAVC's Home A/V Business Unit Manager and Ichiro Kawamura of A/V Technology Center DVD (in charge of DVD recorder development) strictly followed the three basic points in development and production. The first is "Modularized Design Concept." This refers to the standardization of hardware design for sharing, software development modularization, designing, production, establishment of a standardized system involving material purchase, and quality check. The second is a close connection between chipset development and semiconductor devices through close collaboration with Matsushita Semiconductor. The third is the promotion of cell production, an "approach to reform in manufacturing."

Concerning the third point Matsumoto, Manager of the Business Units said:

> *"The following three points are basic to R&D procedures. The first concerns standardization and modularization; the second concerns the integration of key devices and the accumulation of know-how through close links between the Chipset Division and Matsushita Semiconductor and the third concerns black-boxing and other technologies in an easy-to-manufacture process brought about by close links between design and manufacturing. Even when new DVD recorder features are added or old ones are changed, schedules are moved forward, or other events suddenly occur, there is a system in place to absorb these surprises and respond accordingly. Since advanced functions and low prices have passed these three conditions, we achieve our objectives as a result. There is never any compromise. However, we will discuss with the PM Division and change the priority between function and price."*

Cell production at the Kadoma plant in Osaka has had a considerable influence on manufacturing methods. Uniformity in development and manufacturing is essential for accelerating the speed of introducing new products to market and improving quality. Though it takes a little less than a year, starting from the initial concept stage, to bring one DVD recorder model to the market, it is important to improve and overcome problems with cell production at the current plant at an early stage. A unique feature of Matsushita's method is to create close links between plant engineers and technicians from the initial concept stage and finally provide them with details of the design and manufacturing process. Before the die is made, the manufacturing side receives feedback from the development division on a variety of ideas and issues, such as how the product, including prototypes, can be made more easily or how the manufacturing process can be improved. Feedback from technicians is important because this is a part of cell production.

With regard to the development of the system LSI that is also the DVD recorder black-boxed technology, PAVC and Matsushita Semiconductor share the technology road map and hold discussions at various management levels including CEO, manager and development manager levels. Regarding this Matsumoto, Manager of the Business Unit, discussed their collaboration with Matsushita Semiconductor as follows:

> *"We regularly share ideas even on extremely difficult LSI requirements through assigned officers. Almost all the demands for function by the chipset department have been accepted. We have come to understand each other's jobs and business. We try hard to reach the international level for LSIs. Another thing is the schedule. Since we share our mid-term product road map with the chipset department to some extent, we can expect the outcome (product) of a technical process. Chances are that the outcome is almost the same as expected and there are no surprises. We share information about plans for develop next year, including the price range and a product concept at an early stage. This strengthens internal collaboration. There are definitely not as many obstacles as there were before."*

Susumu Koike, president of Matsushita Semiconductor (now the vice-president of Matsushita Electric) has played a proactive role in the assignment of engineers from the chipset department to Matsushita Semiconductor in order to break the barrier between the device (chipset) departments (product design and assembly) and semiconductor department, and promote collaboration among engineers. The significance of such personnel allocation lies in the fact that the future product (chipset) function will be similar to that of system LSIs. In other words, it is important to allocate personnel who are capable of system design for product function, LSI architecture design and software development, and to simultaneously train the semiconductor engineers who understand chipset and the chipset engineers who understand semiconductors. This system has become Matsushita's invisible black-box and conferred a competitive edge.

Koike describes the organizational system at Matsushita Semiconductor as follows:

> *"Semiconductor business has a role in integrating difference organizations in one hierarchy by transferring technologies across business domains. Therefore, Semiconductor's organizational system has to be open and capable of collaboration." Thus, the capable chipset department*

> *engineers were transferred and assigned two roles by Koike: gatekeeper (Allen and Cohen, 1969; Allen, 1971) or boundary spanner (Allen and Cohen, 1969; Tushman, 1977; Tushman and Nadler, 1978), and system design, architecture design, or software development field manager.*

Koike also mentions semiconductor strategies as follows:

> *"To compete with system LSI, we need better technologies and development capacity to deliver a product before anyone else does. Once we aim at a field, we have to capture 40% of the world market share. Obviously, we sell LSIs in order to direct the investment to LSI development, but black box, or knowledge, exists in the software inside LSI. Such tricks are used for the LSI design concept. We have to compete during the system LSI period not with small production of various products, but with the mass production of a small range of products. Here, speed matters. No one buys outdated digital household appliances like DVD devices. Therefore, we should release the latest product before anyone else and win over as many customers as possible. This is a key to a successful worldwide simultaneous vertical launch."*

Matsushita's strength in chipset development, and production and semiconductor development is presumably the essential part of the current DVD recorder technological innovations. A noted characteristic of Matsushita's DVD recorder business is that the sophistication of the product function and the product price reduction conflicting with each other are made simultaneously possible due to the company's technological capacities in system LSI development and sophistication in high-density mount technology.

DIGA, released in March 2003, has key devices such as the system LSI, that are designed to support any voltage and signal format, enabling simultaneous worldwide release or vertical launch. To dominate the world market with another successful simultaneous vertical launch, marketing and technological capacities to continuously design and create new products are required. In relation to this, Tokikazu Matsumoto, BU manager, suggests the importance of organizational unity:

> *"Being in the front line, the PM Division is concerned with the current needs of customers. On the other hand, engineers have their own ideas. We hold discussions with the PM Division and deal with this. It is not very*

difficult to predict technology trends (CPU performance, core technology, process development, chip components). Whether or not this technology is used for a product is a different story. We need to hold discussions with the PM Division on this. The chipset department makes proposals based on predictable technologies. It is important to discuss with the PM Division and decide the combination of technologies used for a product. Unlike the analog era, nothing is impossible with digital products, if technology and functions are combined. It is important to the market, and needs of customers before looking to technological trends. The chipset department and Matsushita Semiconductor should be prepared for new product development. If something unexpected happens, fix it immediately. Someone should accept the responsibility. The problem is who accepts it among the many possible groups. It is important to combine all ideas from the PM Division, chipset department and Matsushita Semiconductor."

Matsushita has successfully completed the simultaneous worldwide vertical launch and emerged as the leader in terms of the world market share for digital household appliances such as DVD recorders due to the formation of various ToB across the groups, specialty boundaries and the project team network. Ohtsubo, the current president of Matsushita Electric, states that the success of their project teams is the result of always setting difficult goals for project members:

"No one thinks about failure. Set the hurdle slightly high and everyone in the project team will aim for it. Highly motivated teams can succeed if they are given such goals."

Ushimaru of the PM Division disregards any success that a project team has experienced and emphasizes the importance of continuous commitment to creating a new hit product:

"If you are satisfied with one hit product and do not release a new product, your competition will soon take over. So, you have to forget the hit product. Once you have succeeded, you become unvigilant. You have to put pressure on yourself so that you can continue to release outstanding products before anyone else does. This remains the biggest challenge."

An important aspect of the digital household appliances strategy is time-pacing, wherein you apply strategies at a certain pace to achieve specific goals set for the future (several times a year, for each significant event, dozens of product models). Thus, "shared strong motivation" is required for "actors" on project teams encompassing several groups.

The president, Nakamura, insists that a mechanism needs to be created within the organization in order to respond automatically. In Matsushita Electric, there are different project teams from unofficial cross-organizational project networks such as the ones with DVD recorders to project teams working closely with the president.

> *"A project team does well when it is not of a "pure breed." Obviously, this means it should be of a "mixed breed." Project teams are useful in solving important issues. Because it is a project team, it can achieve such goals as catching up with a leading digital camera manufacturer in one year." (Nakamura)*

6.3. Project Network by the Formation of a Flat Hierarchical Organization and ToB Network

The problem with Matsushita's old business department system was that with the hierarchical organization, it was difficult for employees to become familiar with the users. The important factors in organizational innovation, part of this Nakamura reform, is the abolishment of the old business department system and the introduction of a flat, web-style organization that is flexible and efficient. The pyramid structure with a peak of 13 hierarchical layers was flattened to four. The main purposes were, in addition to efficient management through introduction of IT, information and knowledge sharing, as well as speedy decision-making.

New posts in the middle management layer in PAVC include the BU manager category owner, group manager, and team leader. BU managers supervise categories such as product area and their responsibilities are similar to those of business department manager. They are given the authority to strategically allocate and make decisions on cross-categorical resources, and solely manage the facility investment and recovery that are related to all categories. Category owners manage each product category and their responsibilities are similar to that of a group manager (who is in charge of investment, recovery, sales, income and expenditures and market share). From the viewpoint of business promotion, the leaders join forces with professional group members on a daily basis. The role of

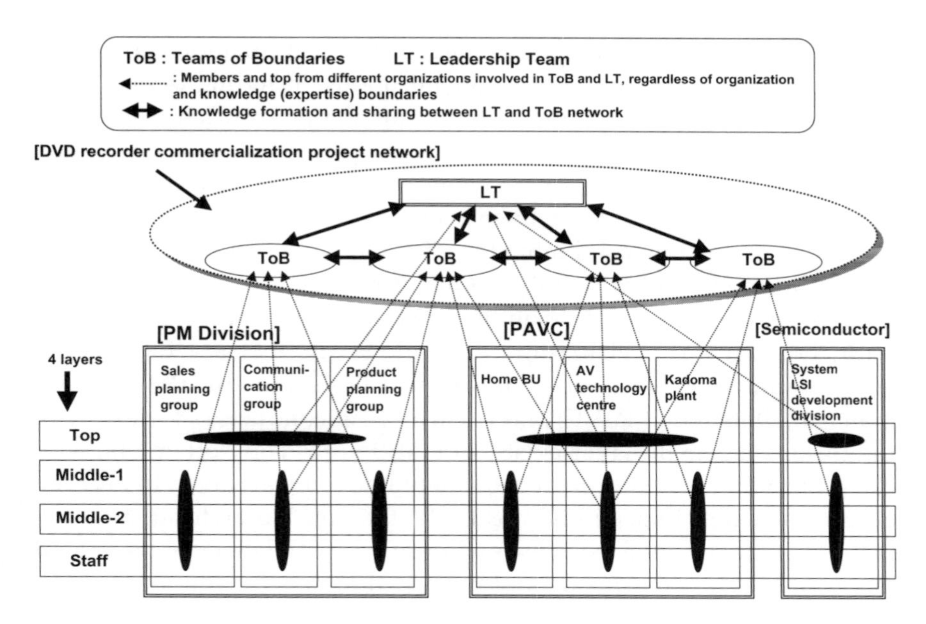

Figure 6.6: Project network and flat hierarchical organization.

group managers (or general managers) is to help the professional groups achieve maximum efficiency and coordinate strategic allocation across BUs and categories. Team leaders (or assistant general managers) are responsible for their respective teams in implementing category promotion.

As shown in Figure 6.6, the four hierarchical layers in the flat, web-style organization consist of two middle layers (Middle-1 and Middle-2), the decision making top layer above, and the staff layer that consists of rank-and-file employees at the bottom. For instance, the four hierarchical layers are simply the PM Division manager, group manager, team manager and rank-and-file employees respectively in the PM Division, while the AVC president, BU manager, category owner, and rank-and-file employees are in the PAVC. The middle management layers are given more responsibilities than before, resulting in boosted employee motivation and commitment to projects.

According to Matsushita, the web in flat & web refers to information transfer and sharing within and among organizations which occur in an open environment like the Web (www) and suggests that multi-layered intra/inter-organizational ToBs be organically networked. These networked

ToBs add a new implication to the interaction of information and knowledge with customers, and among organizations, including partner companies, and become the center of the formation of knowledge in a new dynamic context.

If a business needs a time-pacing strategy to be continuously in place due to changing environments such as market structure and technological innovation, combining the characteristics of a flat hierarchical organization and network ToB is a major requirement. A network ToB guarantees creativity and flexibility in completing tasks in accordance with the company's vision and strategic goals. It has a hierarchical structure in which the leadership team (LT) (Ushimaru, PM Division manager, Ohtsubo of PAVC, and Koike of Semiconductor) consisting of the top management layer exists, in addition to many other LTs, with each consisting of a middle management layer or staff layer. In order to efficiently achieve speed and creativity, the ToB hierarchical structure helps to achieve context sharing and creation, with key persons located in various hierarchies inside and outside the organization. A flat hierarchical organization guarantees efficiency and speed in completing tasks. The key to adapting to changing environments is to utilize the hierarchical organization or the ToB network, depending on the situation, or changing the organizational structure flexibly by simultaneously implementing both the hierarchical organization and the ToB network. The achievement of maximum synergy through the integration of an internal ToB network and a flat hierarchical organization is unique to Matsushita.

6.4. Canon's Innovations

6.4.1. *Behind Canon's management reforms*

Company reforms by Canon in the 1980s with a company vision worth ¥1 trillion were designed to change the product business department system (from five business departments to six business divisions and 20 business departments); strengthen R&D (from an R&D ratio of 6% to a ratio of 10); expand the business categories (e.g. a wider range of products including photocopiers, printers, faxes, computers and word processors); and improve sales. Under the leadership of the then president, Kaku, there were several successful cases as the business department system worked well for new product development empowered by the engineering team. Thus, Canon succeeded in rapidly expanding its manufacturing product range to photocopiers, printers, faxes and computers. Consequently, Canon continued to release hit products, boosting its sales from ¥200 billion to ¥1350 billion during 1977 to 1989. The main office, however, started losing control in the late 1980s, as this business department system was over-used.

For instance, one of the issues with the business department system was inefficient human resource allocation. As each business department recruited employees, itself some departments with resource shortages increased the number of new employees, despite the fact that others had excess personnel. In addition, with a deepening division among business departments, information and knowledge sharing rarely occurred. Although individual business departments might have been optimized, the company could no longer utilize these intellectual and human resources. As a result, cross-business departmental development of new products and technologies was made inefficient and the overall capacity to dynamically respond to the market was weakened. From an overall optimization perspective, these issues implied that the business structure in Canon was no longer capable of achieving synergy as a company. Furthermore, the company could no longer respond to market changes promptly due to the lack of a speedy management process. With its net profit plunging, there was a need for a further review of management style.

Five main management policies were launched as company reforms (under the leadership of president, Fujio Mitarai, 1995–) in the 1990s. The first step towards the transition was to favor sales to profits (profit-minded). The second was the withdrawal from non-profitable businesses (management with choice and focus). The third was a review of the business department system (management with overall optimization). The fourth was innovative production (the introduction of a cell production method). The fifth were the choices and focus on R&D. Eversince he became the president, Fujio Mitarai has been promoting management reforms and efficiency, along with strengthening the business structure at Canon.

Mitarai described the review of the business department system as follows: "When I was newly appointed as the president, we had existing problems such as highly independent business departments with different ways of investment and recruitment. For example, the office equipment group selling photocopiers and printers ignored the deficit in the personal computer business because they were still making an overall profit. This is why the company was in ruins. We made the company office-driven and centralized, based on the idea that the company was more important than individual business departments."

Furthermore, Mitarai radically changed the mindset of employees. In 1996, he began to communicate with employees and explain profit-oriented management. He visited plants across Japan, as well as overseas, to promote this vision of "profit orientation." As a part of profit-oriented management, Mitarai decided to withdraw Canon from unprofitable businesses. In 1996, Canon withdrew from seven businesses including personal computers, electric typewriters, FLC liquid crystal display, and optical cards. Withdrawal, however, met criticism from within, as Canon was a technology-driven company. In fact, the plan to withdraw from the personal computer business met some resistance from within the company. Canon always gave top priority to unique technologies. The core competence of Canon was to make new products through its unique technologies, thereby create new business.

This core competency enabled Canon to launch and expand various businesses such as cameras, photocopiers, laser printers, bubble ink jet printers and semiconductor production devices. The basics of this management system exist till date. Yet, the knowledge of unique path-dependent technologies often have a negative impact such as the competency trap (Levitt and March, 1988; Martines and Kambil, 1999) or core rigidity (Leonard-Barton, 1992, 1995). Once hailed as an important technology both inside and outside the company, its development receives all attention and tends to continue, regardless of profitability or competency. This situation often arises not only in the development phase, but also at some stages after the business is launched. There are several cases in which the opportunity to withdraw from a business is missed due to a strong belief in the power from the bottom (field).

Despite this, Mitarai continued to explain the company's new values and principles at meetings and while communicating with his employees. Eight hundred employees in management positions from across Japan attended his monthly lecture. The management strategy committee was a place for fierce discussion on cross-organizational issues. Management meetings for division managers were held a few times every month, and board meetings were held once in a month. Mitarai visited all branches, including plants and dealers across Japan every year. He actively participated in international and marketing meetings which enable him to exchange views with managers from each management hierarchical layer. Thanks to such repeated dialogues and discussions the resonance of value (Kodama, 2001), that is, value sharing, became popular among employees who had a common goal. Under the leadership of Mitarai, the reforms gradually showed some effect and the company's values and mindset changed radically.

While finalizing the review on the business department system and the withdrawal from unprofitable businesses, Mitarai attempted to unite the employees under one goal and achieve synergy in the company through a management with a new concept, "overall optimization." First, the "Individual Business Division Consolidated Performance Evaluation System" was incorporated into business management. Under this system, losses and capital were recorded and evaluated at each production stage (all business processes including development, production, sales and services) for individual business departments. Even though they have increased the number of new products specified to achieve goals and manufactured the products at lower costs in plants to impress the dealers, a business department was still responsible for the unsold stock. Thus, the management in the business department had to control the entire process including development, production, sales and service. As a result, the they stopped the production of unnecessary products, thereby reducing their inventories and improving cash flow in the company. Moreover, Mitarai transferred finance and human resources personnel from the main office to each business division. As a result, the main office was given more control and even regained its control over business strategies, and resource and budget allocation, thus allowing this vision to optimize overall profit. With these reforms, the division was gradually removed from occupational status and specialized areas (development, production and sales).

Furthermore, Mitarai, in a bid to achieve "overall optimization," used matrix management with the "horizontal" division among business departments. Thus, the "Management Reform Committee" was launched. The purpose of this launch was to integrate business activities in each "diagonally"-run business department. In addition to production areas such as development, distribution, finance, and company policy were covered. Under the "Management Reform Committee," eight committees in the areas of production, development, distribution and finance, including the "Development System Committee," and the

"Production and Distribution Committee," were established. These committees were further divided into smaller groups. In Canon, this practice of integrating diagonally-divided organizations is known as "matrix management."

Mitarai's approach to assigning the heads of the eight committees in order to fully exploit the influence of these committees was innovative. He assigned the business division managers as the heads of the committees. It was important that a manager who was new to an area held the position. Consider the example of the development system committee. If an assigned head of a committee, who is also the image communication division manager, visits each business department to negotiate to solve an issue, the business department managers have to cooperate with him. If not, the business department managers may not be able to convince the head of committee to cooperate with the tasks of the committee. Thus, each business department managers pays attention to other reform committees, while handing the responsibilities of their respective business areas. The managers share issues, regardless of differences among their departments, and cooperate with each other. As a result, communication and collaboration was encouraged. This was one step forward towards the goal of "overall optimization". The "Management Reform Committee," established in 1998, was active until 2000, and resumed its activities in 2001 under a new name, the "Management Strategy Committee".

At present, many companies have such a committee. Yet, most of them only facilitate information sharing among departments, or for meetings between management and managers. Matsushita Electric's president, Nakamura, commented on committee style meetings as follows:

> *"Unless the members decide that the committee will not conclude without solving the issues, the committee might end up being a place for chatting. Sometimes, the participants, controlled by their respective business departments, might exploit the committee for their own interests. So, we have to accept that the role of the committee is to help circulate information throughout the company."*

In comparison, however, the committee, run by Mitarai, has a far more difficult challenge. The committee is not only for information meant sharing, meant but also for promoting the understanding and tackling of the issues involving business departments and departments, and important decision-making. Thus, it is appears that the committee in Canon, as ToB, is more like a project.

In January 2005, Canon announced that, in 2004, its sales increased by 8.4% from the previous year to ¥3467.9 billion and the net profit by 24% to ¥343.3 billion. This led to Canon's increase in revenue and profit for the fifth consecutive quarter. At present, despite facing competition and radical changes in the market and technologies, Canon, with a stable performance achieved, is steadily improving profitability, and the financial structure.

One of the reasons behind Canon's ability to maintain its competence is, as mentioned earlier, the implementation of business process reforms involving development, production and sales. This section analyzes and examines the boundary management for one of Canon's hit products — digital cameras.

6.4.2. *Canon's digital cameras*

Canon manufactures approximately 10 million cameras of 20 different models every year. A new product is released every month. Canon's strategy is to meet the needs of consumers by constantly introducing products with new functions to the market. The digital camera market has grown four-fold in size over the past two years, and every year, 40 million cameras are sold worldwide. With the release of products with a higher level of performance and smaller size, the interest of consumers in purchasing cameras is growing. The price for a digital camera begins to fall two months after release and is reduced to half after six months. Digital camera companies can only expect a high profit for the first few months. Canon continues to acquire 20% of the world share by constantly introducing new products to the market (see Figure 6.7). This is similar to Matsushita's "vertical launch strategy" for DVD recorders.

> *"The market trend changes very fast. Since we compete there, the competition further accelerates changes in the market trend. It requires complex, efficient business management." (President of Canon, Fujio Mitarai).*

Approximately 2,600 employees in the Oita plant where cells for digital cameras are manufactured dedicate themselves to saving time to constantly release new products that meet market demand. True to the principle,

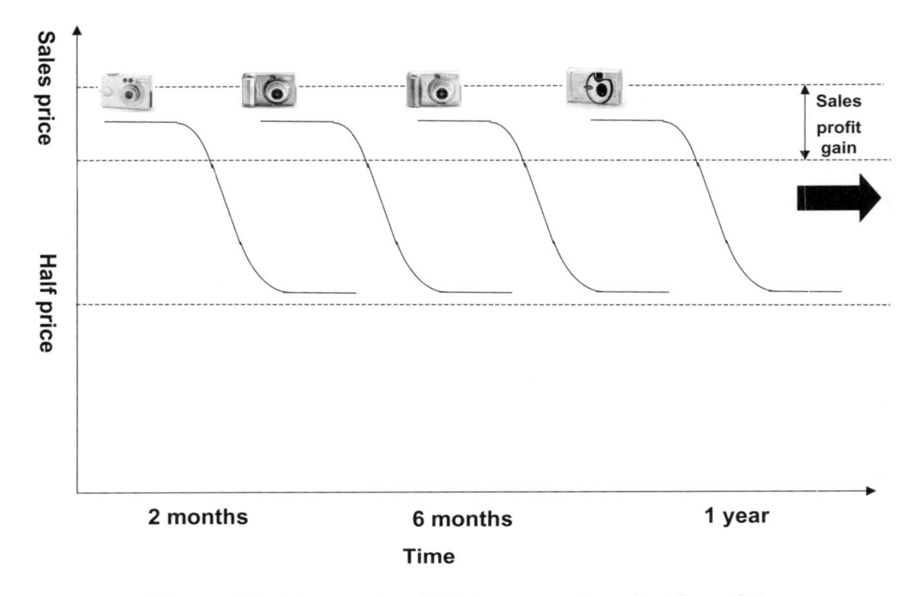

Figure 6.7: Strategy for digital camera "product launch".

"Do not waste time even when walking", the company calculates the walking speed of employees using censors installed in the corridors around the plant. Walking slower than a specified speed prompts a warning sound. This is their attempt to raise awareness for efficiency. The time spent in assembling the cell production lines is saved as much as possible. To set up a production line, the desks on which the production and check devices are positioned are lined up, in one hour. Canon no longer uses belt conveyers for digital camera production. The length of the belt required for making one camera was approximately 100 meters. Thus, changing the production line for a new product was troublesome and time-consuming. Cell production allows flexibility in changing or setting lines for a new product. Canon has reached unprecedented digital camera productivity, after making continuous efforts to find the most efficient, cell setting.

The cell production process of a camera consists of approximately 1,000 different steps. About ten people work as a group to assemble one camera. Since each day's affects profitability, individual workers strive to save time in assembling, and improving productivity by focussing on achieving the production targets. Team leaders help to solve problems that arise in the plant by working together. When productivity does not improve, this leadership team (LT) calculates working hours for individual workers to figure out in the specific assembly process that the caused the bottleneck in production time. This is followed by a review of the relevant cell assembly (e.g. change of work desk arrangement from a line to a circle) to meet the target assembly time.

As digital cameras are increasingly getting smaller in size and more sophisticated, a high density of parts need to be installed. Thus, several problems arise in the assembly of new products. Even mounting a single, tiny spring requires a high level of assembly expertise. Faced with such problems, Canon's production technology department located in a plant developing product devices would share its experience and knowledge, and consider devices and tools for the original assembly of new products. It would also transfer its knowledge to the assembly department. The aim for efficiency in production technology and the capacity to respond flexibly provide the competency to survive in the competitive digital household industry.

> *"More than two thousand people are involved in the process from digital camera development to production. We do not move our production sites overseas just because labor costs are cheaper. Moving overseas for cheaper labor costs is a temporary, not a permanent solution. The key is how to establish the most efficient production system in Japan under the given condition of high labor costs. It is important that we help grow what we have, that is, the technologies and knowledge that are associated with development, production technology and production" (Mitarai).*

6.4.3. *Innovations in digital camera development*

Despite being at the top in the digital camera market, Canon actually withdrew from the business once. Its presence in the field of digital cameras was weak until 2000; it was not among the top five in 1999. It was IXY Digital, a hit product, that changed this situation. IXY Digital was popular then for having the smallest, lightest body in the industry and, was a huge hit when it was released in May 2000, capturing the top market share for the model group. IXY Digital was appreciated by consumers for its size, weight and classy stainless appearance, and more significantly due to the conventional silver salt camera output technology used for IXY Digital.

Unlike silver salt cameras, digital cameras do not require film and, thus, the lens does not need to be positioned at the center. Obviously, this flexibility in lens position reduces the difficulties in technology designing. The earlier versions of digital cameras had lens positioned at one side, rather than in the center. Such designs, however, did not look like conventional cameras. Thus, IXY Digital become hugely popular among consumers with its body design as a digital camera and unique look as a (still) camera. This design was allowed by Canon's unique image engine (semiconductor chip) and one-yen coin technology. Despite being forced to change the organization on several occasions in the past, the team members of the digital camera development team had become familiar with "common determination" to develop potential hit digital cameras.

Canon started its digital camera business in 1984. Initially, the digital camera business at Canon was not successful. While the Los Angeles Olympics were being held, Canon made a joint effort on a test commercial camera with Yomiuri Shimbun. The experiment was capable of commercialization and the world's first commercial electric still camera system was commercialized two years later. With the limited increase in demand, Canon decided to target households. Sales, however, did not increase, due to the immaturity of the market. The product was temporarily withdrawn, and the development team was moved from the camera business division to the R&D department in the main office. Then, the team was transferred from the peripheral equipment business division back to the camera business division.

After being transferred from the camera business division to the R&D department, and withdrawing from the market, the team shifted its focus to element technologies and key component development. The transfer from the peripheral equipment business division back to the camera business division suggested that the digital camera was no longer regarded as peripheral computer equipment. This posed a challenge for the camera market. With the definition of the organization changed, Canon could take advantage of the intellectual properties of cameras built by the development team.

Before 1998, the digital camera development team was not accepted by some employees. There was disagreement among few employees regarding investing more funds and effort in digital camera development, as it was not a well-established business. In this situation, Mitarai worked closely with the development team to avoid the dissolution of the development team. This helped to retain the human resources (intellectual property) and knowledge of digital cameras.

Digital camera development at Canon was also an internal corporate venture. An independent organization supported by top management was partly needed to avoid criticism from and conflict with the existing organizations in the company (e.g. O'Reilly and Tushman, 2004; Tushman and O'Reilly, 1997). Similarly, as mentioned in Chapter 5, the PlayStation development team at SONY received strong support from the top management. In early 1999, Canon launched a project team for the development of IXY Digital.

"New development" is always risky, as its future is uncertain. Therefore, members of existing mainstream organizations are often critical about other members with different views. This is why the top management at Canon had to take control of the development team. In addition, it had to determine the direction of new projects in future and support project activities with patience. The engineers in the team might have been transferred to other sections across the company, if the development team had not worked closely with the president. If it had not worked closely with the president, IXY Digital might not have become a hit product in May 2000, and Canon, might not have been the top player in the digital camera market.

6.4.4. *Systematic approach to digital camera development project*

6.4.4.1. *The "common determination"*

The chief manager for the IXY Digital development project team was Masaya Maeda, then head of the DCP development center of the image communication business division. In Canon, cross-organizational project teams follow a systematic approach to development. The digital development project team consists of about 10 members from various departments. The members are specialists in different areas including system design, electric circuits, software development, mechanical design, production technology, designing, product planning and market launch. The development project forms are similar to the matrix form (Galbraith, 1969) in Canon; the members are involved in a project, while being a part of the group in their own specialized areas. Furthermore, development project members work in one part of their office for both the projects and the group to which they belong. In other words, members do their project tasks (except for trials and experiments) at the work area in the group to which they belong, rather than in a separate area.

At Canon, the criteria for appointing a project leaders are skill and experience and not their age or occupational status. Some of the technology development issues require an experienced section manager to work under a chief project leader. Yet, status or position does not play a role in causing conflicts among project members. With a "culture for educating workers" and a "culture of unity", individual team members proactively show collaborative leadership (Chrislip and Larson, 1994; Bryson and Crosby, 1992). Development projects at Canon are based on the idea that supporting others helps oneself to grow.

Maeda, who has supervised many project leaders, points out that "honest, detailed dialogue and unity among project members" are important in development projects. Such a culture had been gradually accepted in the IXY Digital development project over the previous decade of the electric still camera era, uniting the experienced members, educating the younger generation and the younger generation appreciating the advice of the experienced. Yet, the knowledge boundaries among specialists with different technological backgrounds (Brown and Duguid, 2001) could be an obstacle, as well as a force for innovation in successful development in an unexplored area (Carlile, 2002). In the IXY Digital development project, a common interest in "cameras" among team members was common knowledge (Carlile, 2004), allowing the team to solve difficult, pragmatic issues, and successfully develop new products.

Common interest is undoubtedly important as common knowledge among team members (Carlile, 2002; Cramton, 2001; Star, 1989) in relation to pragmatic boundaries, as knowledge boundaries allow innovation (Carlile, 2002). A more important factor, however, is the presence of a "common determination" among members. Strong motivation and enthusiasm among members to develop a new product, giving birth to this "common determination," is a significant enabler of successful innovation involving pragmatic boundaries. In this case, engineers were not motivated by monetary rewards; "satisfaction through achievement," or intrinsic motivation, (Osterlof and Frey, 2000) was the key motivator.

6.4.4.2. *Formation of "inter development project ToB"*

Maeda, puts his effort into engaging in communication with project leaders and strengthening the collaboration among project teams (see Figure 6.8). Once a month, project leaders and sub-leaders involved in digital camera development take part in a meeting. Project leaders also attend a weekly

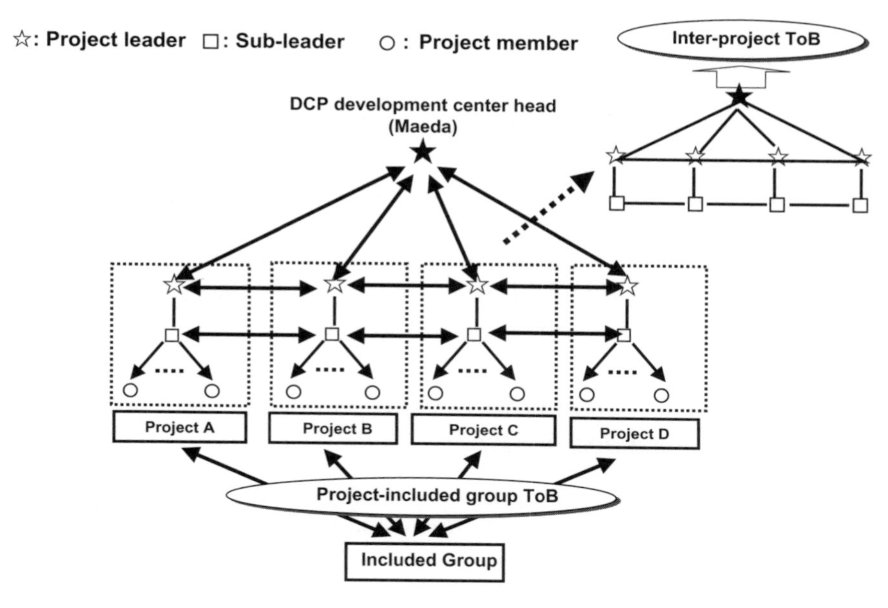

Figure 6.8: Formation of ToB between project and included group in Canon.

or semi-monthly meeting to discuss technical issues. Canon focuses on information and knowledge-sharing among project teams and inter-project collaboration, as well as the optimization of individual projects. This is because inter-project collaboration allows flexible, efficient progress in development due to similarities in technical issues involving the development of digital household appliances like digital cameras. For instance, the image engine made universally suitable for digital cameras was adopted as a platform for different models, resulting in efficient development. Such an inter-project collaboration allows the solving of pragmatic issues and knowledge-sharing. "Creative collaboration" for a constructive, and productive solution (mentioned in Chapter 1) is used in project management at Canon.

Thus, inter-project ToBs are prominent in the systematic approach to development at Canon. Given the presence of such "inter-project ToBs", Canon forms ToBs as and when they are needed. Thus, they can combine the ideas and knowledge of engineers in different areas of expertise by listening to the views and perspectives of specialists and encouraging knowledge-sharing. This allows the solving of various issues that arise during the development process and the production of unique technologies at Canon. Unlike the analog generation, the digital generation requires technology that can be used for different products. Thus, higher quality is required for inter-project collaboration. If the development process reaches a deadlock, closer contact and collaboration can often lead to a solution from an unlikely part of the team, thus allowing for an efficient problem solution. The formation of "inter-project ToBs" as a part of project management is essential in a constantly-changing competitive environment and leads to "creative collaboration" that can respond to dynamics of the market and changes in technology.

6.4.4.3. *The formation of ToBs between development project and included groups*

Another important aspect of project management at Canon is the formation of ToBs between a project and the included group of project members (see Figure 6.8). This ToB is formed on the basis of work areas for both projects and activities of the included group, and the sharing of content and knowledge among members. The project team facing pragmatic boundaries attempts to solve various issues and secures a strategic position, that is, in the commercialization of a new product. Despite having to make radical changes to technology, project team members will often be advised on difficult issues by other engineers in their group. In other words, project members revisit the knowledge that is embedded with in the "community of practice" (Wenger, 1998) to which they belong. Then the members deal with the project tasks using the new tips.

As the development team in an included group makes incremental progress, its members, as a part of the "community of practice," have to continue with the learning, as in the past. Here, the key factors are "common language" and "shared meaning", which are shared as "common knowledge" by the engineers who work in a particular field (Carlile, 2004). Focusing on the strengths and weakness of different viewpoints, they discuss the views of a project member and the analysis of new technical issues from the perspective of a colleague or senior officer in the same field. The dialectic analysis and consideration of the technical issues by several engineers provide a new solution. Here, "harmonized knowledge" is formed as a result of the integration between "distributed knowledge" and "decentered knowledge" — the characteristics of ToB are mentioned in Chapter 1.

In Canon, the ToBs formed among the projects, or the project and the group to which members belong are provide a basis for organizational learning and achievement of innovation. Canon's case in point gives an insight into project management that contradicts suggestions by existing research (e.g. DeFillippi, 2001; Keegan and Turner, 2001; Grabher, 2002; Newell *et al.*, 2003; Prencipe and Tell, 2001; Middleton, 1967), which states that continuous group learning (including knowledge-sharing and transfer between projects or organizations) is difficult in temporary projects.

6.4.4.4. *The formation of ToB networks between development projects and other organizations or group companies*

As mentioned earlier, the reform initiated by Mitarai is characterized by a strong linkage in the ToB network in the development, production and sales processes at Canon (see Figure 6.9) The digital camera development project team and the production technology department constantly hold discussions

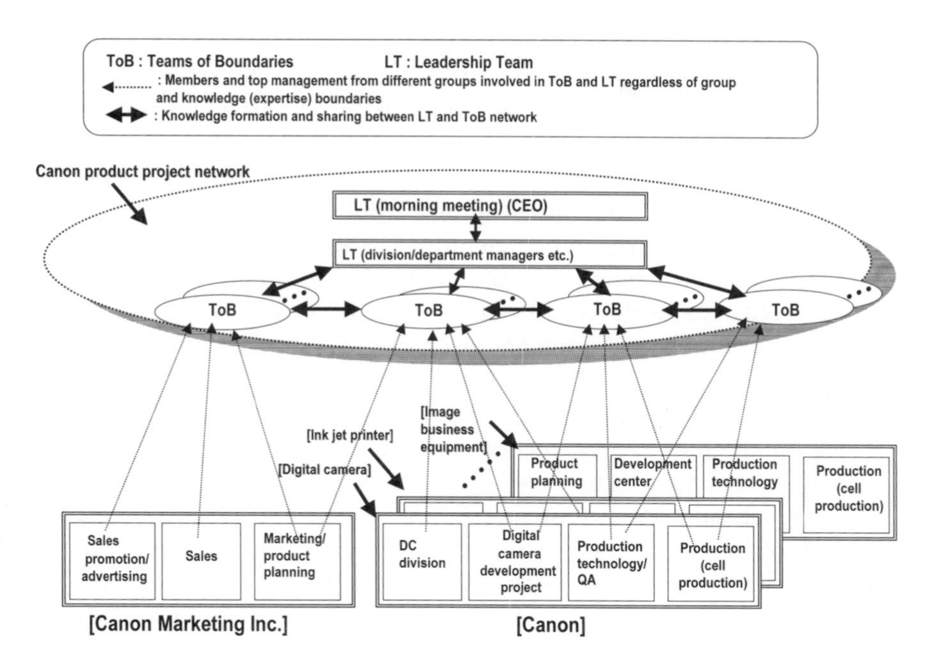

Figure 6.9: Canon group project network.

on a design policy that aims at simplicity in assembly and improved productivity. The development project team and product technology department from the main office in Tokyo and the product technology department from the Oita plant hold face-to-face discussions during every phase of new product development.

The discussions among the development project team, product planning department and designers focus on marketing. The 3-D CAD (computer-aided designing) IT tool plays helps reach team members consensus or boundary object (e.g. Star and Griesener, 1989; Star, 1992) in discussions involving the designer, the product planning department, development project and the production technology department issues.

The introduction of 3-D CAD has facilitated innovative designs at Canon. 3-D CAD can provide ideas on product output without a prototype and run computer simulations of product functions and performance. In addition, 3-D CAD can calculate the cost of final products using the input data on all material costs. The software also enables product data sharing among relevant departments, and simultaneous progress in development and production. Moreover, with clear 3-D images, it is possible for anyone to get a real picture of a product, not only designers and specialists in the area. This IT tool improves the efficiency in inter-organizational coordination and collaboration, and helps to make as much progress as possible in product specification and discussion during early phases such as designing and development. This 3-D CAD, as a boundary object, has been constantly improved by Canon system engineers to bridge the pragmatic boundaries among employees with different areas of expertise as a creative, and efficient way to achieve innovation.

Canon has been trying different approaches to improve productivity and creativity, as well as efficiency in inter-organizational business processes. A number of Canon engineers describe Canon "as a company with well-coordinated departments and a business policy for team work". Members in the development department in Canon find out, thoroughly discuss and attempt to solve technical issues in a casual atmosphere akin to chatting. There is a tactic called "revelation tactics" by Canon employees, in which all technical strategies are revealed to discover various issues. Another tactic, "involve-all tactics," has long been used at Canon to get many departments (e.g. sales and marketing, production technology, quality assurance, business planning, and sales promotions and advertising) to be involved and exchange specialist views on a variety of issues identified by the development project team. Such cross-organizational activity leads to heated discussions in which all members express their honest opinion. Such activity improves inter-organizational communication as well as efficiency, productivity and creativity in the company.

In addition, the formation of project networks among group companies is unique to Canon. One of the Canon group companies, Canon Marketing Japan Inc., works closely with the Canon's main office regarding new businesses. Canon Marketing Japan Inc. is responsible for marketing, sales, advertising and sales promotion in Japan for all products of Canon. The role of the company is to provide a high-level support, through intensified field service, and improved procedures for customers who visit the service stations for repair and respond promptly to the needs of professional photographers. Such close contact with customers in business and service activities allows immediate, precise understanding of market information. The company then reports without delay such information to the product planning and development departments.

By having direct contact with customers, Canon Marketing Japan Inc. employees not only report problems to the main office, but also present their concepts for new products that are based on potential market needs and trends through discussions with the relevant department from the main office. The issues are discussed thoroughly until both sides are satisfied. Before the development of a new product begins, Canon Marketing Japan Inc. thoroughly discusses the specification, price and release date with the product planning department and development project team from the main office. Both parties, without any compromise, commit themselves to finding the best solution.

Such project networks covering Canon and Canon Marketing Japan Inc. are formed not only for the business process involving development, production, and sales of digital cameras, but also for all Canon products (ink jet printers, photocopiers, peripheral equipment and image business equipment) in respective product projects. Canon can constantly launch new products at the right time (see Figure 6.9) by responding to changes in the market and technologies, and by sharing the content and knowledge through ToB networks that are platforms for project networking.

6.4.5. *Leadership team (LT) at top level*

CEOs attend a daily "morning meeting" in Canon (see Figure 6.9). Before Mitarai took up his position as president, the meeting was a mere formality. With few people attending, these discussions lacked enthusiasm.

Mitarai does not accept any reason for a CEO not attending the meeting except for business trips and overseas-based CEOs. Inspired by Mitarai's enthusiasm, other CEOs proactively attend the meetings, thereby adding the much-needed excitement to the meetings. Mitarai describes the morning meetings as follows (Mitarai and Niwa, 2006):

> *"I think that enthusiastic discussions are a part of Canon's company culture. CEOs attend a daily morning meeting at 8 a.m. and I think that this meeting plays a role in cultivating this culture. We exchange information and views on a variety of issues over a cup of tea. The atmosphere is very relaxed. There is no specific agenda, so we do not need to make a proposal or conclusion. We do not have a chairman or organizer.*
>
> *The morning meetings result in discussions on important topics that are beneficial for the Business Strategy Committee. A significant benefit of the morning meetings is that the CEOs get to know each other on a personal level and this creates a relationship of trust. After attending the meeting to discuss almost everything on current affairs for one year, understand the personal opinions and judgments of other attendees on various issues. As a result, they share their values with other people.*
>
> *It seems to me that this is the reason behind the fact that everyone freely expresses their opinions at other meetings in Canon. Perhaps people feel comfortable with expressing their opinion without being concerned about what others think about them after all these years. Even though someone may disagree with your opinion, you can avoid emotional conflict by understanding the reason behind their disagreement. Sharing values helps you, even if you have to make a decision yourself, while visiting overseas, for example. The decision you make not contradict the company's position in most cases.*
>
> *Another benefit of the morning meeting is improved efficiency in management. We often have a first discussion of the issue related to daily tasks in the morning meeting. With most CEOs attending the meeting, the formal meeting efficiently leads to a conclusion after enthusiastic discussion. This dramatically improves the collaboration among business departments."*

"Leadership Teams (LT)" during such events as "morning meetings" (described in Figure 6.9) raise new issues to be dealt with and discussed at a business strategy or development meeting involving business departments. The outcomes of these meetings create a basis for decision-making regarding important matters and new business projects. Then, inter-department LTs mainly comprising the managers from relevant business departments and departments, are formed to create a new project. ToB networks, thus formed comprise of the project leaders and middle managers who are directly-involved in business activities.

As shown in Figure 6.9, the ToB network consists of both project networks of Canon and Canon Marketing, which are responsible for a series of business processes including sales, sales promotion, advertising, marketing, product planning, development design and production technology. Through this ToB network, actors share context and knowledge, and create new technologies, products and businesses. Moreover, the LT's connection with the ToB network is always close due to the level of communication and knowledge. Also, actors use this network to make correct decisions.

6.5. Boundaries (ToB) Synchronization

This section gives a new insight into the new product development processes that are common to Matsushita Electric and Canon. In the project networks formed by Matsushita Electric and Canon, the project does not focus on product development. Rather, a number of actors work through close interaction between the sections such as sales, product planning, development design, development design, production technology and production. The manufacturing of digital household appliances such as DVD recorders and digital cameras is subject to extreme environmental changes including market change and technological innovation. Matsushita Electric and Canon could only acquire world market share by continuously delivering new products to the market at the right time. To make this possible, both companies continue to use the global "vertical launch strategy" as a time-pacing strategy.

On the other hand, in order for actors in different groups and with different expertise to form a project network, it was important to form a ToB network that is a platform for context and knowledge-sharing. As shown in 6.10, the "R&D ToB", the "Product Development & Production ToB", "Product Planning ToB" and the "Sales ToB" are formed within a project network.

In the "R&D ToB", Matsushita Electric and Canon invent the black-boxed core technologies for digital household appliances (system LSI for DVD recorders, image engine chip for digital camera) that are difficult to copy and give the companies an advantage over their competitors. In the "Product Development & Production ToB", dvelopment based on new product design concepts and production technologies provide an advantage over the competitors in terms of quality, cost and speed. The link between these ToBs leads to the optimization of the whole business process involving R&D, development and production.

Furthermore, the strong link between "Product Development & Production ToB", the " Product Planning ToB" and the "Sales ToB" results in strengthened collaboration between sales and marketing powers; the launch of new unique product concepts based on potential consumer need; and the combination of speed and capacity to add variety to the successfully-developed products based on this concept, enabling Matsushita and Canon to dominate DVD recorders and digital cameras, markets respectively.

I consider the formation of ToBs and network interaction as a source of product development capacities of Matsushita and Canon. Instead of viewing the firm as a bundle of resources (Wernerfelt, 1984; Barney, 1991), it is viewed "as a bundle of different boundaries in which knowledge must be shared and assessed" Carlile (2004, p. 566). According to my field observations, actors from different organizations are engaged in tasks for worldwide "vertical launch strategies" (or practice time-pacing strategies) mainly in their own ToB to launch a new product. Actors, in their own ToB, make decisions regarding the details in the strategies and tactics, and complete their roles specified in the strategies to achieve their goal of product launch.

However, the optimization of all ToBs not occur will if each ToBs, does not complete their tasks at the same time, or some of them do not finalize their tasks. Project leaders and middle managers in management positions in ToBs are especially required to participate in several ToBs, and encourage the transfer and sharing of information and knowledge among actors from different groups and areas of expertise. In other words, their role is to not only dynamically share the context and knowledge ToBs and complete their own tasks, but also to support others showing "collaborative leadership." Such "creative collaboration" allows the optimization of all ToBs through the link among ToBs, or rigid networking, as well as the optimization of individual ToBs.

In other words, if the ToBs interact and are synchronized at the same pace, the level of task achievement in each ToB enables the optimization of individual ToBs and the network ToB. Figure 6.10 shows a model of this synchronization.

So, what is this concept? Synchronization needs to be looked at in terms of micro-strategy — strategizing and organizing in relation to the daily business of actors (e.g. Whittington, 1996, 2003). In this case, actors from different groups discuss the actions needed for success in the worldwide "vertical launch strategies" of new products. Then, the countless action items comprising the overall strategies and tactics are broken down to items that are assigned to different sections such as marketing, sales promotions and advertising, sales, product planning, development, production technology, manufacturing and distribution. Among these action items, the ones that a single organization cannot achieve independently are especially important. Such action items need to be dealt with by the coordination and collaboration with other groups, or by one group incorporating the output from other groups.

All of these action items that cannot be completed by one group have to be executed through the formation of ToBs beyond group and knowledge

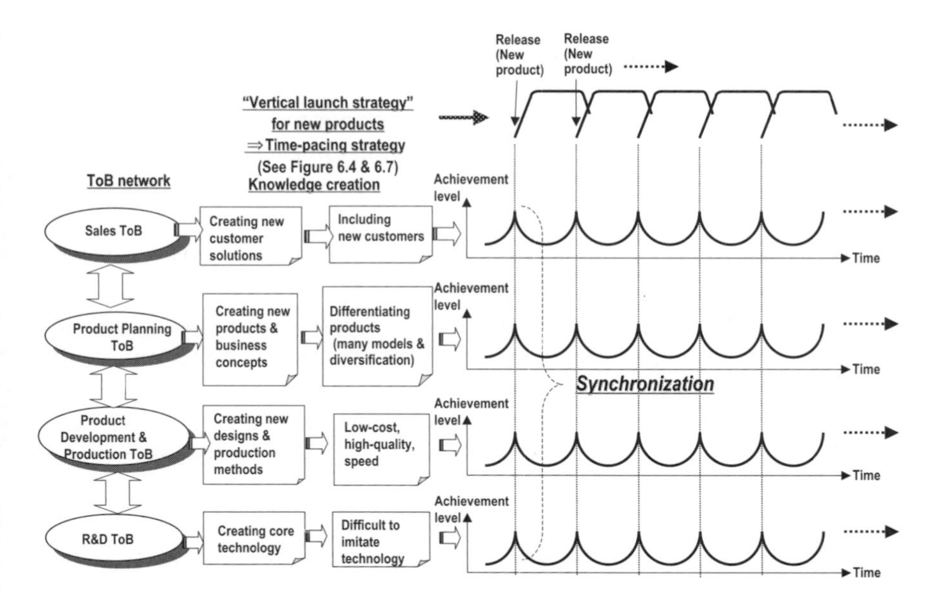

Figure 6.10: Boundaries (ToB) synchronization.

boundaries. In the ToB, actors discuss and reach an agreement on "what (action items to be executed)", "why", "when", "whom", and "how", or the detailed target, meaning, timing and means. This is "strategy as action" by the actors who are the micro unit in the formulation and implementation of the detailed strategies and tactics. For the actors, "strategy-as-action" has a dynamic element means that which they execute the strategy after changes overtime, which are carried out through struggle. Actors need to have a dynamicview of strategy, and execute not only deliberate strategies, but also emergent strategies with flexibility (Kodama, 2004). In addition, they have to improvize to deal with radical situation changes.

In a ToB, actors execute the action items closely related to other groups by sharing the context and knowledge through constructive dialog and "creative collaboration". While executing the items for "the strategy-as-action" that each ToB decides on, actors are always monitored for their level of achievement in the execution process. Furthermore, the items for "strategy-as-action" to be executed in individual ToBs are interdependent on other ToBs. In other words, the items, "when," "whom" and "how", require coordination and collaboration with actors from different groups.

Thus, the committed actors, especially the top management, participating in several ToBs have to ensure that the achievement of all tasks (target) for the strategy as action progress at the same speed and rhythm in each ToB, in order to achieve the goal for the entire project (successful "vertical launch strategy" for new product development). Synchronization is the mechanism by which "strategy as action" in each ToB is simultaneously achieved through completion of task by actors who work at the same speed and rhythm in each ToB.

To actors, ToBs and ToB networks are platforms to share dynamic context and create new knowledge. ToBs provide the time and space for sharing and creation of tacit and explicit knowledge, dialog and pragmatic practice. A new characteristic found in new product development by Matsushita and Canon is that diverse, multi-layered ToB and ToB networks with various contexts and knowledge always exist. Actors have been forming and uniting these ToBs by proactively encouraging others within the environment (e.g. consumer) and the group. Actors are actively engaged in the formation and unification (networking) of ToBs. Yet, importantly, ToB and ToB networks collectively consist of actors from different areas of expertise, and always provide knowledge boundaries that are potentially a source of innovation.

These knowledge boundaries possess the characteristics of pragmatic boundaries, as uncertainty in new product development and novelty factors increase (Carlile, 2004). The "common determination" of actors is required to convert the energy generated by pragmatic boundaries into innovation. The "common determination" of the actors rooted in shared values (Kodama, 2001) is more important than boundary objects as a tool for encouraging innovation and common knowledge, (Carlile, 2002; Cramton, 2001; Star, 1989) including common language, meaning and interest. In Matsushita and Canon, this "common determination" of actors helps to form the rigid ToB network and the LT, and leads to a success in the worldwide "vertical launch strategy" immediately after the development of new products.

7

Use of Project Formation to Stimulate Innovation in a Traditional Big Business A Case Study of Communications Businesses in Japan

This chapter presents a case study illustrating how a traditional corporation created new digital communication service markets and managed to establish a dominant position in the competitive field of ICT (Information and Communication Technology) in Japan. To implement radical innovation, this corporation adopted a large-scale, project-based organization that was imbued with an entrepreneurial spirit supported by different types of personnel. This chapter considers processes to manage discord and friction with the existing organization, which promotes mainstream businesses in order to implement market-creating strategies.

7.1. Management Change in Corporation

The punctual equilibrium model proposed mainly by the research group involving Tushman *et al.* and Nadler *et al.* (Tushman *et al.*, 1985, 1986, 1997; Nadler *et al.*, 1989, 1995) has been used so far to analyze corporate innovation and organizational change, and to report the innovation mechanism of a large number of business types and categories.

Organizational change is of two kinds: incremental and discontinuous. Incremental change is a stable change with assured efficiency, while discontinuous change is change-oriented change in which the emphasis is on effect. For a corporation to achieve discontinuous change, strategy, structure, competence and process must be transformed together.

In view of the complex and uncertain environment that the high-tech industry face in the future, it is essential that companies gain a competitive edge through market-creating strategies. This is to facilitate a complete revamping of strategies, structure, culture, competence, business processes and other factors, which constitute the basic framework of an organization in order to effect radical change. To generate the discontinuous and radical change stressed by Tushman and Nadler, the larger and the more complex an organization, the greater the paradoxical nature of the reform process.

Paradoxes can be seen internally at every level throughout the organization, in every business unit, each department, each project and other structural elements of the corporation. Specific examples include the "management paradox" (Thompson, 1967) of flexibility and certainty, "the organizational culture paradox" (Pascale, 1985, 1990) of autonomy and socialization of organization members, the "strategic paradox" (Mintzberg, 1987) of deliberate and emergent strategies. If such paradoxes can trigger a radical change, they can also greatly influence the content and quality of radical change. Thus, it may become increasingly important to know that the paradox phenomenon is the driving force for radical corporate change (Quinn *et al.*, 1988).

The objective of this chapter is to consider how traditional corporations innovate in the increasingly competitive field of ICT. It concerns the mechanisms by which different project-based organizations give rise to various paradoxes within a corporation(s) achieve radical change and aims to build a radical change model for corporations facing reorientation (Nudler *et al.*, 1995).

7.2. Digital Communication Revolution at NTT

On January 1, 1994, then-president of NTT Masashi Kojima declared that the company would transition itself from a telephone company to a multimedia company. During this time, NTT was facing a significant transition from a 40-year existence as an analog telephone business to a new one utilizing multimedia technologies. Following privatization in 1985,

NTT implemented incremental changes by spinning off group companies (the data communications section in 1988 and the mobile communications section in 1992); entering new business fields; and introducing voluntary retirement and other in-house streamlining policies. As a result, by the beginning of 1994, the company had reduced its personnel from around 300,000 to 180,000. The company's business operations were also subject to major changes. Income from analog telephone sales, the core of the company's business, began to decline owing to the liberalization of the telecommunications market in 1985, which allowed new common carriers to enter the market, thus leading to a reduction in telecommunication fees. On the other hand, the demand for non-voice services such as data communications gradually increased, primarily from corporate users. By 1994, the multimedia boom made its presence felt in the US but the telecommunications carriers did not know anything about the strategies to be implement and services to be created for the unexplored territory.[1]

---

[1] In June 1994, the NTT head office created a "service production and planning department", a small project-based organization that was a precursor of the MBD. Its mission was to create a new business after the telephone service. The author was, at this time, a project manager, and was shifted to this organization in the NTT head office building in Hibiya in Tokyo. He recalled many heated discussions in an office facing the park. This was before the Internet really started to take off and nobody, at that time, realized how fast it would grow.

Ikeda (2006) recalled "Microsoft CEO Bill Gates visited the NTT Hibiya head office at 9 a.m. on 9 December 1994. I took part in the meeting as a multimedia representative. In this meeting, Bill Gates asserted that the Internet would never develop into anything significant. It was for volunteers, amateurs and academics. It will not have any business potential. The Internet was not guaranteed by anyone and, therefore, not reliable, and businesses will be reluctant to use it. He said that PC networks were where the future lay."

Soon after this, the situation in the US changed completely. Ikeda recalls the following. "At 11 a.m. on June 23, 1995, Bill Gates visited the Hibiya NTT head office the second time. This time, he asserted that the Internet would grow very quickly and that businesses should target the growing Internet population. He said that Windows 95 to be released later that year would naturally come with Internet capability."

While the World Wide Web (www) had started its rapid growth in 1994, neither Bill Gates nor NTT could predict its popularity. Microsoft's battle with Netscape in the browser business is well-known (e.g. Cusumano and Yoffie, 1988), but starting from 1995, Microsoft its new Internet strategy implemented under the strong leadership of Bill Gates. Incidentally, Bill Gates had also expressed that multimedia needed optical fiber. This was an opinion that NTT shared and has been proven right by the current-broadband businesses.

7.2.1. *Top management builds project-based organization*

The two people who felt the greatest sense of crisis over NTT's future were Mr. Kojima, then president, who made the "Multimedia Declaration" in 1994, and Mr. Junichro Miyazu, the then vice-president and also responsible for technology, who became the president in 1996. They were working towards a business structure for the multimedia business by radically changing the NTT culture and business style. They concluded that they had to introduce a new department to the head office to implement multimedia strategies for the future. Mr. Ikeda, a board member and director who became managing director of NTT in 1996, was incharge of this task. Launched in June 1994 with about 50 staff members, the new department came to be known as known as the Multimedia Business Department (MBD) (initially, it was named as Service Manufacturing and Planning Department). In 1997, the department had grown into a large project-based organization with about 850 staff. Top management members Mr. Kojima, Mr. Miyazu and Mr. Ikeda shared a common value system, a future vision and a firm belief, as well as a will to dismantle NTT's traditional culture to create a new multimedia business market, based on information and communication technologies.

During this time, Mr. Miyazu told Mr. Ikeda that the NTT organization was steeped in its analog telephone service heritage and would fight any new business venture that breached its corporate culture. When starting something it would be useless to try to gradually persuade everybody at NTT of the need for changing the firm's course; the important thing was to get started. He suggested that a new organization be set up and used to drive a wedge into the NTT structure. The people forming this wedge would have to take considerable flack, but that would be worth it, if they could get the new business going (MBD, 1998).

Miyazu repeatedly told Ikeda that the new organization must be based on a new ideology that allowed it to take new initiatives. This dialogue between the top management regarding the shared vision of taking NTT from a phone company and into the multimedia business, and similar values, assisted Mr. Ikeda in laying the groundwork for MBD. Utilizing his experiences as a former personnel director at NTT, Ikeda assembled a multi-faceted staff from among the 180,000 of NTT's domestic employees. These included researchers and engineers with more than a hundred patents and industrial new designs to their credit young employees who had started businesses as, students, and the top engineers in Kansai.

Many of the project leaders for MBD were selected from domestic branch managers group, in the higher management. The 830-strong personnel thus selected brought with them exceptional skills and experience.

MBD had the freedom and flexibility similar to a project-based organization that set it apart from NTT. Ikeda felt that a smaller organization within a large corporation would facilitate information sharing and innovation. He thought that the old idea of "man versus organization" aptly captured this predicament. Ikeda experienced the "man versus organization" dilemma, first on "organization" side in various management positions, and later on the "man" side, during his three-year stint as a personnel director. On the "organization" side, he worked towards creating a new organization in which he spent a long time debating the issues involved with the parties concerned and considering minute details to build an ideal organization. However, the person finally assigned to head this organization was far from suited to fulfill the mission for which the organization had been set up. He still remembers his disappointment on seeing the a different picture of the organization within a gap of two years. Unless the person heading the organization is fully-cognizant of its objective, any framework for an organization, however well-made, will come to naught.

The personnel department provided experiences of a similar frustrating nature. In one case, he had three equally suitable applicants for a post. All were expected to do well in the job and its scope was set to expand. Any of the three, who was appointed, would benefit the organization, but there was only one post. What made matters worse was that the two applicants who had to be passed over were not really suitable for any other post. "Project-based" was the only rather commonplace solution he eventually could come up with.

Starting with ISDN[2] as a digital infrastructure, MBD used the same process that comprises a large number of streams was launched. It was a complex task to be handled on a structural basis. Since the organization was affected by changes, it was important for it to conform to dynamism and flexibility. In this kind of environment, a project-based set up seemed appropriate to handle change.

MBD that started as an ISDN digital communications infrastructure made available a large number of streams in the application sector.

[2] A digital network service (Integrated Services Digital Network) established by the telecommunications standardization sector of the International Telecommunications Union (ITU-T).

On the first of April 1997, 830 employees of MBD were involved in the following projects: GR, GR Homenet, Phoenix, WNN-C, multimedia investment, 3V, business application, G-Net development, ATIS, JUST, FamilyMart, Rainbow, China, marketing, new cellular phone models, Phoenix, NOD student net, WNN-S, HCN, satellite, ISDN-AP, line business, multchinetto, aiai, zenkokuren, yarima, SHOW mulchi, system sales, NOW-ISDN, mulchinetto ai, Twin-VQ, CCi, A&M, NTT fan planning, energy, Okinawa branch, MS, computer telephony, contents center, G-Square, ITV, NPS, WNN-A/Z, etc. Keeping in view the numerous projects, it must have been a tightrope walk for the employees (Ikeda, 2005).

These newly-formed project-based organizations differed from the previous technically-oriented NTT projects in that they were "post-independent development" oriented, market-oriented. They involved many of the world's leading IT companies (many of which are still competitive) for example, Microsoft (VOD, security, MSN and other business alliances), General Magic (alliances in agent communications and other fields), Silicon Graphics (VOD Business alliances), PictureTel (joint development of TV conferencing systems), Apple, AT&T, Inktomi and other companies in strategic alliances as partners in new business alliances (development of products, services and joint ventures).

MBD project-based organizations differed from NTT's traditional existing line organization (number of employees: 170,000). In those days, income from analog telephone services contributed a lot to NTT's earnings, and the line organization employees cautiously guarded existing business processes, conventions and other factors, which constituted their corporate culture. They had deliberate strategies (a planned strategy for each functional division covering business plans, equipment planning, customer service and maintenance service) in place for their telephone services, and a track record of reliable service to users throughout the nation spanning several decades. It was an orderly line organization (below, we will refer to this existing line organization as the traditional organization) where incremental refinements and improvements were carried out on a daily basis, and information and technological know-how disseminated from the main office to the branch offices and vice versa. As expected, friction and conflict within MBD, due to the original business practices based on a new concept, and the traditional organization, could not be avoided.

An organization or system is already obsolete by the time it is established. A new business should do away with the existing systems and concepts, and must be able motivate its employees. When the fringes of the industry were changing (for example, the fusion of communications and broadcasting), NTT simply had to change, and function and conflict were bound to occur (MBD, 1998).

Figure 7.1 compares the MBD project-based organizations with the existing traditional organization. Both organizations differed distinctly in their hierarchy. The traditional organization had between 8 to 10 levels between the president and the rank-and-file employee whereas in MBD, there were only 4 or 5 levels between the president and the regular project staff. MBD was an organization with a flat hierarchy. While MBD held conferences to settle important issues, many issues at Ikeda were settled through informal talks, which led to fast decision-making. This facilitated faster decision making. In traditional organization, the administration and decision-making processes were of great importance. In this organization, issues were dealt with depending on their degree of importance, investment capital, etc. in various conferences — a process seen by many employees as a regular ritual.

A comparison of the strategy-making processes of both organizations is discussed here. MBD continuously pursued emergent and entrepreneurial

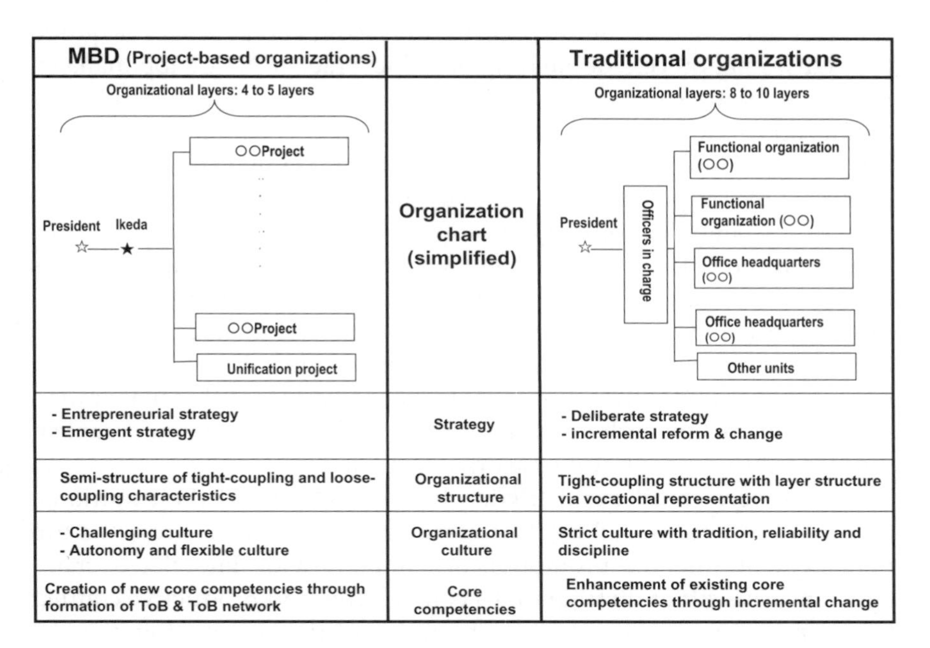

Figure 7.1: Comparing project-based with traditional organizations.

strategies, and was able to generate interest in ISDN digital communications among an increasing sector of customers and infuse life into the dormant ISDN market. MBD looked around for and created new business concepts and ideas, pursuing emergent and entrepreneurial strategies to stir new life into stagnant markets. Simultaneously, MBD formed ToBs within the traditional organization, promoted knowledge management, and aggressively and persistently set up forums for communicating the vision and values shared by both top management teams. These efforts gradually changed employee attitudes resulting in a nation-wide deliberate strategy that rapidly increased the ISDN market, and by 2000, ISDN subscriptions had surpassed Deutsche Telecom (Germany), to become a world leader in ISDN subscriptions.

MBD formed various internal and external strategic business communities within its challenging organizational culture, created new core competencies, and continuously promoted emergent and creative measures aimed at long-term innovation. In contrast, the traditional organization implemented carefully-planned measures aimed at short-term efficiencies, in which importance was placed on stability and control through a traditional and reliable organizational culture that was nurtured by reforms and improvements from core competencies acquired through a long process of building on achievements. NTT's top management team with Miyazu and Ikeda deliberately maintained paradoxical organizations, strategies, cultures and competencies within the company, activated and integrated these different systems simultaneously, and thus enhanced the output of the entire company. This concept is similar to the idea of the ambidextrous organization reported by academic research (Tushman and O'Reilly, 1997; O'Reilley III and Tushman, 2004), but differs from it in one respect. In an ambidextrous organization, business-level interaction is thoroughly restricted and the general manager supervises both organizations. In this case, each management level (top, middle and lower) stimulated interaction (knowledge sharing and collaboration through interaction and discussion) between the project-based organizations and the existing traditional organization.

The severe conflict and friction between MBD and the traditional organization was caused by the top-down vision transfer from the top management, and the promotion of company-wide knowledge management. This situation triggered a constructive and productive conflict between the organizations. The integration of the emergent and entrepreneurial strategies launched by MBD and the deliberate strategy launched by the traditional organization led to the creation of new markets, and services.

7.2.2. *Project-based organization characteristics and emergent and entrepreneurial strategies*

MBD business strategies were implemented by incubating the important ideas and actions of project leaders and project managers through joint development and ventures in the form of strategic alliances with outside partners and customers to produce tangible results. At any given time, MBD handled 20 projects simultaneously. Each project formed multiple ToBs and ToB networks through strategic tie-ups with outside companies, or partnerships with specific customers. Each project leader comprehensively managed and promoted more than one ToB and ToB network. Each project team consisted of about 30 to 40 employees. In ToBs with outside partners, or specific customers in each project, Internet and videoconferencing were freely utilized for project management in joint development, or as a means of sharing information or knowledge related to joint incubations with customers. Project leaders aggressively configured an adhocracy organization that was deliberately networked (Nohria, 1997).

MBD projects promoted businesses that were based on quick decision-making and action, as if they were small ventures. Thus, each project was of a loose-coupled nature that permitted both flexibility and autonomy. While dialogs and discussions with Ikeda, the top leader of MBD, allowed the concepts, strategies and tactics of the project leaders to take concrete form, the resulting close relationships among project leaders helped to generate new strategies and tactics. Ikeda and the MBD project leaders shared the vision and values, which help them work towards their mission of digital communications and the broadband business. Although strategically, the MBD had a strong emergent aspect on the whole, the deliberate, planned strategic factors identified by the executive team, and the tightly-coupled organization that resulted from close cooperation between the project leaders under Ikeda, made it possible to channel the results of experimentation or incubation into the formation of actual businesses.

The organizational structure of MBD, was designed to handle a complex environment characterized by both tightly-coupled and loosely coupled organizational elements, i.e. strict control among executive team members, while at the same time, granting flexibility and autonomy to each project (see Figure 7.2).

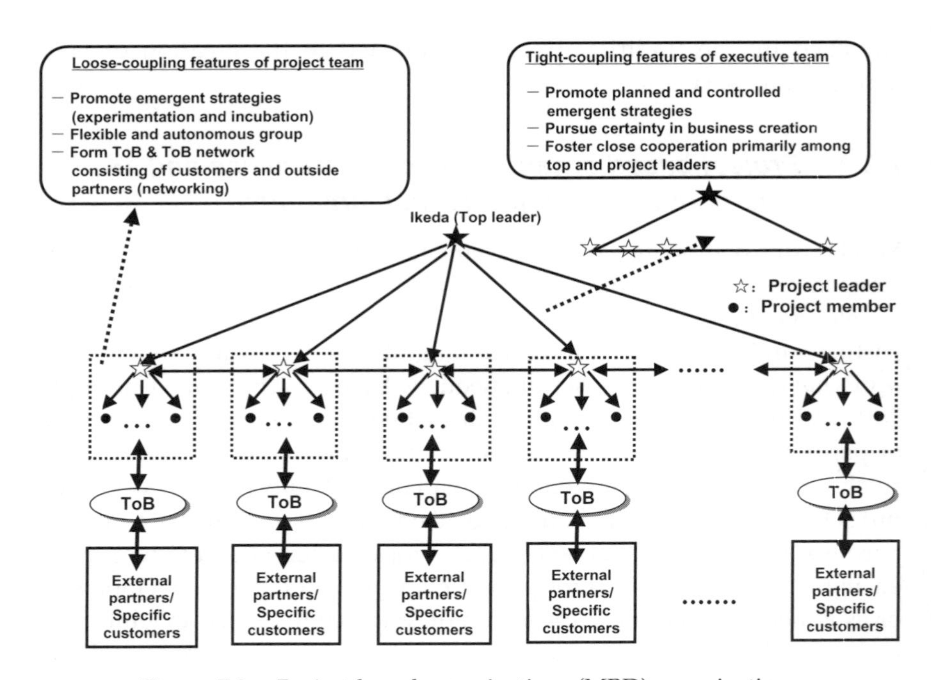

Figure 7.2: Project-based organizations (MBD) organization.

However, market and technological changes often necessitated the merging or abolition of project organizations. More people were hired for successful projects while the not-so-successful ones were either merged or revised. Several project leaders managed multiple projects. For example, a project leader in charge of product development also handled formulating solutions for corporate customers using this particular product. Such project leaders had to always remember the synergy effect of project tasks, and determine resource allocation, strategy and tactics.

As already stated, Ikeda considered that this collaboration with a large number of talented staff members was an everyday tightrope act. MBD's work environment encouraged project leaders to present new ideas on a regular basis. Though some project leaders presented similar ideas, Ikeda gave project-based organizations the maximum possible organizational slack (Nohria and Gulati, 1996; Bourgeois, 1981) as this provided a forum to share project ideas.

These project-based organizations were very productive; some of the results achieved are described in the following sections.

7.2.2.1. *Terminal adapter development*

The first ISDN product was the MN128 terminal adapter, a bestseller that set an example for other products to follow. The development of this product broke the established NTT product development conventions in that it was a joint development with BUG, an entrepreneurial startup (now a listed company) headquartered in Hokkaido. Product development at NTT at that time had to follow a strict internal protocol that determined procedures for product development and procurement. In addition, gaining the go-ahead for any product development project required numerous company conferences. The MN128 development project team emphasized on 'speed' as their strategic goal was quick development and rapid market entry. The existing traditional organization had a functional organization in charge of developing terminal adapters. Friction and conflict between the traditional organization that observed and honored the strict internal business process protocol, and an organization that put greater store on meeting strategic goals and speed of execution, were therefore inevitable.

After many heated in-house discussions, an understanding was reached after some changes in internal procedures — a clear definition of roles and the allocation of the risk of the entire project were made. The project members started several business simulations, and finally managed to bypass the strict in-house protocol to speed up the process. Collaborating with an NTT subsidiary and group member (called NTT-TE at the time), they started joint development with BUG. Communications between Tokyo and Hokkaido relied solely on ICT (telephones, e-mail, TV conferencing systems, etc.). Product specifications, detailed functions and development schedules were determined and managed in this manner. TV conferencing, in particular, turned out to be a useful tool for discussing issues and problems, as well as aligning attitudes. It served as a boundary object (e.g. Star and Griesener, 1989; Start, 1992). After facing many difficulties, team managed to release a terminal adapter at a surprisingly low price of ¥27,000.

In November 1995, Microsoft released Windows 95. This product simplified the PC interface and became popular in homes where they could be connected to telephone lines and the Internet. The PC had now turned into a multimedia terminal, which greatly changed its functional role. Many Internet websites were created and attracted the attention of customers as they were capable of representing text, images and sound. But still images took a long time to download on slow analog modems and the demand for fast and convenient ISDN lines, and for the MN128. The number of users who switched to ISDN steadily increased.

7.2.2.2. *NTT and Microsoft cooperation: MSN, the Microsoft Network (MSN); April 1996 service startup*

NTT and Microsoft agreed to cooperate in building, operating and providing content for an MSN network in Japan (Nihon Keizai Shinbun, 1966b) in March 1996. The startup of MSN was timed to coincide with the release of the Japanese version of Microsoft Windows 95 in November 1995, and was the first nationwide online service. NTTPC Communications, an NTT group company, provided the Japanese network with the service. NTTPC provided 45 MSN access points throughout Japan, which were gradually increased to cope with the increasing demand.

In partnership with Microsoft, NTT assisted in expanding the range of content, and providing web sites with exciting content, online phone services that allowed map searches, online ordering, etc. In addition to cooperating in Internet services, NTT and Microsoft pursued a number of business openings geared toward promoting ISDN and the merging of communications and computing.

7.2.2.3. *Promoting business through joint ventures — establishing GrR HomeNet Corporation*

NTT, Sega, Sony, Yamaha and Victor jointly formed GrR HomeNet Corporation in November 1995 to boost the ISDN demand (Nihon Keizai Shinbun, 1995b) by providing customers with easy access to the Internet, online shopping, online gaming, chatting and other services from their homes. Service started in November 1996 (Nihon Keizai Shinbun, 1996c) under the name of "plala". "Plala" provides online shopping, interactive gaming, karaoke, music-on-demand and other services for home users, and is an influential ISP in Japan (see http://www.plala.or.jp/index.shtml).

7.2.2.4. *G-Square for Internet shopping and goo, the search engine*

To provide the end users with an attractive content via ISDN, NTT corralled content providers (CP) in many industry and business sectors, and started G-Square, an Internet and hosting facility.

What this facility did was similar to that of Google, goo, Yahoo and Rakuten's current services. G-Square supplied a convenient Internet guide that contained goo, a leading search engine with access to customized information.

Recognized for its speed and high-quality search functions, goo was the product of Inktomi USA (later, it became the foremost US search engine and was eventually sold to Yahoo), a company famous for its outstanding search technology and user-friendly interfaces. NTT brought its Japanese processing technology to make goo a high-quality Japanese search engine with the largest Japanese database and the world's fastest data collecting and processing performance (see http://www.goo.net.jp/).

Shopping malls that included Takashimaya, a large Japanese department store, that provided high-quality music distribution services, went online by 1997. Customers were free to use prepaid cards, direct debit or credit cards to pay for their shopping. They were now able to search and order a product online and select their preferred method of payment.

7.2.3. *New projects arising from mixed projects*

In 1997, MBD started expanding the optical fiber network to accomodate the broadband business. With its MBD activities, NTT took communications starting from the introduction of ISDN in 1994 through the three phases of hop (analog circuits), step (digital circuits: ISDN) and jump (optical fiber) (see Figure 7.3). Thus, the road to ISDN did not end there, but it was a step towards optical fiber. During this time, the cost of optical fiber had dropped, and the systems and devices required for building fiber networks were progressing. By 2000, NTT had reached 20 million lines, and had already taken the decision to lay the groundwork for optical fiber networks. The ISDN service business was now firmly on track as exploratory activities had given way to exploitive activities. MDB was now ready to start an "optical fiber business", another exploratory activity designed to develop future strategies using resources garnered during ISDN development. Exploration and exploitation (March, 1991: Holland, 1975) are not mutually-opposed strategies, they are pursued by firms to maintain balance and complement each other (He and Wong, 2004).

The "Broadband via fiber business" formed by the MBD was referred to as the PHOENIX project. The project included members who were involved in other projects. New members were assembled, regardless of positions in business planning, marketing, sales, research and development, technology,

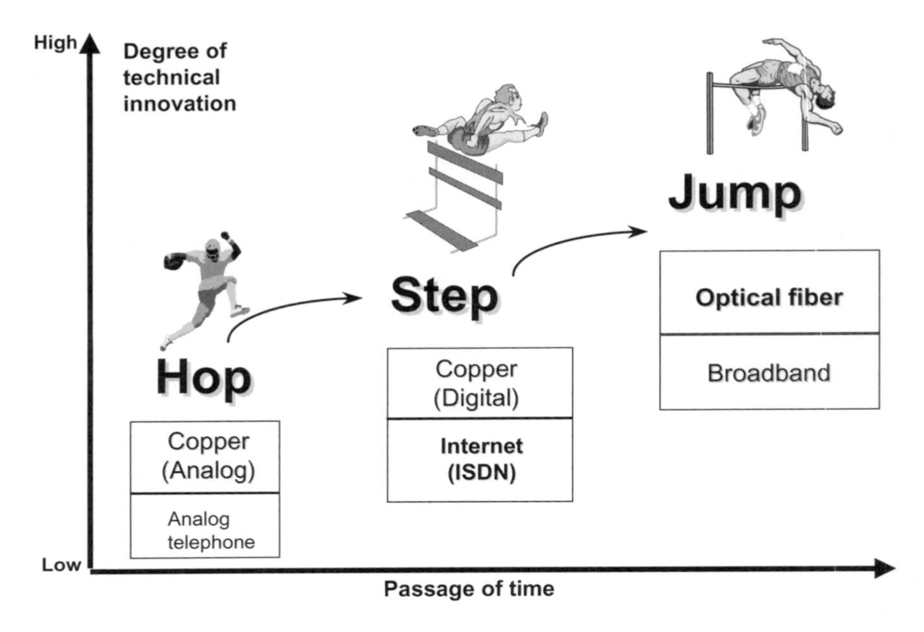

Figure 7.3: NTT multimedia & broadband strategy.

equipment investment, service planning, investment, and public relations. These members had to handle existing project tasks alongside the PHOENIX project. The dialog and relationship among the project members, including the project leaders, were directed towards the common goal of implementing a future strategy. In other words, the PHOENIX project was a project network in itself — a manifestation of inter-project relations (see Figure 7.4).

PHOENIX project meetings were held everyday and were mandatory. As the outline of the PHOENIX project became clearer, it become a "NTT policy" and "NTT strategy" to present to the president and the top management all the details the title of "Use of fiber optics." Ideas from the top management were incorporated and with more meetings were held. Finally, the PHOENIX project was submitted at a multimedia strategy conference and turned into an official policy. Further meetings followed to gain the support of employees of the traditional organization. In December 1997, a "Council for promoting PHOENIX" was formed, with participation from around 250 firms. New services such as B2E (Business-to-Enterprise) and B2B (Business-to-Business) employing optical fiber

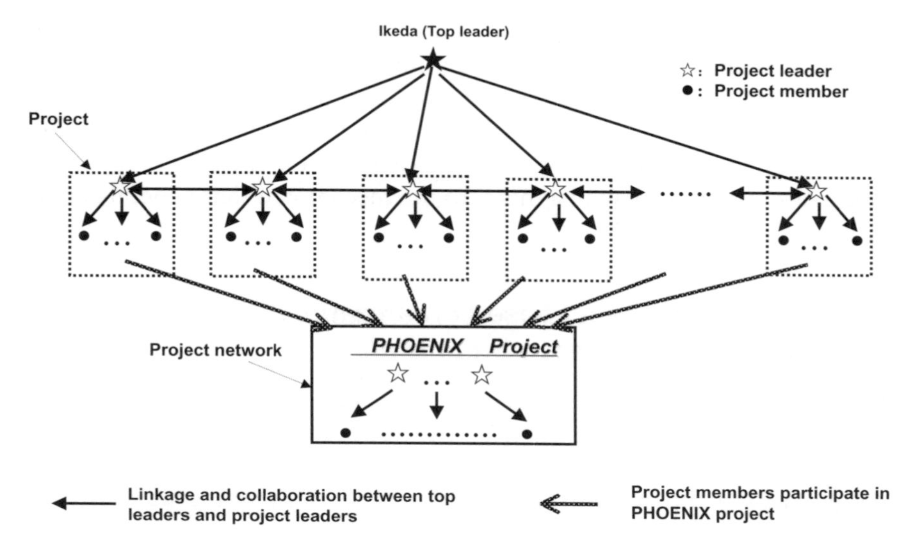

Figure 7.4: Using project network to form a new project.

were introduced. At the time of this writing (October 2006), the NTT Group is the largest provider of optical fiber broadband solutions, which have found their way into regular homes, and have turned Japan into a country with the highest proliferation of optical fiber connections in the world.

7.3. New and Practical Insights into this Case

This section discusses about the factors that made radical change successful, and the discussion is based on recently-obtained practical insights. Two similarities in the ideology of Van de Ven and Pool (1995) regarding the change process explain the radical change in NTT. The first similarity is the dialectic model. Working toward a future re-orientation, NTT used the new values and methods of operation of the MBD, to obliterate old values. It also introduced company-wide knowledge management to deal with its discord and conflict with the traditional organization and to generate constructive change.

The second similarity is the teleology model. The strategic and tactical competences that the project-based organization and traditional organization build to gain competitive advantage in spreading and expanding digital communications — the objective of the entire firm — builds a consensus between the two organizations and stimulates radical change to achieve this goal. The merging of these two models is the closest model for explaining the radical change process achieved in the NTT. NTT's case study also provides new insights into the mechanism that generates radical change in corporation.

7.3.1. *Creating project-based organizations in a heterogeneous organization*

To implement radical change, the top management can build a project-based organization that differs from the rest of the corporation. In NTT's case, the talented members of the project-based organization were supported by the top management, and given considerable authority in determining future corporate strategy.

The project leaders in charge of the organization needed innovative leadership and provided the organization's members with flexibility and autonomy. They created ToB networks with internal and external partners including customers to enable emergent, continuous experiments and incubation for future strategies. Their creative thinking and ideas on networking made it possible to promote emergent and entrepreneurial strategies (Nutt *et al.*, 1997). This case resembles the ideas proposed by Hamel (1999) in *Bringing Silicon Valley Inside.* In this book, project-based organizations are used to create innovative ideas through the entrepreneurial spirit present in a project-based organization to implement change in a traditional organization.

7.3.2. *Radical change of organization culture*

The new organizational culture of a project-based organization eventually obliterates the old organizational culture of the traditional organization. A new organization used as a driving force in implementing radical change in an corporation became a separate organization or subsidiary that was physically separated from the existing organization. This allowed the new organization to pursue innovation at its own pace (e.g. Tushman *et al.*, 1997). This approach though effective in implementing change, is not free from problems. Pursuing innovation affects the merger of the new and old organization culture, and the maintenance of harmony (Markides, 1998). The new organization refreshes the organizational culture and produces innovations, but leaves the problem of changing the attitudes of employees with an old mindset untouched.

This case shows that such problems can be overcome, if the top management maintains a positive attitude in dealing with the new and existing organizations to deliberately create a paradox in the corporation. While conflict and friction cannot be avoided, the pursuit of extensive knowledge management in both organizations, including the top management, by providing employees with a forum for interaction and mutual understanding, can help to gradually turn conflict and friction into constructive and productive results.

This case used a project-based organization that differed from the existing organization, and the ideas and actions of the new members caused chaos and fluctuations in the corporation. The resulting attitude changes in the employees and the merging of strategies generated a new order.

This corresponds to the self-organization process that occurs between corporate elements (the different project-based organization and the traditional organization) (Ulrich *et al.*, 1984). Self-organization allows the corporation to establish strategies, organizational structures, organization culture and competence, as well as maintaining their congruence to control two different and paradoxical organizations in order to achieve radical change.

7.3.3. *Integrating strategies*

Project-based organizations pursue future business opportunities, through external knowledge, creativity, innovative thinking, as well as promoting experimentation and incubation, by creating ToB networks. Through trial and error, they promote emergent and entrepreneurial strategies. At the same time, the traditional organization with its tight-coupling and functional structure distributes new products and services created by project-based organizations according to deliberate strategies that are well-planned in terms of efficiency and certainty. The integration of these two strategies enable the project-based organization and the traditional organization to pay close attention to time linkages to address the current and future business needs.

7.3.4. Leadership by project leaders

Leadership is required not only in the top management team, but also at each level in the project-based organization and the traditional organization. Each organizational level (top and middle) in a corporation has its own functions and must train leaders who think innovatively and are action-oriented. It is essential that they execute strategy and tactics within their own organization, promote knowledge management, and construct a management system that permits a leader to demonstrate their abilities.

The project leaders of the new organization who continuously produce creative and emergent strategies must have the capability and leadership to build new knowledge by forming ToB networks with external partners including potential customers. It is vital that the company who hire leaders project can create new businesses in new markets, and thus help to maintain the company's competitive edge. Tichy *et al.* (1997) calls the mechanism of a firm, which enables it to bring forth successive leaders, the leadership engine. This mechanism allows an organization to have a constant competitive advantage and, is also a necessary to implement radical change, as seen in this case study.

8

Innovation by Project-Based Organizations

8.1. Exploitation and Exploration by Project-Based Organizations

As shown by the case studies throughout this book, the conventional definition of project management is not sufficient to explain the nature of a project-based organization. The top management invests the resources required by the project to achieve the preset goal by executing the project based on a deliberate strategy (Mintzberg and Walters, 1985) within the given time limitations, but this is not limited to the functions of performing a project task as an exploitative practice. Chapters 2, 3, 7 and 5 dealt with DoCoMo, Vodafone, NTT's development of new services and Sony's game business, respectively. The corporate project teams in these firms transcended industry and business sector boundaries to form ToBs with customers and external partners to create project networks. The project-based organizations in these corporations carried out exploratory practices to establish a future strategy.

Project teams that pursue an exploratory practice emphasize on a strategy-making process (Mintzberg *et al.*, 1998) based on an emergent strategy, or entrepreneur strategy, rather than a strict and deliberate strategy. An emergent strategy does not mean that projects are entirely devoid of planning. The execution process to achieve the target is based on trial-and-error and the project itself consists of emergent characteristics.

As the case study in Chapter 2 points out, project tasks contain both exploitative and exploratory practices. Projects involve exploitation that pursues the refinement of existing knowledge (resources or competence) and exploration, a quest for new knowledge that involves risk-taking and experimenting, and therefore filled with uncertainty and novelty. Exploitation contains strong elements of organizational learning where incremental changes improve daily routines and refine the existing knowledge (March, 1991).

Exploration uses radical or discontinuous change to discover new knowledge and has a strong element of innovation. In other words, exploration changes existing routines to find new markets and technologies, and create new routines in a corporation (Nelson and Winter, 1982). Radical change, especially in science and technology, must rely on the slow refinement of knowledge through daily research and development efforts to enable project members to transcend large hurdles in facing a challenge.

It is important that the result of innovation and newly-obtained knowledge (new routines or specific technologies in the form of know-how or skills) be subject to knowledge transfer, or sharing, not only to specific project members, but also to other projects and other organizations. The smooth transition from exploratory practice to exploitative practice is thus an essential phase in deploying new know-how and routines throughout the corporation. To ensure that current and future businesses are within the same striking distance, the top management has to creatively use project characteristics, as dictated by project and strategic content, or simultaneously establish projects that exemplify exploration and exploitation in the corporation.

This chapter will first discuss the formulation and implementation of the project strategy process from the viewpoint of market-creating strategy and market-adaptive strategy. Then we will point out that the network strategy (creating ToB networks) of the project will create new knowledge and promote learning. Second we will discuss that the top and middle management teams of ToB need to adhere to a dynamic project formation chain model to continuously create new projects targeted at exploitation and exploration in the corporation. Third we will discuss the relationship between boundaries and knowledge integration (technology integration and new business model formation). Innovation as a corporate competitive edge is derived from boundaries and the integration of boundaries. I would like to consider the formation of ToBs and ToB networks, the source of boundaries and innovation, from the point of view of the knowledge integration process.

8.2. Strategy by Project-Based Organizations

8.2.1. *Formation of project-based organizations*

First, we will discuss the process of forming a project-based organization in a corporation and methods of executing strategies. As described in Figure 1.2 in Chapter 1, the project formation process and project type differ. Project type is used by the top and middle management practitioners to execute market-created strategies and market-adaptive strategies by interacting with the environment.

Market-creating strategies here refer to strategies for creating new products, services and business models, to embody them and establish a position in new business areas. DoCoMo in Chapter 2, Vodafone and Sharp in Chapter 3, Mitsubishi Electric in Chapter 4, Sony in Chapter 5, and the NTT case in Chapter 7, are examples of cases in point.

Market-adaptive strategies involve developing customized products or solutions for a specific customer and developing products to adapt to market or technical changes. The context in many project management situations discussed so far have mainly been project tasks for specific customers within a given time span. For the development of products and services in the high-tech industry where markets and technology change at a rapid rate, adjustment and integration are deep-rooted issues (Lawrence and Lorsch, 1967). Creating project networks that transverse the functional organizations is an advantage, as project networks deal with deep-rooted issues in a fast and flexible way. This is especially true in the case of Matsushita Electric and Canon described in Chapter 6, whose digital home appliances have a very short life cycle and are offered in a broad product lineup. They require a time-pacing strategy using an in-house project network.

The decision-making process for projects vary with the corporation, but top management involvement increases as project importance rises and resources (staff, equipment, capital, etc.) are determined according to the strict, but appropriate in-house consensus before the project is initiated.

An informal project network that transverses functional organizations and business departments is often formed by the middle management. (The product development process at Sharp described in Chapter 3 is a case in point.) However, the informal consensus building (or the formal consensus building between organizations) that the top management of a functional organization or business department implements to achieve a pre-determined goal facilitates the smooth operation of the project network.

The improvement activities of daily routines and other temporary projects (also referred to as a task force) are often determined by the middle or lower management.

8.2.2. *Microstrategy formulation using project-based organizations*

The project members including the project leader or chief handle the concrete formulation of strategy. How do the project members formulate a strategy? (See Figure 8.1.). A market-creating strategy must consider new products, services and business models, that are decided upon during the brainstorming sessions are held in the course of the project to build a new business concept for the product, service or business model.

An analytical approach (e.g. Porter, 1985) for examining the competitive advantage of positioning a new strategy in a project is performed alongside the analysis of traditional marketing procedures that segment or target customer groups, or e-marketing (e.g. Kotler, 1999).

The project members are a group of specialist staff members who turn the business concept of a targeted strategy into documentation (spelling

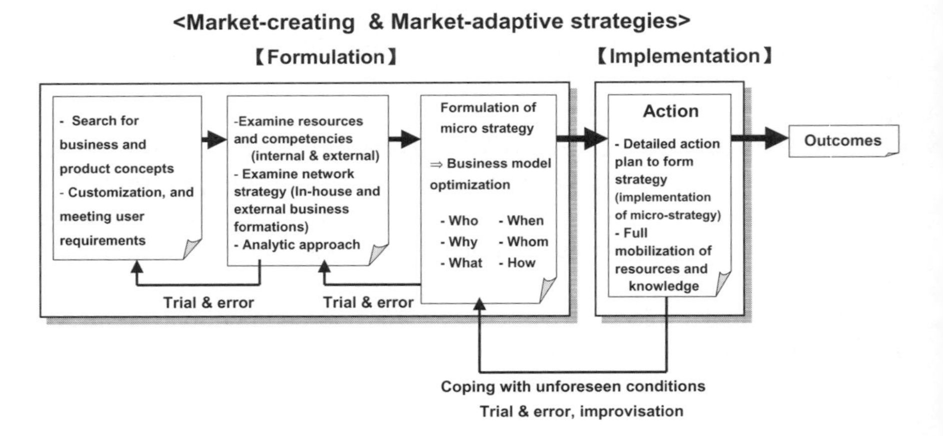

Figure 8.1: Microstrategy formulation and implementation.

out the nature of a new product or service, and the mechanism of a new business model). Since the costs (development, manufacturing, PR and other costs) required to formulate a new business in a market-creating strategy are not evident from the start, not only the conditions (product functions, service specifications, etc.), but also the costs required to implement a new business must be considered.

In addition to the above issues, the project members must express new business, consider internal and external knowledge (resource and competence), and consider network strategy for new internal and external business formations.

Of course, this does not exclude development prior to the project or the new development process undertaken by in-house research and development departments, which are essential in keeping core competencies alive. But recent product development by the high-tech industry is not limited to in-house innovation, but relies also on first-class external knowledge. R&D approaches such as open innovation (Chesbrough, 2003) and the *Connect and Develop* (Huston and Skkab, 2006) method used by P&G in the USA are not uncommon.

Especially in recent high-tech firms, projects that perform exploratory practices are expected to not only to enable development of best-selling products, but also to reduce development costs and development periods. But the one's use of only own or in-house resources does not guarantee the success of a new development task.

The case studies of DoCoMo in Chapter 2, Vodafone in Chapter 3, and NTT and other communication carriers in Chapter 7, describe the development of new consumer services — their final target. Communications carriers without an equipment manufacturing division must conduct joint development of a new system (hardware and software platform) with an external partner. This indicates that access to external knowledge is an important issue. Development projects of manufacturers that conduct joint development with telecommunication carriers have to develop and manufacture complex new systems (hardware and software platforms) within pre-determined timelines.

Thus, manufacturer development projects, regardless of the suitability of core technology, development and manufacturing costs, development periods and other factors must be duly considered. This requires that internal and external developer partners including group corporations be related in order to build a dynamic knowledge network (Kodama, 2005).

I would like to call this dynamic internal and external knowledge network the network strategy of the project-based organization in this book. The LSI that is the core engine in Sony's PlayStation, described in Chapter 5, is manufactured by a project network operating as a knowledge network comprising of Sony, Toshiba and IBM.

Access to external knowledge and capturing it is not limited to technology. The cellular phone business at DoCoMo or Vodafone, Sony's game business and the broadband business at NTT made it essential to build a service business model, in addition to a technical one. This required business information generated by a partnership that traversed across different industries and business sectors. Thus, project networks operating as knowledge networks had to be built with multiple partners. These project networks must be dynamically rebuilt to suit corporate strategy.

Until now, networks with external partners have been assessed only on transaction cost as corporations have mainly targeted project efficiency (Williamson, 1975, 1981). Thus, the knowledge-integration process (Kodama, 2006) — searching for, assessing and quickly incorporating excellent knowledge from outside the corporation — and making it part of its core competency is very important. As stated earlier, product development projects at P&G USA generate best-selling products through effective access to and integration of external knowledge. This improves R&D efficiency and lowers development costs (Huston and Skkab, 2006).

Projects that execute market-creating strategies and market-adaptive strategies require strengthening and maintaining traditional core competencies, as well as promoting an aggressive integration of external knowledge and capabilities to flexibly handle market changes in a fast-moving market environment (Brown and Eisenhardt, 1997; D'Aveni, 1994, 1995; Chakravarthy, 1997; Eisenhardt and Sull, 2001). The resource-based view of the firm (Wernefelt, 1984; Barney, 1991) — a strategic theory analyzing corporate competitive advantage — is a static theory. It lacks a dynamic approach with regard to the deployment of resources by a corporation to achieve competitive advantage (Priem and Butler, 2001; Mosakouwski and McKelvey, 1997). By contrast, the dynamic capability (Teece, Pisano and Shuen, 1997; Eisenhardt and Martine, 2000) concept adds the intangible resource of knowledge and its dynamic configuration elements to knowledge as a resource-based view.

'Dynamic capabilities' are defined as an organizational process by which members manipulate resources to develop new value-creating strategies. Teece *et al.*, stated that competitive advantage is achieved by a firm's "ability to integrate, build, and reconfigure internal and external competences to address rapidly-changing environments" (Teece *et al.*, 1997, p. 516). But their theory does not provide a detailed process for the dynamic tasks of formulating and implementing it at a practical level.

The case studies presented in this book deal with industries and corporations in a rapidly-changing competitive environment. Such entities refine and deepen internal knowledge (path-dependent resources), dynamically take in external knowledge (path-breaking resources), and integrate internal and external knowledge to create new products, services and business models. To do this, knowledge distributed throughout the corporation must be integrated, and projects require a dynamic process that reconfigures this knowledge to suit conditions. This indicates that the vertical and horizontal boundaries, which constitute the corporate business model, must be continuously reconfigured to adapt to environmental changes (or deliberately create new environmental changes) (Eisenhardt and Bingham, 2005; Kodama, 2006a).

To identify new business opportunities and ensure the growth of existing businesses, the skillful combination of path-dependent and path-breaking knowledge through strategic alliances, M&A and industries and business sectors, regardless of business lines, will require the ability to enthusiastically and persistently capture new knowledge for future projects (e.g. Karmin and Mitchell, 2000; Graebner, 2004; Kodama, 2006).

All the case studies presented in this book indicate that corporations engaged in the cellular phone business, game business, digital appliances and broadband business cannot just rely on deepening and refining in-house knowledge, but must also possess a dynamic view of strategy (e.g. Markides, 1997; Eisenhardt and Sull, 2001).

Projects with a dynamic view of strategy, use hypothesis and repeat business simulations and trial-and-error experiments to narrow down the field to the optimum condition required to implement a new business (a concrete business model, product, service specification, business formation or the like) (see Figure 8.1).

In this trial-and-error process, the project members as experts ask the usual questions of "Who", "Why", "What", "When", "Whom" and "How" to formulate a micro strategy (see Figure 8.2).

As stated in Chapter 1, a project as a ToB possesses the four elements of "shared thought worlds", "harmonized knowledge", "creative collaboration" and "boundaries penetration." "Shared thought worlds" and

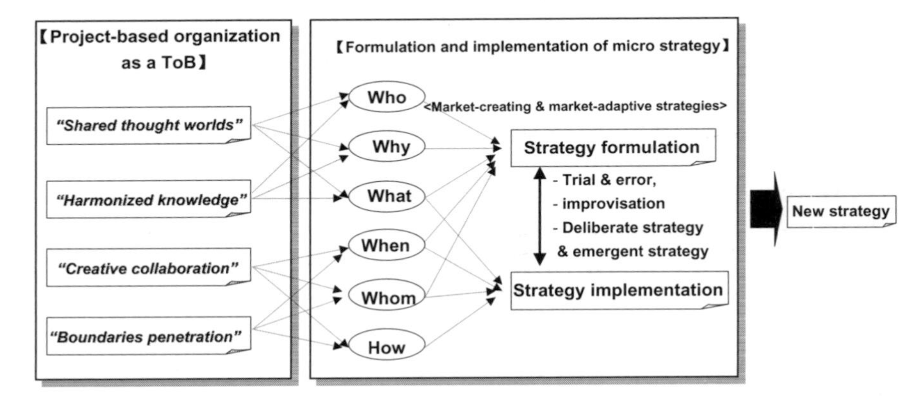

Figure 8.2: Strategy formulation and implementation in a project-based organization.

"harmonized knowledge" provide the context necessary to determine the "Who", "Why" and "What" for the formulation and implementation of the targeted strategy. "Creative collaboration" and "boundaries penetration" provide the context necessary to determine the "When", "Whom" and "How" for the formulation and implementation of the targeted strategy. The project members in the ToB complete the micro strategy, the detailed and optimum business content intended to embody a new business, and determine the external and internal knowledge, and the business formation required to implement it. The detailed business content includes an action plan to implement strategies using "Whom", "What", "When" and "How". The project members pinpoint the network strategy (business formation) to capture the internal and external knowledge required in the knowledge-integration process described above.

The project members determine a goal in the exploratory process, called a market-creating strategy. For example, in the DoCoMo case described in Chapter 2, the goal was the new business strategy that they intended to implement. In the Vodafone and Sharp cases described in Chapter 3, the goal was the creation of a karaoke cellular phone culture. In the Mitsubishi Electric case described in Chapter 4, the goal was the creation of a cellular-phone-based TV phone culture. However, realistic business activities must involve essential processes such as "How" and "What", which work toward the building of a detailed micro strategy. Therefore, project members in case studies in Chapters 2–4 used trial and error in a set hypothesis to arrive at the best solution.

As stated above, while projects that pursue market-creating strategies require deliberate analytic strategy, emergent strategy and entrepreneur strategy become equally important. The thought and action process of the project members must follow a more complex business model in a business environment, which is not limited to their corporation, but involves an external environment as well. The project members need to be physically and mentally strong to cope in such an environment. Project-based organizations pursuing market-creating strategies as a means of exploration are also an important engine of the internal corporate venture.

Market-adaptive strategies involve orders to specific users, customization and solutions, as well as consumer product development to cope with changes in markets and technology. Customization and solutions have to match specific user requirements, while consumer products must be targeted at a customer segment, and a product lineup strategy must be targeted at a splintered market. These market-adaptive strategies rely on exploitative practices where project teams closely monitor changes in markets and technology to continuously refine in-house knowledge. Project members who execute exploitative practices also need an accurately targeted and analyzed deliberate strategy. They need the mindset and conduct required to match user requirements and "counting backward marketing" (used by Matsushita Electric described in Chapter 6) linked to a time-pacing strategy. Projects intended to implement market-adaptive strategies have fewer emergent characteristics compared to market-creating strategies. However, this requires that project members often have to use a trial-and-error approach to cope with issues (access to and integration of technical aspects, project resources and external knowledge) as the strategy formulation process progresses. As a result, problem-solving projects with emergent-strategy elements appear even when market-adaptive strategies are used.

If all the strategy formulations and implementations in the customization and solutions targeted at specific users can be accomplished using project resources, the load on network strategy that has to use internal and external knowledge would be minimal. But when some tasks in a project are outsourced, the competence of the outsourcing partner should be thoroughly analyzed to ensure that the best partner is selected.

Knowledge-sharing and organizational learning corporate networks (i.e. ToB networks) must be built to deploy the result of projects (new know-how or skills), described in detail below, and apply them to other in-house projects and existing organizations. Consequently, any strategy (market-creating and market-adaptive strategies) should have a "network mindset" as its important component.

8.2.3. *Implementing a micro strategy through project-based organizations*

The next step is to implement a micro strategy that has been formulated. However, strategy formulation and implementation often overlap. For example, since the result of adjustments and negotiations with internal and external partners influence the details of strategy formulation, the formation of internal and external partners, or ToB networks, which accompany the strategy formulation process, are often executed by the project members. They have to consider the "Who", "Why", "What", "When", "Whom" and "How" in the strategy implementation process. Discussions between the actors and shared values that transcend the boundaries between different organizations and specialized niches are very important elements of a ToB network (Kodama, 2001). But unforeseen events (problems or new issues) can occur during the implementation process. Then the project members should use a trial-and-error process or work towards micro strategy implementation and formulation (see Figure 8.1).

8.3. The Strategy Dynamics of Project-based Organizations and Project Formation Dynamic Chain Reaction

Figure 8.3 shows the series of strategy dynamics from strategy formulation to implementation, as well as the accumulation of intellectual assets in the innovation and learning process in a project-based organization. The practitioners (top and middle management) in a corporation (organization) look for new business strategy, or customer cultivation opportunities. Projects that have been established through formal or informal consensus formation by the top or middle management test, and build the ToB network formation as a network strategy in the strategy formulation and implementation process described above. The knowledge-integration (or knowledge-creation) (for example, Grant, 1996; Nonaka and Takeuchi, 1996), or knowledge-sharing process geared to generate innovation and learning, are integrated in the strategy and implementation process by the

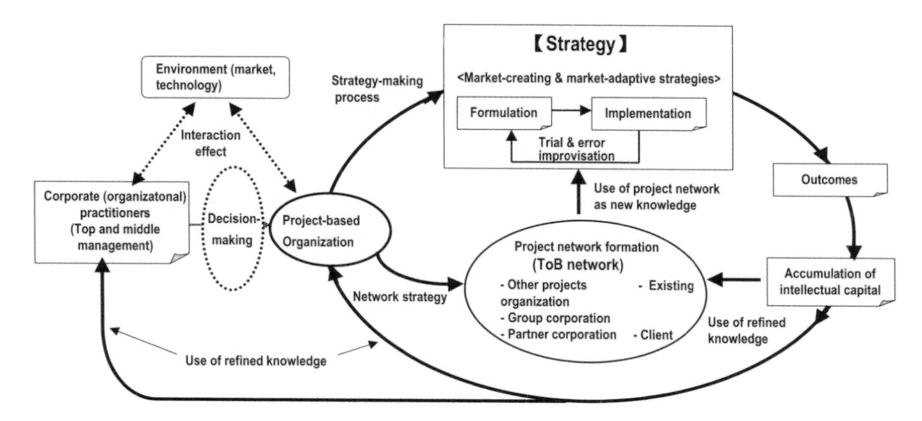

Figure 8.3: Strategy dynamics in project-based organizations.

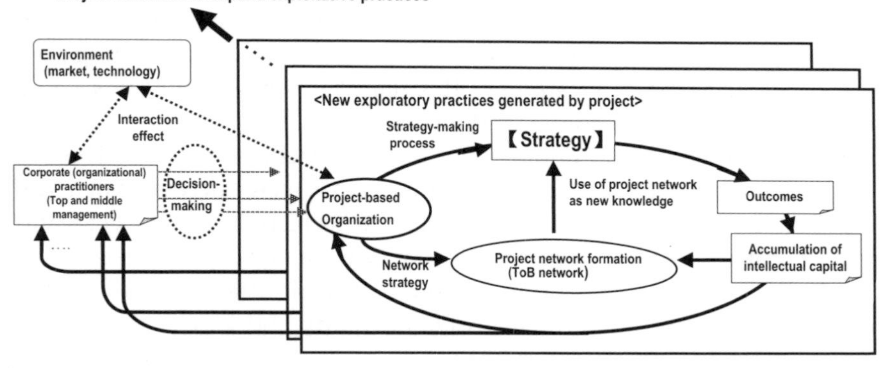

Figure 8.4: Dynamic chain of project formation.

project team. The results of strategy implementation, in addition to know-how and routines for the implementation, become deeply embedded in the project and the ToB network. The project members and organization's practitioners identify and employ knowledge or routines in the form of know-how and skills refined by the project results. They then repeatedly perform exploratory practices to find new business and exploitative practices to uncover best practices. This is referred to as the dynamic chain of project formation in this paper (see Figure 8.4).

In Figure 8.4, the knowledge assets accumulated as a result of exploratory practices generated by the project that was formed first produce exploitative practices as routines based on new know-how and skills. These new exploitative practices are either generated during the extension of a project, or are created during the formation of new projects.

The former type, an exploitative practice generated by a project is of the following type. In a market-adaptive strategy, this occurs when solutions based on newly-obtained know-how and skills are supplied to another customer via the same project. This is often the case in the customization and provision of solutions in the IT field. In a market-creating strategy, this applies to projects concerned with the development of new products and services such as upgrade tasks (incremental improvements) provided to consumers. The project members involved in the initial development accumulate skills and know-how through handling the product and the service, and they can thus ensure the effective promotion of business, rather than transfer a project task to another project, or organization. These were the project members who built the project networks in Matsushita Electric and Canon described in Chapter 6. The project members of emergency projects at Sharp, described in Chapter 2, took over an existing project. In a market-adaptive strategy, this happens when routines based on newly-obtained know-how and skills are learned in another project and stimulate the horizontal deployment of best practices. This involves the deployment of customization and solutions that were successful in a specific sector to customers in the same sector, it corresponds to project teams in corporate marketing departments in many global corporations.

In this case, the execution of a company-wide strategy or top-down project-based learning becomes essential (Brady and Davies, 2004). In a market-adaptive strategy, this applies to projects formed elsewhere for newly-developed products and services such as upgrades (incremental improvements) provided to consumers. The clear division of roles in the functional organization (sales, technology, services, etc.) for handling the development of new products and services will effectively promote the business such as business deployments by telecommunications carriers described in Chapters 2, 3 and 7. These corporations separate the execution of projects that promote exploratory practices, or market-creating strategies, and the execution of exploitative practices to promote and establish newly-created organizations, and implement strategies into different organizations. The specific conditions will determine whether projects or a functional organization should be used to execute an exploitative practice.

For example, when a new product or service is not selling well, emergency projects that transcend functional organizations are often formed, or else, new projects that aim to expand sales are formed. It is the top management that determines the implementation of such projects.

The knowledge assets accumulated in the exploratory practice in the project are used in the execution of new exploratory practices in the same project, or in other projects. In market-adaptive strategies, exploratory practice is used when the same project provides a customer with new solutions geared to obtain new know-how and skills. In market-creating strategies, this is exemplified by a project that focuses on innovation. The project team at Sony in charge of PlayStation development (see Chapter 5), which had to develop the next-generation game device and core engine is an example of this. The Mitsubishi Electric case described in Chapter 4 where the video development project core members formed ToB networks with related organizations in the corporation to develop new systems is another case in point.

The following is an example of the latter case i.e. an exploratory practice generated by a project. In a market-adaptive strategy, this is when an innovation task is executed by a project organized elsewhere. In a market-creating strategy, this is when a project organized elsewhere is used to develop an innovation task. The project formation of the telecommunications carriers (DoCoMo, Vodafone, NTT) described in Chapters 2, 3 and 7, new projects tended to be formed depending on an innovation task. This is because cellular phones and the broadband business require diverse service strategies and this makes it important to gain internal and external knowledge. This is the lifeline of the communications carrier business.

Then why do these projects form a dynamic chain? The reason is the special character of projects ToB. As shown in Figure 1.2, the corporations mentioned in this case study possess a project culture that makes it easy to form the strategy required by the environment. For example, at Sharp (Chapter 3), not only emergency projects, but also project networks that informally transcend business departments are formed at all times. Matsushita Electric and Canon (Chapter 6) have a similar project culture. This is because "shared thought worlds" exist in the top and middle management layers at these corporations. As stated in Chapter 1, the crossover carrier path peculiar to Japanese corporations has provided a breeding ground for shared values and resonance of value (Kodama, 2001). As a result, this has created a corporate culture at Japanese corporations, which has facilitated the sharing of tacit knowledge as a community practice

(Nonaka and Takeuchi, 1995). Top management employees at Sharp have handled emergency projects, and the understanding of project formation among Sharp employees is high.

At Canon, ten or more product development projects are formed for each project and project leaders and project members handle different tasks. After the completion of a project, the project members return to the function organization group as a community of practice to which they belong but they participate in many projects depending on conditions. These crossover experiences between projects and communities of practice are embedded as harmonized knowledge in an employee. This harmonized knowledge connects different fields of expertise, or knowledge boundaries (Brown and Duguid, 2001). In addition, harmonized knowledge gives birth to new meaning and viewpoints at the knowledge boundaries between experts and become the pragmatic driving force to solve problems (Peirce, 1989; James, 1907; Bourdieu, 1977). The pragmatism in the corporation will give rise to a project culture that transcends objectivism.

The "shared thought worlds" and "harmonized knowledge" form a breeding ground that facilitates the creation of "creative collaboration" among employees. The formation of ToB networks at the top management or middle management layers results in the formation of a top management team or a middle management team. At Canon, the top management team plays an important role at morning assembly. Constructive dialog and creative abrasion (Leonard-Barton, 1995) via ToB networks generate the collaborative leadership (Chrislip and Larson, 1994; Bryson and Crosby, 1992) in top management and middle management, and cross-functional projects between functional organizations and business departments are formed depending on top and middle management conditions. As in the DoCoMo, Sony and NTT cases, the collaborative leadership of leaders between corporations that transcend different industries and business sectors generated "boundaries penetration" characteristics of projects. The project network between corporations promotes a win-win relationship to implement network strategy.

8.4. Knowledge Integration through ToB Network

This section analyzes the relationship between organizational and knowledge boundaries on the one hand with knowledge integration (technology integration and formation of new business models). The author believes that the organization's capability create innovation and learning — the competitive edge of a corporation — comes from boundaries, or from the integration of boundaries. The capability that arises from the networking (i.e. ToB networking) of boundaries by actors, or boundary (also ToB) integration, is the "hidden competitive edge" of a corporation, a factor I would like to call "integrative competence".

One of the lessons provided by the case studies in this paper is that the productive friction and creative abrasion elements between actors in the knowledge and organizational boundaries between the project team, the functional organization and the external partner promote "creative collaboration" between the actors, which leads to new product and service development, and a business model. This results in "creative collaboration" and creates ToB (Team of Boundaries). The second lesson is that project leaders, functional organizations and other organizational actors execute the networking of the knowledge boundaries (ToB) distributed inside and outside the corporation by "creative collaboration". And the existence of knowledge boundaries, which connect the inside and outside of the corporation permits the integration of specialized knowledge of different kinds to implement the development of new products and services, and business models.

8.4.1. *'Internal integrative competencies'*

A project is a group consisting of actors from different fields of expertise and multiple knowledge boundaries exist between the project members. Project networks that transcend functional organizations and business departments have knowledge boundaries created by actors participating in the project network and possessing diverse domain-specific knowledge, and also have organizational boundaries rooted in the friction and a competitive spirit within an organization (especially among different departments). I would like to discuss the meaning and benefits of integrating boundaries that exist both inside and outside a corporation.

In the Sharp case described in Chapter 3, president Machida emphasized the "importance of increasing the vertical depth and horizontal width of technology and creating a chemical reaction in the firm." From the viewpoint of knowledge integration, increasing the vertical depth of technology signifies that each expert should deepen his/her domain specific knowledge and deepen their knowledge in, e.g., communications technology, computer technology, software technology, imaging technology, lens technology, semiconductor technology, high-density packaging technology, or production control technology. Horizontal width means that an engineer who has deepened his vertical knowledge should also make an effort to study technologies that are similar to his area of expertise. For example, an expert in imaging technology should study semiconductor technology or software technology; a designer of communications technology should study digital appliance design, while a designer of digital cameras or digital video cameras should study communication technology device design. As described in Chapter 3, linking adjacent technologies can result in the technical integration or chemical reaction that gives birth to entirely new products such as the camera cellular phone. In 2006, Sharp brought out the AQUOS cellular, a phone with terrestrial digital TV capability, which merged cellular technology with Sharp's proprietary LCD TV technology. This new product was a result of another "Kin pro" chemical reaction.

As stated in Chapter 3, about Sharp, this is an example of an integration of deep domain-specific technological knowledge with a different adjacent technology, and corresponds to knowledge boundaries integration among experts. The project network at Sharp that transcended business departments formed multiple boundaries (ToB) (see Figure 3.3). The project network leaders integrated (network) these boundaries (ToB) to implement technology integration (knowledge integration) and develop a camera cellular phone. As stated in Chapter 6, about Matsushita Electric and Canon, this was a case of integration of knowledge boundaries of different experts among functional organizations (marketing, sales, development, design and manufacturing) (see Figures 6.6 and 6.9).

When the actors in each field of specialization belong to different organizations (functional organization or business department), there are also organizational boundaries in the form of friction between organizations and vested interests. These organizational boundaries cause abrasion and conflict between the actors. One of these is the initial sense of discomfort the actors experience in having to transform accumulated path-dependent knowledge (Carlile, 2002). The friction and vested interests of business departments has a negative influence on organic links between business departments. Many actors have a strong dislike for transforming existing knowledge, power, control, structures, etc.

However, new knowledge integration will not be possible without boundary integration through a ToB network. To do this, a top management, a middle management teams and a custom management team (a team that has no official designation) must be set up as a ToB to network that spans business departments and fields of expertise, and forms shared values and resonance of values through dialogs and discussions (Kodama, 2001). Shared value and resonance of value elements stimulate dialogs and debates based on creative abrasion (Leonard-Barton, 1995) and productive friction (Hagel III and Brown, 2005) within and between ToBs.

These ToBs will, through a formal and informal ToB linkage (networking) of each management layer internally, link different management layers (network) to enable the sharing of deep knowledge, thus providing a linkage to prepare for future action (see Figure 8.5). In Figure 8.5 LT, which, also refers to the executive team that includes the board members or a business team that includes the president. Canon's morning assembly described in Chapter 6 is a good example. Networked ToBs like these have also been reported in TQM promotion activities and in new product development (Amasaka, 2004). Toyota Motors have several ToBs that build a vertical and horizontal network. These ToBs are also linked to outside suppliers to enable the creation and sharing of knowledge within the Toyota Group.

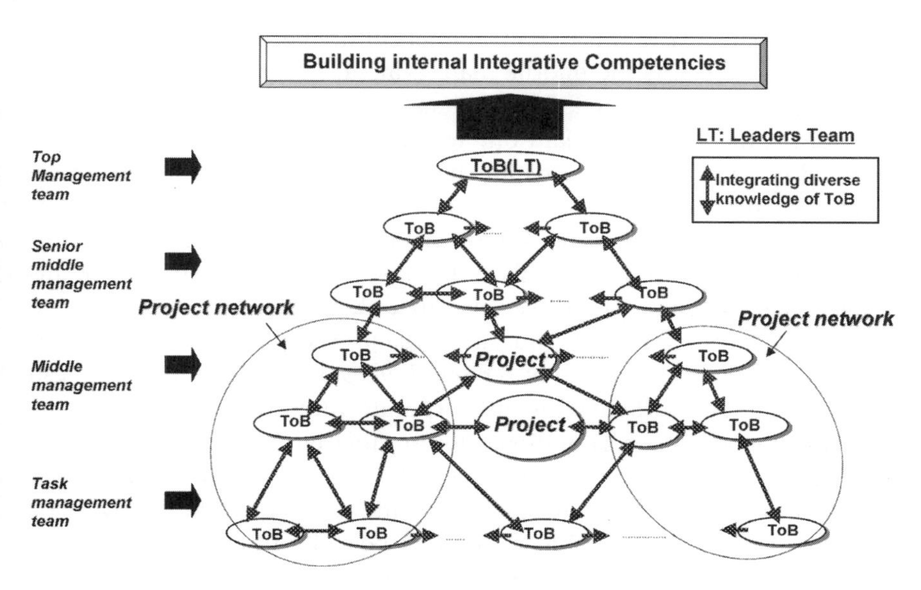

Figure 8.5: "Internal integrative competencies" through in-house ToB network.

Research so far has shown that innovations can be successful in ambidextrous organizations (O'Reilley III and Tushman, 2004) where a business startup is initiated in a new organization separated from the existing organization, and where communications between the organizations is minimized, while the general manager would oversee operations of both organizations. In contrast, another research has indicated that general managers are a source of friction so that the interchange between the organizations in the form of a mutual general manager should be limited, while the interaction at a practical level should be increased (Govindarajan and Trimble, 2005).

This research contains valuable information, and as the Sony PlayStation case, described in Chapter 5, shows, SCE, a new subsidiary, was responsible for the hit product, PlayStation. There was no collaboration between Sony and SCE executives. In this sense, the Sony case shows innovation through an ambidextrous organization. However, ambidextrous organizations are not trouble-free. For example, long-term, merging and harmony between the "old corporate culture" and the "new corporate culture" is a problem (Markides, 1998). Even if the new organization is imbibed with a new culture and is successful at innovations, most of the employees in the organization still possess old values and this results in reforming the values of all employees.

The problem with this organizational culture becomes serious among the employees below the middle management. The viewpoint of the top management in many US firms is that managers and employees who hold onto old values should be laid off, and that the new business should be ushered in by new employees imbibed with a new spirit, using new routines to ensure the renewal of the entire corporation. Experiences of many traditional Japanese enterprises show that laying off people does not completely solve this problem. This is because they recognize that "manpower is intellectual property," and that their tacit knowledge is the source of competitive edge. Thus, at a Japanese corporation, the problem is how to make the best use of the employees. Employees in a Japanese corporation are instilled with the corporate philosophy and values as soon as they join the corporation after graduating from school and they receive plenty of on-the-job training (OJT) (e.g. Okazaki-Ward, 1993). Employees who are posted in suitable positions will gradually show their worth and they will be assigned different posts in different departments to improve their coordination skills. As described in Chapter 1, employees will gradually acquire "shared thought worlds" that will strengthen a sense of solidarity between them. Assigned to posts, they will gradually rise to the ranks of upper management. This is how employees are trained at Japanese corporations.

Thus, this paper supports the view of existing US mainstream research (O'Reilley III and Tushman, 2004; Govindarajan and Trimble, 2005) regarding the merging of the "new organizational culture" and the "existing (old) organizational culture". Project leaders in new organizations with projects and project networks emphasize an organization with strong lateral linkage. This is the reason for the deep collaboration between project leaders (mainly the middle managers in a Japanese corporation), and other project leaders and middle managers in the existing organization. The general managers, directors and senior executives must have an understanding of the management in the existing organization and be able to bond with them.

As previously mentioned, it all depends on how ToB networks are used in the corporation to build top and middle management teams. In contrast, the constant presence of ToB networks at each management layer provides a breeding ground that facilitates the creation of projects to flexibly respond to changes in environment and strategies. The creative strength of the ToB network constitutes an integrative competence as hidden competitive edge in the corporation, which is difficult to observe from outside. This integrative competence generates routines such as new actor skills, know-how and core technologies such as black box, and helps and accumulate intangible intellectual assets (see Figure 8.5). Here, integrative competences are used to indicate the capability embedded in a corporation and will be referred to as "internal integrative competencies" to distinguish them from the capability to capture external knowledge described in the next section.

8.4.2. *'External integrative competencies'*

ToB networks extend both inside and outside the firm. As seen in the DoCoMo, Vodafone, Sony and NTT cases, project networks as ToB networks were built to link different business sectors and industries. The cellular phone business, game business and the broadband business use new value chains (Porter, 1985) and value networks (Christensen, 1997) not present in conventional businesses to build different linkages. The communications platform for cellular phones built by DoCoMo and Vodafone is not limited to distributing content and applications, but also provides new businesses such as mobile e-commerce (referred to as "wallet phones" in Japan). In this field, many firms offer B2B (Business-to-Business) or B2C (Business-to-Consumer) to enable marketing, PR activities, sales etc. The game business has witnessed an explosive growth — home users to networks to content delivery — and consumer usage is expanding across business sectors. Cellular phones and game devices are thus breaking down the conventional boundaries between the consumer and businesses in the network world of ICT, which is having an impact on various business sectors and industries.

A strategy shared by DoCoMo, Vodafone, Sony and NTT is an attempt to build a network strategy that integrates internal and external core knowledge. By building ToB networks involving many influential external partners and specific customers, these strategies enable the creation of business models. In the value chain, the developments of cellular phone, game device and broadband technologies and services impact not only one's own firms, but also businesses in entirely different industries. DoCoMo, Vodafone, Sony and NTT affect other businesses, and it has, therefore, become essential to form partnerships based on ToB networks that establish win-win relationships between firms. Consequently, these corporations will have to reconfigure these ToB networks to suit strategies or conditions. Businesses operating in competitive environments (e.g. cellular phone business and broadband business) require a task that can dynamically build or revise relationships with external partners. This task is executed by project teams made up of various expert groups (business planning, marketing, sales, technical development, etc.). These project teams build a ToB network that interacts dynamically with external partners to absorb useful knowledge, and build new and creative business models. The manufacturers introduced in this paper, i.e. Sharp, Mitsubishi Electric, Sony, Matsushita Electric and Canon, also do this. Of course, refining technology derived from the black box of in-house core technology and technology integration is important. However, as the system architecture evolves (including improvements and other product upgrades), it is equally important to absorb useful knowledge from outside and integrate it with one's own corporate knowledge through ToB networks with external partners (including joint development partners or component manufacturers). Especially as the product development span for cellular phones, portable data terminals, game devices, communication devices, digital home appliances and other high tech products is constantly becoming shorter due to technical innovations and changes in user demand. As a result, the system architecture requires frequent revisions.

The system architecture for broadband and mobile multimedia products frequently needs revising. Corporate research centers and departments with core knowledge such as communications technology (broadband and wireless technology), or core knowledge that includes computer technology, middleware software and application software, are specially in need of deep collaboration through a technical integration process. To rapidly develop products and introduce them to the market, a firm must integrate elemental technology from influential partners all over the world with its own elemental technology and use this technology to develop new products. At the same time, the elemental technology obtained from other sources must be thoroughly studied and refined to convert it into the corporation's own core technology.

Members of the marketing and sales department should form ToBs with large customers to acquire customer knowledge that can be used to inform in-house engineers on what is happening on the customer side. An important strategy for a group corporation is building ToBs to achieve group synergy between group corporations so that the group corporation can act as one entity and share knowledge regarding market and R&D strategies, and develop new technology strategies. Project leaders and leaders in each organization must share the deep knowledge in the ToB and build networks centering on each in-house ToB to deeply embed and integrate knowledge. NEC, a large Japanese communications manufacturer, uses the term "dynamic collaboration" to refer to the business formation that promotes the dynamic sharing and integrating of external partner knowledge through building ToB networks.

In the increasing intensity of corporate competition, corporations are further progressing along the path of "selection and concentration" to seek a new model that will deploy businesses dynamically through collaborations that combine the strength of a corporation with external strengths. This new business model conducts flexible collaborations with corporate clients and customers to create new corporate values that merge multiple strengths and boost competitive edge. It will require the capability to withstand wrenching environmental changes and may require changing partners. It dynamically changes the collaboration format to optimize the value chain: NEC refers to this as dynamic collaboration (Nihon Keizai Shimbun, 2003).

As stated above, the salient feature and similarity of the communications carriers and manufacturers described in this case study is that they creatively and effectively import external knowledge through the formation of externally-integrated ToB networks. We will refer to this capability as "external integrative competencies" (see Figure 8.6). The synthesis of these "external integrative competencies" and the previously discussed "internal integrative competencies" become "integrative competencies" that operate as a driving force to simultaneously generate market-creating and market-adaptive strategies.

The case studies presented in this book show that simultaneously building these two disparate ToB networks made it possible to obtain the organizational capability to implement products, services and business models. I believe that, in a practical business context, the "integrative competencies" concept provides a micro viewpoint, and a more detailed and dynamic description of the mechanism for obtaining organizational capability than the "dynamic capabilities" concept of Teece *et al.* (1997, p. 516) ("ability to integrate, build, and reconfigure internal and external competences to address rapidly-changing environments").

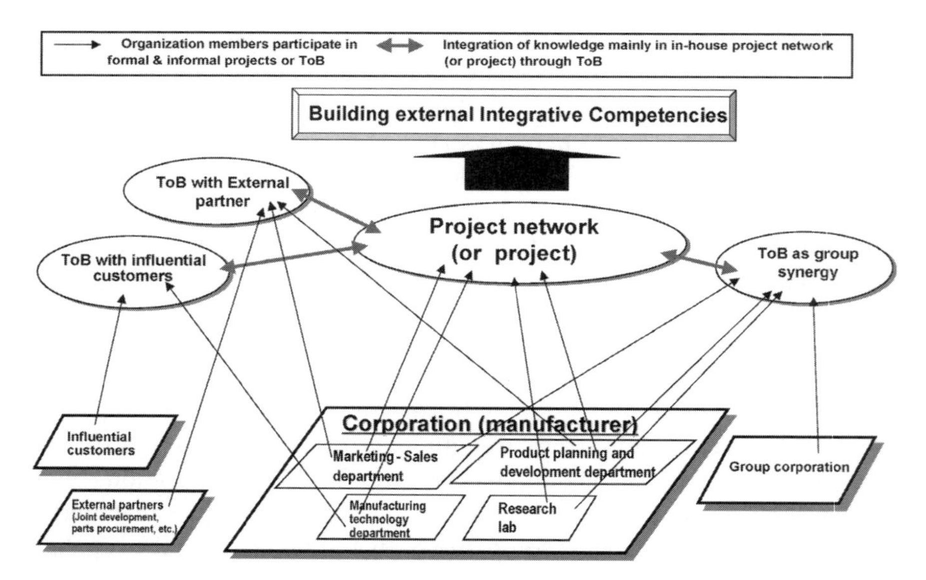

Figure 8.6: "External integrative competences"through external ToB networks.

8.4.3. *Dynamics of ToB and ToB network formulations — strategy practices process performed by practitioners*

In this section, I look at how ToBs or ToB networks are formed and new knowledge is created, from the viewpoints of practitioners (project leaders, project members, middle managers, and staff), organizations, and practices. As shown in Figure 8.3, the members of projects form ToBs with various internal and external organizations and network these ToBs in order to formulate and implement new strategies. As a result, new knowledge is gained. Practitioners implement the strategy practices process which accumulates this new knowledge and of utilizes the knowledge for a strategy-making process. How practitioners think and act as they perform their day-to-day tasks can be revealed by studying, this strategy practices process performed by practitioners from a micro point of view. A thorough studying of practitioners' strategy practices and processes also helps to determine why a business innovation process has succeeded, or failed at a practical level.

The importance of research on practitioners' activities has been reported by many scholars: managerial work (Stewart, 1967; Minzberg, 1973; Kotter, 1982; Whittington, 2003; Jarzabkowski and Serle, 2004), product innovation (Dougherty, 1992; Kodama, 2005), learning and knowledge (Nonaka and Takeuch, 1995; Orr, 1996; Wenger, 1998; Kodama, 1999; Carlile, 2002, 2004; Orlikowski, 2003), practice-based view of knowledge (Bourdieu, 1980; Orlikowski, 2002; Brown and Duguid, 2001), strategy-making (Grant, 2003; Floyd and Lane, 2000; Dutton, Walton and Abrahamson, 1989; Huff, 1990), and technology and information management (Orlikowski, 2000; Kodama, 2003). In actual business sites, new knowledge is born from day-to-day practices performed by practitioners (Orlikowski, 2003). This is why it is meaningful and important to study what and how managers think as they execute strategies.

Whittington (2006) has proposed an integrative framework wherein practitioners' activities are chronologically analyzed based on three concepts: strategy praxis (Reckwitz, 2002), practices and practitioners. However, this micro practices process varies from industry to industry, and from company to company. It is, therefore, important to first derive a common strategy practices framework within a specific industry. An important challenge, in the future, is to discover and propose a framework common to all industries and companies. As a sample of a micro strategy practices process, we will now look at how a development-to-market project for a new service is carried out at a communications carrier.

The following is a chronological description of a strategy practices process framework common to all processes of a new-service development from planning to implementation at a communications carrier, as explained in Chapters 2, 3 and 7.

8.4.3.1. *Phase 1: project startup*

The first step in the Phase 1: Project Startup shown in Figure 8.7 is the formulation of strategies (market-creating strategies and market-adapting strategies) that the development project members selected from various organizations aim for. Some companies often have a service-planning organization responsible for designing new services and business models, and a development organization responsible for technical reviews. For simplicity, I will combine these two organizations into one development project ("the project").

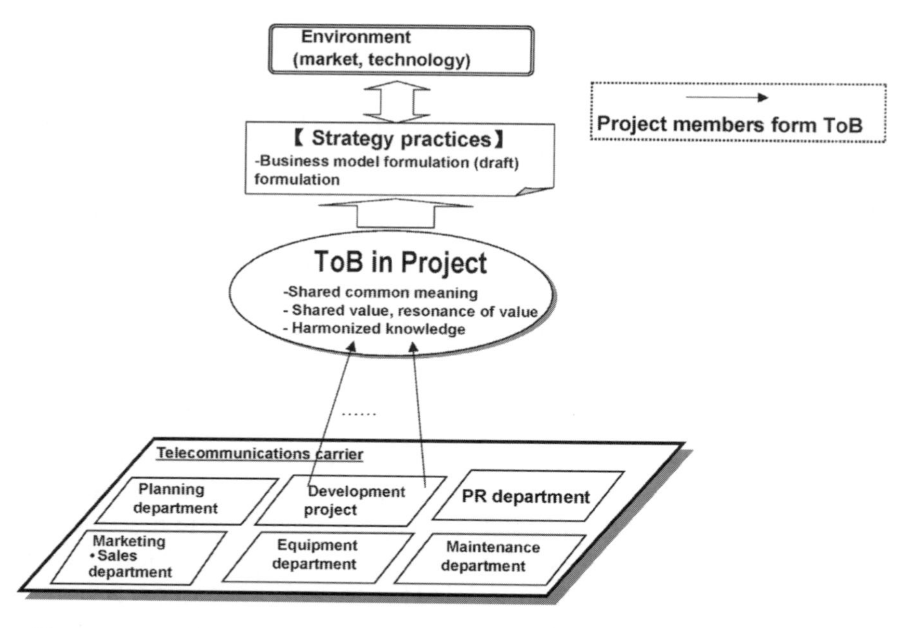

Figure 8.7: Strategy practices process (phase 1: development project startup).

In the project, a preliminary proposal of the business model for a new service is produced as explicit knowledge, using the inspiring tacit experienced knowledge accumulated by individual project members. Many interactions occur between members before explicit knowledge is produced. When viewed at a micro level, tacit and explicit knowledge is repetitively exchanged rapidly among project members, as they think and act. This is referred to by Nonaka and Takeuchi (1995) as the high-speed spiral in the SECI model. The business model is not easily produced, as numerous documents on the business model as explicit knowledge are repeatedly discarded and rewritten by project members. Each time a document is discarded, project members go back to the starting point of their thinking process as reflective practitioners, think about strategy formulation again, and document the thinking process. The provisional business model includes forming business through exploiting knowledge both within and outside the company as a network strategy. The analytical strategy approach tools by Porter (1985) and others are also used in this preliminary proposal formulation process. In some cases, leading companies seek advice from external consultants (Kipping, 1999; McKenna, 2006).

As the preliminary proposal is completed, project members determine common meanings in the business model (Carlile, 2004; Dougherty, 1992). Meanings shared by project members are a characteristic in a community of practice. As explained in Chapter 1, a project as a ToB has the characteristics of a community of practice (Carlile, 2004, 2002; Jantsch, 1980; Shannon and Weaver, 1949). It also has a pragmatic aspect that positively solves problems for the challenging implementation of a new service.

8.4.3.2. *Phase 2: intra-organizational activities*

In the next step, project members perform actions to seek agreement from other internal organizations on the preliminary proposal, as explicit knowledge, of a business model for the new service. In general, numerous tasks at communications carriers are allocated to the planning, marketing & sales, PR & advertising, development, equipment, maintenance and services departments. In addition, a division is usually provided for each type of service. As discussed in Chapters 2, 3 and 7, on the development and commercialization of services at communications carriers, a service cannot be implemented without involving organizations for technology platform development, sales and maintenance, or without commitment from specialists. It is neither efficient nor possible for the project alone to perform all tasks involved in implementing a new service. The next important step for the project, therefore, is to obtain agreement from the relevant organizations through coordination and negotiation efforts (see Figure 8.8).

Project members present a preliminary proposal for the new service to the relevant departments. Presentation is made in formal/informal meetings with the members of the relevant departments. Project members receive ample professional feedback from the members. Sequences of episodes and events (Hendry and Seidl, 2003) are repeated, and heated discussions are held. Great knowledge boundaries exist between the project members who are in charge of performing exploratory new service development and the members of other departments who perform routine tasks for the existing mainstream businesses. By providing a development proposal for the new service to other departments, the novelty in knowledge boundaries among practitioners increases dramatically. These boundary characteristics are called pragmatic boundaries (Carlike, 2004, 2002; Jantsch, 1980; Shannon

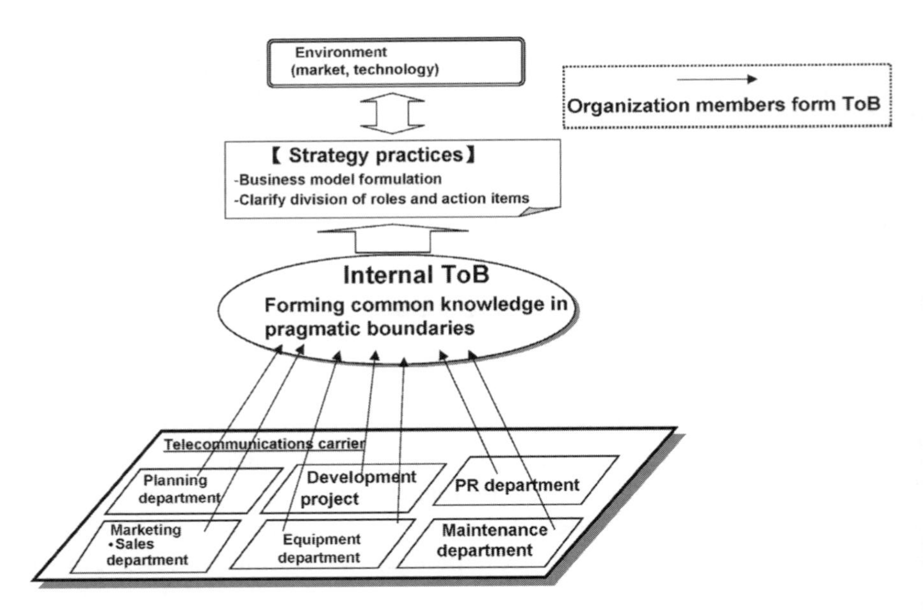

Figure 8.8: Strategy practices process (Phase 2: intra-organizational activity: forming internal ToB).

and Weaver, 1949), and the project leaders are responsible for solving problems in pragmatic boundaries. Differences in individual opinions seen in practitioners' pragmatic boundaries need to be transformed in a positive way to reach agreement among members. Only then does it become possible for the business model scheme to receive company-wide acceptance.

How should project members coordinate the knowledge boundaries between themselves and the existing department members to reach agreement? In many companies, not only top management, but also project leaders and middle managers in existing organizations, are deeply involved in the agreement-seeking process (Whittington, 2006; p. 619). The decision-making process varies from company to company. In general, however, either an agreement is reached at the middle-management level where the relevant departments are involved, or the decision is made at the top-management level (in a development planning or management meeting). As middle managers and practitioners under middle managers carry out the actual strategy formulation and implementation, it is important to reach agreement at the middle-management level. In agreement-seeking meetings, project leaders should actively promote the mission of the company, and of the project, and the need for the new business model to other departments.

As discussed in Chapter 6, it is important for members to first recognize and understand various issues and problems in order to form a consensus in pragmatic boundaries. Project members should think objectively and accept others' opinions, instead of being tunnel-visioned in trying to accomplish their mission. Project leaders must respect the viewpoints of other project members. Problems and issues pointed out by those other than project members include development cost and time reduction, and global optimization. Project leaders must make an effort to address issues presented by relevant departments and to provide satisfying answers. In other words, project leaders are required to have a dialectical thought to "aufheben" contradictions (Kodama, 2005). Top management, on the other hand, needs to create an environment that encourages constructive, productive discussions at the middle-management level, including project leaders. Top management and project leaders must have a deep understanding of a decision-making process consisting of apparently conflicting elements: encouraging and stimulating different opinions, and seeking and reaching consensus (Reberto, 2005).

As a result of the agreement-reaching process based on vigorous discussion, the pragmatic boundaries between practitioners from different organizations positively affect each other, helping the members of other organizations to be aware of their roles and tasks for achieving strategic goals. Furthermore, common knowledge interest in tasks to create a new market is generated among the organization's members (Carlile, 2004). Another important element for practitioners in forming positive pragmatic boundaries is a strong common intent, as explained in Chapter 6. These kinds of common knowledge trigger the renewal of the knowledge of project members from other departments. As a result, ToBs are formed as positive-action pragmatic boundaries centered on the project and incorporating related organizations. Within the ToB, the practitioners of the project and relevant organizations define and perform detailed action items.

8.4.3.3. *Phase 3: extra-organizational activities*

After internal agreement is reached, the project team searches for the knowledge possessed by the external partners (depending on the nature of the proposal; this is concurrently done with the internal agreement-reaching process; see Figure. 8.9). External partners for communications carriers usually include communications equipment manufacturers and/or IT vendors that develop technology platforms (system development) required to realize new services. The project chooses the best partners through discussions and negotiations with potential partners. Communications carriers often attempt to explore potential manufacturers or suppliers using a global competitive tendering system. Success in the tender, therefore, provides a great business opportunity for manufacturers to establish partnerships with communications carriers and to provide them with solutions that satisfy their technical requirements (Brady and Davies, 2004; Davis, 2003).

The project at the communications carrier selects the best manufacturer and carries out the actual contract negotiation process. After a contract is signed by both parties, a formal development project is formed at the manufacturer, and a ToB is formed between the communications carrier and manufacturer projects, and the development specifications including each party's responsibilities and action items are defined. In case the development proposal is complex or involves more technical areas than usual, the manufacturer's laboratory staff and/or production management specialists at the factory join the the ToB. As the terms and

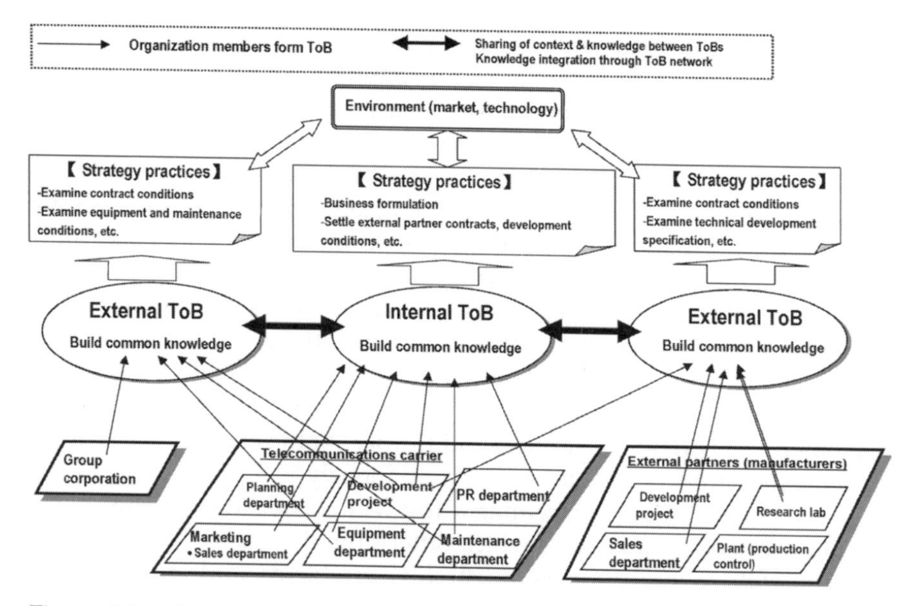

Figure 8.9: Strategy practices process (phase 3: extra-organizational activity: forming external ToB).

conditions in the contract are important to both parties, the manufacturer's corporate sales staff is always involved.

The strategy practices in the processes of contract negotiation and the definition of detailed development specifications are totally different from those in the internal ToB mentioned above. The project leaders and managers at the communications carrier must try to lead the external ToB with the manufacturer, and the internal ToB, to share the same context in tasks. Specifically, the communications carrier project must have detailed business and technical terms and conditions defined in the internal ToB reflected accurately in the contract agreement with the manufacturer, and the development specifications. At the same time, the project team needs to supply in a timely fashion the agreement-reaching process in the internal ToB with any business and technical requests, or restrictions specified by the manufacturer. Project leaders and managers must commit themselves to both the internal and external ToBs to ensure that the two ToBs share the same context and knowledge. Many episodes and events concurrently occur in different contexts in the two ToBs. Project leaders and managers need to understand and fuse these different contexts.

Synergy strategies with group enterprises as extra-organizational activities are also an important issue for communications carriers. To actualize new services, it is important for the internal development projects — the equipment, maintenance and marketing sections — to form a ToB to establish contract conditions, as well as cooperative reactions on the technical side and marketing side concerning new businesses with group enterprises and outside cooperating sales companies. Items concerning the method for selling services to consumers, after support, and the maintenance at the time of failures related to continuous repetitive use by customers are also important tasks for communications carriers to improve customer services. The concept of "service" differs from "products" in the sense that the business does not end upon the completion of sales to the customer. The "brand" of services and further? of the enterprise is formed by having customers use the service continuously.

As described above, in forming a ToB with an outside company, there are many episodes and events which differ from those in the context of an internal ToB; so practitioners must solve problems and subjects with improvisatorial strategy practices by fully understanding the information and the context in these formal and informal episodes and events. Project leaders and middle managers in communications carriers understand and share the context and knowledge in each ToB by committing to both internal and external ToBs. Project leaders and middle managers mutually transfer the context and knowledge that differs between each ToB through forming a ToB network. And they form a shared common meaning in the ToB network and, at the same time, construct and share pragmatic common knowledge for a new challenge, i.e., the actualization of new services.

The roles of the project leader and middle managers in strategy practices are designed for the actualization of a business model consisting of new services, and they must implement micro strategies that are formalized minutely. For that purpose, they must implement a network strategy by forming external ToBs, as shown in Figure 8.1. However, in the process of this strategy implementation, there may be cases in which an unexpected problem occurs from a technical aspect. In such cases, practitioners must make final decisions by providing feedback to the formulated micro strategy, or through trial and error. In internal and external ToBs shown in Figure 8.9, knowledge produced from new strategy practices by practitioners is integrated (Grant, 1996). Knowledge, in this context, means not only explicit knowledge, but also practitioners' new tacit knowledge acquired through new strategy practices. Such knowledge corresponds to business model ideas and technical platforms; that actualize new service function and new manuals for the technical, maintenance and marketing sections; new employee routines to implement new services; and routines for public relations and advertising.

It is not the case that knowledge integration by forming a ToB network shown in Figure 8.9 occurs only in external ToB networks shown in Figure 8.6. In each ToB, in Figure 8.9, ToB networks along the vertical hierarchy in the company shown in Figure 8.5 (for example, the case of Mitsubishi Electric in Chapter 4) exist simultaneously. And the knowledge integration process is performed by practitioners' strategy practices in multiple ToB networks that cross organizations in each enterprise vertically and horizontally. These knowledge integration processes that cross inside and outside the enterprise vertically and horizontally produce "integrative competencies" as an enterprise.

Although a series of strategy practices processes by practitioners is outlined above, actual processes are more complex. The reason is because strategy formulation and implementation activities in enterprises are produced by interactions between individuals when viewed from a micro viewpoint. By observing the processes of strategizing and organizing (Whittington, 2003) more minutely, it can be understood why managers of enterprises and organizations take such actions, and why the business fails or succeeds.

In the previous sections, I showed complex processes ranging from the development of a new business (new product, new service, new business model) to its implementation in a step-by-step manner. Individual episodes and events that are repeated everyday involve various problems and subjects, where there is diverse friction and conflict between practitioners and furthermore invisible discord among organizations. However, many of the wise middle managers whom I know decide their will improvisatorially in each situation that they face and implement business strategies, while repeating trial and error methods. There are few cases where matters advance along the initially-imaged strategy and as described previously, any strategy-making process involves many emergent factors.

As the size of an enterprise increases, there are practitioners having more diverse senses of value, and also there are differences in subjectivity and competency between individual businesspersons; so many managers spend much more time on the consensus-forming process that exists at each management level. In the decision-making process of pragmatic boundaries, however, positive opinions of many members are not always correct, but arguments from a negative viewpoint based on the assumption of a diverse competitive environment, uncertainty accompanying forecasts of future trends, and further discussions on business simulations, are also important. And the role of project leaders, middle managers and those of higher rank is to establish dialectic discussions comprising thesis, antithesis, and synthesis within a consensus-forming process.

8.5. ToBs and ToB Network as Macro-Micro Linkages

I consider that a project as a ToB or a ToB network to be an intellectual platform for practitioners to share a dynamic context (relationships with time, places and persons) and produce new knowledge. ToBs and ToB networks correspond to a temporal space generated or changed when practitioners share contexts with others through interaction and the changing of contexts. The temporal space for sharing tacit knowledge, dialogue and discussions, and strategy practices is a ToB or ToB network. Organizations and individuals are in a dialectic relation, and practitioners change the organization with the human power they possess, while the temporal spaces of "here and now" as a ToB, or ToB network, and the dynamic practical consciousness, are cyclically related to the organization. As discussed in the case of DoCoMo in Chapter 2, practitioners possess the practical power to transform the organization or environment with their own acts, while being restricted by the organization or the environment that they themselves produced (Giddens, 1984; Giddens and Pierson, 1998).

The platform that bridges practitioners and organization (enterprise) is the ToB or ToB network. In other words, the temporal space where practitioners assemble for intra-organizational and extra-organizational strategy practices, and spend intellectual power and practice, are ToBs and ToB networks. New dynamic contexts are produced from various episodes and events occurring daily in the ToB or ToB network, and practitioners share these contexts. Practitioners implement strategy practices continuously for knowledge integration (or knowledge creation) by refining existing knowledge and searching and acquiring for new knowledge, through formal and informal strategy practices (see Figure 8.10). Practitioners' micro strategy practices impact the entire macro structure of the organization, company, or industry through the formation (or elimination) and consolidation of ToBs.

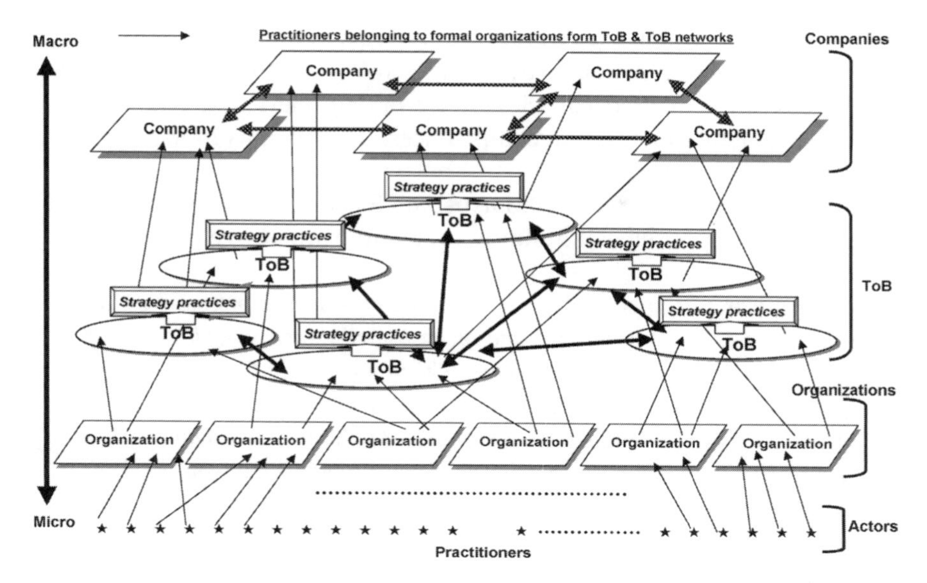

Figure 8.10: Practitioners, organizations and companies centered on ToB & ToB networks (image).

Therefore, with regard to ToBs and ToB networks, not only their important positioning in social networks as micro-macro linkage, but also how practitioners influence enterprise performance by forming and linking ToBs with practitioners, organization, ToBs and ToB networks, enterprise, industry, and further, through the generation and accumulation of social capital (Coleman, 1988; Burt, 1997; Nahapiet and Ghoshal, 1998; Cohen and Prusak, 2000) is important. On the contrary, ToBs and ToB networks become important for the analysis from the viewpoint of how they influence practitioners. In knowledge management, social capital, as valuable as knowledge capital, is generated from ToBs and ToB networks. Also, ToBs and ToB networks are important from the viewpoint of clarifying the process in that various items of knowledge are integrated by the ToB network beyond the borders of ToBs. Furthermore, ToBs and ToB networks have practical significance from the viewpoint of how practitioners generate new items of knowledge by forming and linking ToBs.

A new viewpoint obtained from several case studies in this book is that diverse and hierarchic ToBs with different contexts, and further, a network structure of these ToBs always exist. These are formed and linked by practitioners through their independent activities of working with others in the environment (market, technology, etc.) or organization. Knowledge-creation activities by forming ToBs and ToB networks, which have been implemented consciously by practitioners and taken root as routines, generate integrative competences, described as hidden competitive power of enterprises.

The current president of Matsushita Electric Fumio Osubo (2006) suggests the importance of building up latent competitive power.

> *"The apparent competitive power of an enterprise is expressed by clear indexes as viewed from the side of customers, such as sales, market share, and ranking of brand image. The problem is hidden competitive power, which is hardly visible from the eyes of customers but is an essential part of manufacturing products. Daily work and teamwork of employees constitute the basis of hidden competitive power...It is important to connect operations of design, development, production, and quality control and re-integrate them into a single operation. European and American IT enterprises have strong features of management of distribution of functions. Sections in charge of personnel affairs, design, and development are independent of each other and are connected by strong leadership. In Japanese manufacturers, however, designers may move to the production and production may place orders with the development section. Data from various functions overlap, but the organization overall displays great power. This is a feature of the Japanese manufacturing industry and is its essence. Most Japanese enterprises have a culture in which the design, manufacturing, and purchasing sections work together, thereby accumulating knowledge." (Otsubo, 2006)*

The current president of NEC Kaoru Yano (2006) suggests the importance of innovation though teamwork.

> *"Currently, all members intend to become a single team by holding up the* 'One NEC' *slogan. Teamwork is important. If members are always thinking about working jointly with the adjacent organization, new possibilities will open unlimitedly. Indeed, cooperation across borders of organization is advancing considerably. ... Teamwork is a special Japanese art. How can we compete with foreign countries by forgetting teamwork? Overseas enterprises are going to mimic the advantages of Japan, namely teamwork. Therefore, if we unite now and give rise to*

synergy through mutual cooperation, we will be able break through the deadlock of growth." (Yano, 2006)

Only by forming ToBs and ToB networks does it become possible to form team power beyond the boundaries of sections and functions advocated by Otsubo and Yano, and construct a value chain of business processes and, as a result, embed integrative competencies as a hidden competitive power in the enterprise.

9

Implications and Conclusions

In the previous chapters, we used various case studies to discuss project-based organizations from the viewpoint of corporate strategies. Many existing books on project management deal with the management of subcontract-based development projects. They mainly discuss technical methodologies that enable projects to produce expected results. Project management was originally considered a management technique for large-scale government-related projects, mainly in the US. Of late it has been employed in the construction industry. More recently, it has been effectively introduced in the subcontract-based businesses of IT and other large-scale information systems and has given good results.

The Project Management Institute (PMI), based in the US, has developed *"A Guide to the Project Management Body of Knowledge (PMBOX)"*, as a *de facto* standard for project management. Targetted at organizations and Practitioners, PMBOX defines the detailed implementation process to ensure that deliverables satisfying customer requirements are produced, using the work-breakdown structure (WBS) technique. In practical and academic areas, a number of research results that bridge practices and theories in project management have been presented in the *Project Management Journal* and the *International Journal of Project Management* published by PMI and the International Project Management Association (IPMA) in Europe.

As shown by the case studies in this book, projects can be used not only in subcontract-based businesses, but also as a management technique for implementing corporate strategies. The top and middle managements of an organization, therefore, need to aim for the formulation and the implementation of a project-based organization's corporate strategies, by utilizing both the projects' mobile characteristics such as autonomy and flexibility, and the loosely-regulated management control for creating new businesses and refining existing businesses.

Routine tasks of planning, marketing, sales, development, production, support, promotion and advertisement, general affairs, and accounting departments, can also be regarded as projects in a broad sense, as these tasks are performed by practitioners within a limited timelines to achieve desired results. Each of the various departments in an organization, therefore, can be considered as a collection of projects.

The most important challenge for an innovative organization is to establish the "dynamic chaining of project formulation" (Chapter 8) in order to continually produce projects to implement market-creating strategies and market-adapting strategies. In this chapter, we will look into the new practical insights obtained from the in-depth case studies.

9.1. Trigger Business "Chemical Reactions" Both Inside and Outside the Organization!

Many studies indicate that traditional practices in existing mainstream businesses and excessive belief in path-dependent knowledge (Rosenberg, 1982; Hargadon and Sutton, 1997) can lead to competency traps (Levitt and March, 1988; Martines and Kambil, 1999) and/or core rigidities (Leonard-Barton, 1992, 1995) in organizational innovation management, when markets, technologies, and other environmental conditions change. There is no guarantee that organizations that are currently performing well will always remain competitive. The top and middle managements of an organization, therefore, must have a dynamic view of strategies (Markides, 1997, 1999; Chakravarty, 1997; Eisenhardt and Sull, 2001) to acquire new strategic positions for future business creations, instead of depending on existing mainstream businesses. True project-based organizations are only those that concurrently carry out market-creating strategies, wherein highly-uncertain new businesses are created, and market-adapting strategies are expanded by refining existing businesses.

When it comes to the actual formulation and implementation of market-creating strategies, however, practitioners, particularly of large-scale organizations, often say, "We have trouble getting internal understanding and cooperation when we try to propose and implement new businesses", "We have communication problems among divisions and departments because of organizational walls", or "Different business proposals from different divisions are creating conflicts." These "organizational walls" are, in fact, created by "mental walls" that exist in practitioners' own minds. Knowledge boundaries caused by these mental walls form mental models specific to practitioners of specific areas or positions. Controlled by their specific mental models within their closed boundaries, practitioners perform their routine tasks, and these tasks give rise to a specific organizational culture.

The "Project Culture" discussed in Chapter 8 can be achieved only after this obstacle of mental walls is removed. No matter how many projects are undertaken in an organization, there will be no active business as long as these mental walls exist. Sharp's commitment to foment innovation activities, discussed in Chapter 3, is a good example of forming an internal mechanism to trigger chemical reactions. Machida, the president of Sharp, explains chemical reactions as follows.

> *"It is important for engineers to expand their technologies while looking deeply into a single one. The ability to create new technologies by fusing different technologies will increasingly be required. It is like a chemical reaction. For example, combining hydrogen with oxygen creates water. It is important for us to fuse different technologies to produce a totally new material. To create new demand, it is necessary to develop a new product by combining completely different technologies."*

This strategic practice based on Machida's chemical reaction concept must have led to Sharp's organizational capability to produce many popular products (e.g. Sharp mobile phones with built-in cameras and LCD widescreen TVs presented in Chapter 3). Formal and informal dynamic chaining for project formulation is established to implement chemical reactions (two or more emergency projects, discussed in Chapter 3, are always in progress at Sharp).

Sharp seems to be the only company to have built a project culture that allows the company to produce popular products consistently. What kind of mechanisms does an organization need in-house to trigger active "chemical reactions," as Sharp does? What should top and middle managements do? Like the DoCoMo, (Chapter 2) or NTT (Chapter 7) cases, one practical answer is to build different project-based organizations with diverse staff to shake up the traditional organizational culture. Companies working on market-creation strategies in search of a breakthrough in their existing business should bring new and different knowledge to trigger "chemical reactions". Large-scale internal/external chemical reactions in knowledge result in new business models that traverse different industries (examples include the mobile phone, broadband and game businesses described in the case studies in this document).

Top management should encourage and promote healthy friction and conflict between different projects and existing organizations. However, it should thoroughly understand the context of a discussion so that hostile conflicts can be avoided.

Transparent discussions with external practitioners from other industries are required. Companies need to clarify what they can do to build good relationships with their partners so that partners can share their strategic vision. Transparent, dynamic partnering (Sull, 2005) and the knowledge integration (Kodama, 2006) created by the partnering process trigger a "chemical reaction of knowledge" both within and outside the organization.

9.2. Building a Foundation for a Project Culture

To remove mental walls between practitioners and cause chemical reactions in knowledge, it is essential to promote the maximum sharing of information and context by practitioners so that a foundation for a project culture can be built. To do this, managers should formal or informal study meetings or committees, backed by top management. However, as pointed out in Chapter 6, "Unless charged with a clear problem solving purpose, a committee can become just a place where people say whatever they want to and produce no results. Departments tend to try to remotely control their representatives on committee and get them to pursue the department's own interests. Committees should be considered merely as a communication mechanism" (Kunio Nakamura President, Matsushita Electric).

Unless core committee members actively deal with proposals (e.g., new businesses), presented in a meeting, committees will become a mere communication mechanism. An important step for forming a project culture is to have practitioners participate in the committee so as to enable the attendees to arrive at a common interest in the proposal. Furthermore, the staff directly engaged in the newly-proposed business should be gradually involved in the committee as core members so that the committee evolves into a project. The Canon case discussed in Chapter 6 wherein product development staff tried to involve staff from other departments is based on a similar concept.

Top management, middle management and leadership teams are essential to built project culture. Leadership teams (LTs) consist of leaders (CEO, executives, division managers, department managers, project leaders, middle managers, assistant managers and other leading staff) of each management level (top-management level and middle-management level of project-based organizations and traditional organizations, and cross-functional teams). LTs serve to fuse and integrate knowledge in projects and traditional organizations, as well as to deliver company-wide integrative competence (internal and external integrative competencies).

In some cases, the top managements might have to appoint senior executives, project leaders and/or middle managers as core members. LTs are cross-functional teams covering the same management level or traversing across different management levels. Each LT, networked in multiple layers, traverse the organizations vertically. The objective of forming LTs is to enable discussions. LTs perform their tasks via committees and formal/informal conferences. Some practitioners insist that internal meetings should be minimized. Meetings that are held merely for information sharing and do not deliver results are not required. Meetings that required trigger dynamic changes as required are needed. Mitarai, the President of Canon, and Suzuki, Chairman of Seven & I Holdings are of the opinion that "meetings with vigorous, positive discussions are essential!" Canon's morning meeting described in Chapter 6 is an example of good LT. As explained in Chapter 8, high-quality strategic meetings (Hendry and Seidl, 2003) that trigger dynamic changes in context, and deliver episodes and sequences of events required to dynamically form ToB and ToB networks, provide practitioners with a base to implement strategies.

Vigorous, intense discussions among LT members help them to gain a good understanding of issues and problems. Through communication and collaboration, LT members can also understand and appreciate each other's role and responsibilities. This enables friction or conflict among the LT members to be transformed into constructive, productive friction or conflict. LT members have to constantly think about actions to be taken and contributions to be made to improve corporate performance. As the final decision maker, the CEO provides top-down leadership from time to time. It is also important that the CEO creates discussion opportunities for interactive collaboration between the CEO and LT members, and maximizes the coherence of each member's leadership. LTs help leaders including the CEO to share and resonate values in the drive toward meeting strategic targets (Kodama, 2001). The integrated synergistic effect of leadership results in both internal and external integrative competence.

LTs should include senior executives and middle managers from the planning, management strategy, marketing strategy, financial strategy and IT strategy departments. This ensures that different viewpoints are discussed during meetings. Discussions within and among LTs can result in both short- or long-term projects that conform to strategic targets and the environment (see Figure 9.1).

Multi-layered LTs between projects and existing organizations exist at each management level in all organizations as discussed in the case studies elsewhere in the book. It is well known that when Carlos Ghosn was president of Nissan Motors, he formed nine cross-functional teams (CFTs) consisting of senior executives and middle managers to implement strategies practices and produce good results in Nissan's revival (Ghosn, 2002).

In Toyota Motors, multi-layered LTs, ToBs in the form of consisting of management leaders are formed at each management level (group, section, department and executive levels). Group-level LTs deal with solving chronic or technical problems, and section-level LTs provide

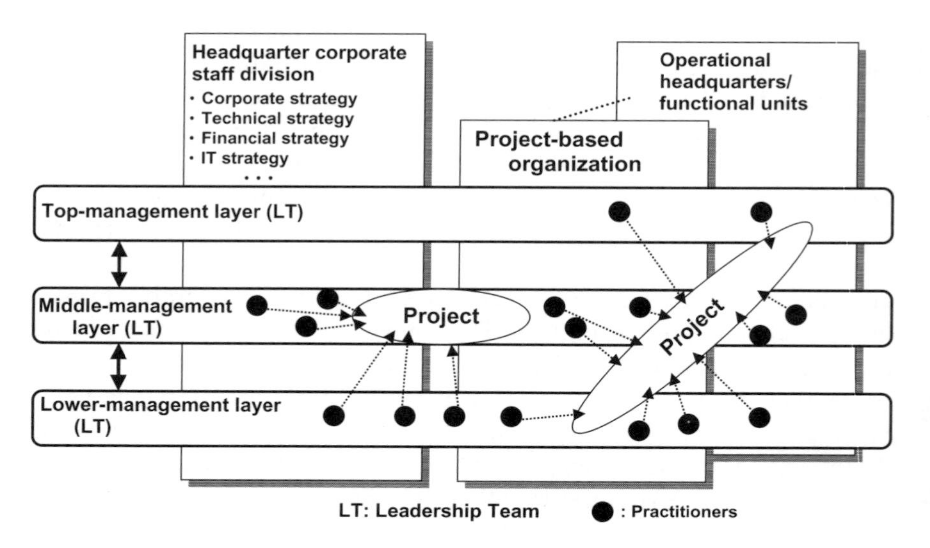

Figure 9.1: Multi-layered LTs formed in businesses.

general solutions that can be applied globally. Executive-level LTs deal with new global production systems, improve relationships among departments, and create advanced technologies. In addition, joint task management teams involving affiliate/non-affiliate suppliers in and outside Japan are formed, providing an LT network to ensure highly-reliable products.

To continually provide its customers with better products Toyota has networked its 13 departments including marketing and sales, development and design, and production. Furthermore, the management departments (technology management, production management, sales management, information technology and quality assurance departments), and general affairs and other departments (total planning, TQM promotion, PR and advertisement, safety, health and the environment, liaison, finance and accounting, overseas business, and personnel and general affairs) are individually networked via LTs in a multi-layered fashion, activating internal resources and capabilities, as well as enabling local and global optimization via organic LT networking (Amasaka, 2004). Multi-layered LT networks exist at various management levels, and involve external partners (see Figure 9.2).

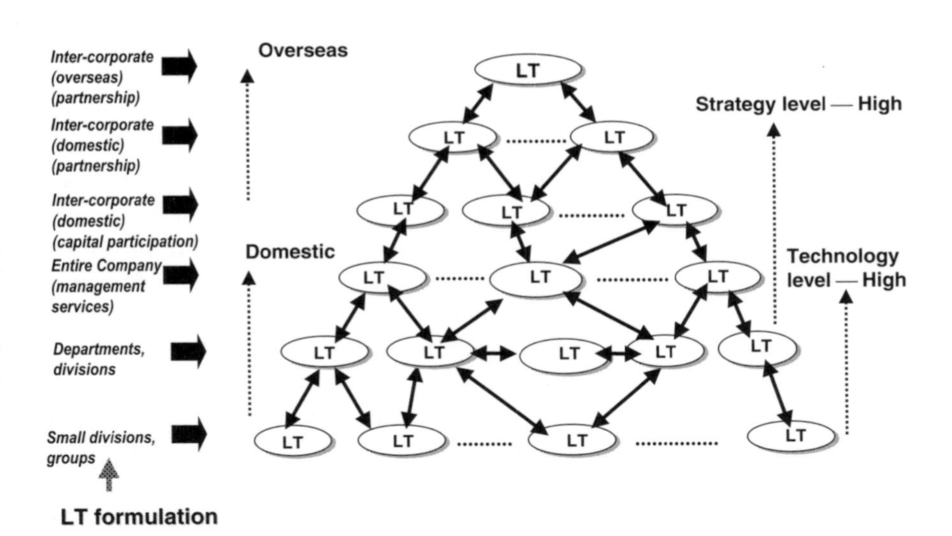

Source: Created by the author based on Ammasaka (2004).

Figure 9.2: Image of Toyota's case of multi-layered LT.

9.3. Form Project Networks for New Innovations!

LTs are project teams (ToBs) formed by leading practitioners. Figures 9.1 and 9.2 illustrate multi-layered LT networks (or ToB networks). These types of project networks play an important role in promoting market-adapting strategies. DoCoMo, Vodafone, Mitsubishi Electric, Sony and NTT, which seek market-creating strategies, have project networks (ToB networks) that have internal projects at their center and extend internally and externally. Canon's network between product development projects (see Figure 6.8) and NTT's new business development project (see Figure 7.8) also have new internal project networks. These project networks fuse different knowledge in individual projects (ToBs) having different contexts, thus triggering chemical reactions in knowledge. Core members including project leaders and managers are always deeply committed to two or more projects (ToBs), and are required to have a clear understanding of the context of each project. These core members link the different contexts of the projects to create a common context for the project network. Core members then create a common meaning based on this common context and disseminate it among project members. Project leaders and managers are responsible for forming the common context and meaning that result from dynamic context changes within the project network. They also need to share a strong common intention and interest with respect to strategic targets, and think positively and solve various problems.

In project networks friction and conflict can occur between project network members who have different knowledge, practices, abilities and specialized skills. To change these conflicts into creative abrasion (Leonard-Barton, 1995) or productive friction (Hagel III and Brown, 2005), project network members need to have a common viewpoint and deep commitment to achieving strategic goals, as well as shared values (Kodama, 2001). Project network members are also required to possess improvisational thinking and acting abilities (Weick, 1969, 1979). Just like dancing to jazz or surfing ocean waves, they need to be able to pick up the faint scent of a business opportunity, and integrate clues for problem-solving and various ideas from different specialized areas, and able to take practical action accordingly (e.g. Kanter, 2001).

Project leaders are also required to have a well-balanced dialectical leadership, as explained in Chapters 2 and 4 (Kodama, 2005). With this ability, they should be able to synthesize inconsistencies in order to solve various business and technological problems. In addition to a coordinating role in and outside the organization, project leaders should play the role of gatekeeper (Allen, 1977) and boundary spanner (Allen and Cohen, 1969; Tushman, 1977; Ancona and Caldwell, 1992), as well as practitioners who can actively commit themselves to the knowledge integration process (Kodama, 2006). In short, project leaders need to have a clear understanding of technology and business to integrate diverse knowledge in project networks that traverse the entire organization and extend externally. In addition to performing internal and external coordination tasks, they must also be able to make appropriate decisions. Of course, it is not easy to find project leaders who bring with them these abilities. By trial and error and self-examination, however, they should be able to gain valuable skills and know-how.

In this book, we have discussed project activities in several organizations to answer the question of the organizational capabilities possessed by top companies in a knowledge-based society. By looking at the formation of project-based organizations, we have provided a framework and insight that is important in promoting core corporate strategies — both market-creating strategies and market-adapting strategies. Creating a project culture is an issue being dealt with not only by executives and managers of Japanese companies but also by those in multinational companies worldwide. How well an organization can organically and innovatively combine different knowledge from various internal and external projects in order to gain integrative competencies as a hidden competitive power is a key factor for success in a knowledge-based society.

Bibliography

Ackoff, R (1981). *Creating the Corporate Future*. New York: Wiley.

Allen, T and S Cohen (1969). Information flow in research and development laboratories. *Administrative Science Quarterly*, 14, 12–20.

Allen, TJ (1977). *Managing the Flow of Technology*, Cambridge, MA: MIT Press.

Allen, TJ and R Katz (1986). The dual ladder: Motivational solution or managerial delusion? *R&D Management*, 16(2), 185–197.

Alvesson, M (1995). *Management of Knowledge-Intensive Companies*. New York: De Gruyter.

Amasaka, K (2004). Development of 'Science TQM', a new principle of quality management: Effectiveness of strategic stratified task team at Toyota. *International Journal of Production Research*, 42(17), 3691–3706.

Ancona, DG and DF Caldwell (1992). Bridging the boundary: External activity and performance in organizational teams. *Administrative Science Quarterly*, 37, 634–665.

Asakura, R (1998). *Innovators in SONY* (in Japanese). Tokyo: IDG Communications Press.

Bailyn, L (1991). The hybrid career: An exploratory study of career routes in R&D. *Journal of Engineering and Technology Management*, 8(1), 1–14.

Baldwin, CY and KB Clark (2000). *Design Rules, Vol. 1: The Power of Modularity*. Cambridge: MIT Press.

Banker, JA (1993). *Paradigms: The Business of Discovering the Future*. New York: Harper Business.

Barabasi, A (2002). *The New Science of Networks*. A Perseus Books Group.

Barlett, C and S Ghoshal (2000). *Transnational Management*. Boston: McGraw-Hill.

Barley, RS (1986). Technology as an occasion for structuring: Evidence from observations of CT scanners and the social order of radiology departments. *Administrative Science Quarterly*, 31, 78–108.

Barley, RS and PS Tolbert (1997). Institutionalization and structuration: Studying the links between action and institution. *Organization Studies*, 18(1), 93–117.

Barney, J (1991). Firm resources and sustained competitive advantage. *Journal of Management*, 17(3), 99–120.

Benson, J (1977). Organization: A dialectical view. *Administrative Science Quarterly*, 22, 221–242.

Bourdieu, P (1980). *The Logic of Practice*. Cambridge: Cambridge University Press.

Bourgeois, LJ (1981). On the measurement of organizational slack. *Academy of Management Review*, 6, 29–39.

Brady, T and A Davies (2004). Building project capabilities: From exploratory to exploitative learning. *Organization Studies*, 25(9), 1601–1621.

Brown, JS and P Duguid (1991). Organizational learning and communities-of-practice. *Organization Science*, 2(3), 40–57.

Brown, JS and P Duguid (2001). Knowledge and organization: A social-practice perspective. *Organization Science*, 12(6), 198–213.

Brown, SL and KM Eisenhardt (1998). *Competing on the Edge*. Boston: Harvard Business School.

Bruch, H and S Ghoshal (2004). *A Bias for Action*. Boston: Harvard Business School Press.

Bryson, J and BC Crosby (1992). *Leadership for the Common Good: Tackling Public Problems in a Shared-Power World*. San Francisco: Jossey-Bass.

Burgelman, RA (1983). A process model of internal corporate venturing in the diversified major firm. *Administrative Science Quarterly*, 28, 223–224.

Burt, S (1992). *Structural Holes: The Social Structure of Competition*. Cambridge and London: Harvard University Press.

Carlile, P (2002). A pragmatic view of knowledge and boundaries: Boundary objects in new product development. *Organization Science*, 13(4), 442–455.

Carlile, P (2004). Transferring, translating, and transforming: An integrative framework for managing knowledge across boundaries. *Organization Science*, 15(5), 555–568.

Chakravarthy, B (1997). A new strategy framework for coping with turbulence. *Sloan Management Review*, 38, 69–82.

Chesbrough, H (2003). *Open Innovation*. Boston: Harvard Business School Press.

Child, J and RG McGrath (2001). Organizations unfettered: Organizational form in an information-intensive economy. *Academy of Management Journal*, 44(6), 1135–1148.

Child, J and SB Rodrigues (2003). Corporate governance and new organizational forms: Issues of double and multiple agency. *Journal of Management and Governance*, 7, 337–360.

Chrislip, D and C Larson (1994). *Collaborating Leadership: How Citizens and Civic Leaders Can Make a Difference*. San Francisco: Jossey-Bass.

Christensen, CM (1997). *The Innovator's Dilemma: When New Technologies Cause Great Firms to Fail*. Boston: Harvard Business School Press.

Clark, KB (1985). The interaction of design hierarchies and market concepts in technological evolution. *Research Policy*, 14(2), 235–251.

Clark, KB and T Fujimoto (1991). *Product Development Performance*. Harvard Business School Press.

Cohen, D and L Prusak (2000). *In Good Company: How Social Capital Makes Organizations Work*. Boston: Harvard Business School Press.

Cohen, WM. and DA Levinthal (1983). Absorptive capacity: A new perspective on learning and innovation. *Administrative Science Quarterly*, 35, 147–160.

Coleman, J (1988). Social capital in the creation of human capital. *American Journal of Sociology*, 94, 95–120.

Cramton, C (2001). The mutual knowledge problem. *Organization Science*, 12, 346–371.

Cusumano, MA and DB Yoffie (1998). *Competing on Internet Time*. New York: The Free Press.

Das, TK and B Teng (2000). Instabilities of strategic alliances: An internal tensions perspective. *Organization Science*, 11(1), 77–101.

Davis, A (2003). Integrated solutions: The changing business of systems integration. In *The Business of Systems Integration*, A Prencipe, A Davis and M Hobday (eds.), pp. 333–368. Oxford University Press.

DeFillippi, RJ (2001). Introduction: Project-based learning, reflective practices and learning outcomes. *Management Learning*, 32, 5–10.

DeFillippi, RJ (2002). Information technology and organizational models for project collaboration in the new economy. *Human Resource Planning*, 25(4), 7–18.

DeFillippi, RJ and M Arthur (1998). Paradox in project-based enterprise: The case of filmmaking. *California Management Review*, 40(2), 125–139.

DiMaggio, P and W Powel (1983). The iron cage revisited: Institutional isomorphism and collective rationality in institutional fields. *American Sociological Review*, 48, 147–60.

Dougherty, D (1992). Interpretive barriers to successful product innovation in large firms. *Organization Science*, 3(2), 179–202.

Dutton, JE, E Walton and R Abrahamson (1989). Important dimension of strategic issues: *Journal of Management Studies*, 26(4), 379–386.

D'Aveni, R (1995). Coping with hypersompetition: Utilizing the new 7S's framework. *Academy of Management Executive*, 9(3), 45–60.

Eisenhardt, K and M Bingham (2005). Disentangling resources from the resource based view: A typology of strategic logics and competitive advantage. *Managerial Decision Economics*.

Eisenhardt, KJ and J Martine (2000). Dynamic capabilities: What are they? *Strategic Management Journal*, 21(10–11), 1105–1121.

Eisenhardt, KM and DN Sull (2001). Strategy as simple rules. *Harvard Business Review*, 79, 106–116.

Eisenhardt, KM and SL Brown (1998). Time pacing: Competing in markets that won't stand still. *Harvard Business Review*, March–April, 59–69.

Fleming, L and O Sorenson (2004). Science as map in technological search. *Strategic Management Journal*, 25, 909–928.

Floyd, SW and P Lane (2000). Strategizing throughout the organization: Management role conflict and strategic renewal. *Academy of Management Review*, 25(1), 154–177.

Forsgren, M (1997). The advantage paradox of the multinational corporation: Nordic contribution to international business research. In *The Nature of the International Firm*, I Bjorkman and M Forsgres (eds.), pp. 69–83. Copenhagen: Handelshojskolens forlag.

Galbraith, J (1973). *Designing Complex Organizations*. Reading: Addison-Wesley.

Gann, MA and AJ Salter (2000). Innovation in project–based, service–enhanced firms: The construction of complex products and systems. *Research Policy*, 29, 955–972.

Gersick, CJ (1994). Pacing strategic change: The case of a new venture. *Academy of Management Journal*, 37, 9–45.

Ghosn, C (2002). Saving the business without losing the company. *Harvard Business Review*, 80(1), 37–42.

Giddens, A and C Pierson (1998). *Conversation with Anthony Giddens Making Sense of Modernity*. Cambridge: Blackwell Publishers Ltd.

Giddens, A (1984). *The Constitution of Society*. Berkeley: University of California Press.

Govindarajan, V and C Trimble (2005). *Ten Rules for Strategic Innovations*. Boston: Harvard Business School Press.

Grabher, G (2002). Cool projects, boring institutions: Temporary collaboration in social context. *Regional Studies*, 36(3), 205–214.

Graebner, M (2004). Momentum and serendipity: How acquired leaders create value in the integration of high-tech firms. *Strategic Management Journal*, 25(8/9), 751–777.

Granovetter, M (1985). Economic action and social structure: The problem of embeddedness. *American Journal of Sociology*, 91, 481–510.

Grant, R (1996). Prospering in dynamically competitive environments: Organizational capability as knowledge integration. *Organization Science* 7, 375–378.

Grant, RM (2003). Strategic planning in a turbulent environment: Evidence from the oil majors. *Strategic Management Journal*, 24(6), 491–517.

Grinyer, P and P McKiernan (1994). Triggering major and sustained changes in stagnating companies. In *Strategic Groups, Strategic Moves and Performance*, H Daems and H Thomas (eds.), pp. 173–195. New York: Pergamon.

Gunz, HP (1980). Dual ladders in research: A paradoxical organizational fix. *R&D Management*, 9(1), 29–32.

Hagel III and JS Brown (2005). Productive friction. *Harvard Business Review*, 83(2), 139–145.

Hagel, J and M Singer (1999). Unbundling the corporation. *Harvard Business Review*, 77(2), 133–141.

Hamel, G and CK Prahalad (1994). *Competing for the Future.* Boston: Harvard Business School Press.

Hamel, G and CK Praharad (1989). Strategic intent. *Harvard Business Review*, 67(3), 139–148.

Hamel, G (1996). Strategy as revolution. *Harvard Business Review*, July–August, 69–82.

Hammel, G (1999). Bringing silicon valley inside. *Harvard Business Review*, 77(5), 70–84.

Hanna, MT and J Freeman (1984). *Organizational Ecology*. Boston: Harvard University Press.

Haour, G (2004). *Resolving the Innovation Paradox*. London: Palgrave Macmillan.

Hargadon, A and R Sutton (1997). Technology brokering and innovation in a product development firm. *Administration Science Quarterly*, 42, 716–749.

He, Z and P Wong (2004). Exploration vs. exploitation: An empirical test of the ambidexterity hypothesis. *Organization Science*, 15, 481–494.

Henderson, RM and KB Clark (1990). Architectural innovation: The reconfiguration of existing product technologies and the failure of established firms. *Administrative Science Quarterly*, 35(1), 9–30.

Hendry, J and D Seidl (2003). The structure and significance of strategic episodes: Social systems theory and the routine practices of strategic change. *Journal of Management Studies*, 40(1), 175–196.

Henrie, M and A Sousa-Poza (2005). Project management: A cultural literature review. Project Management Journal, 36(2), 5–14.

Hobday, M (1998). Product complexity, innovation and industrial organization. *Research Policy*, 26, 689–710.

Hobday, M (2000). The project-based organisation: An ideal form for managing complex products and systems? *Research Policy*, 29, 871–893.

Holland, JH (1975). *Adaption in Natural and Artificial Systems*. Ann Arbor: University of Michigan Press.

Huff, AS (1990). Presidential address: Change in organizational knowledge production. *Academy of Management Review*, 25(1), 45–74.

Huston, L and N Skkab (2006). Connect and develop: Inside Procter & Gamble's new model for innovation. *Harvard Business Review*, 84(3), 58–69.

Ikeda, S (2005). *Shigeru-Net* (in Japanese). Tokyo: CIAJ.

James, W (1907). *Pragmatism*. New York: The American Library.

Jantsch, E (1980). *The Self-Organizing Universe*. Oxford: Pergamon Press.

Jarzabkowski, P and R Searle (2004). Harnessing diversity and collection action in the top management team. *Long Range Planning*, 37(5), 399–419.

Johansson, F (2004). *The Medici Effect*. Boston: Harvard Business School Press.

Kanter, MR (2001). *Evolve! Succeeding in the Digital Culture of Tomorrow*. Boston: Harvard Business School Press.

Karmin, S and W Mitchell (2000). Path-dependent and path-breaking change: Reconfiguring business resources following acquisitions in the U.S. medical sector, 1978–1995. *Strategic Management Journal*, 21(11), 1061–1081.

Keegan, A and JR Turner (2002). The management of innovation in project-based firms. *Long Range Planning*, 35(4), 367–388.

Kim, WC and R Mauborgne (2005). *Blue Ocean Strategy*. Boston: Harvard Business School Press.

Kochanski, JM and G Ledford (2003). People solutions for R&D. *Research–Technology Management*, 46(1), 59–61.

Kodama, M (1999a). Strategic innovation at large companies through strategic community management — an NTT multimedia revolution case study. *European Journal of Innovation Management*, 2(3), 95–108.

Kodama, M (2002a). Transforming the old economy company to new economy. *Long Range Planning*, 35(4).

Kodama, M (2003a). Strategic innovation in traditional big business. *Organization Studies*, 24(2).

Kodama, M (2003c). Strategic community-based theory of the firms: Case study of NTT DoCoMo. *The Journal of High Technology Management Research*, 14(2).

Kodama, M (2005). Knowledge creation through networked strategic communities — Case studies in new product development. *Long Range Planning*, 38(1).

Kodama, M (1999b). Customer value creation through community-based information networks. *International Journal of Information Management*, 19(6), 495–508

Kodama, M (2004). Strategic community-based theory of firms — Case study of dialectical management of NTT DoCoMo. *Systems Research and Behavioral Science*, 21(6), 603–634.

Kodama, M (2006). Knowledge-based view of corporate strategy. *Technovation*, 26(12), 1390–1406.

Kodama, M (2007). Innovation through boundary management — A case study in reforms at Matsushita Electric. *Technovation*, 27(1–2), 15–29.

Kodama, M (2002b). Strategic partnership with innovative customers: A Japanese case Study. *Information Systems Management*, 19, 31–52.

Kodama, M (2002b). The promotion of strategic community management utilizing video-based information networks. *Business Process Management Journal*, 8(5), 462–489.

Kogut, B and U Zander (1992). Knowledge of the firm, combinative capabilities and the replication of technology. *Organization Science*, 5(2), 383–397.

Kotler, P (1999). *Kotler on Marketing*. New York: The Free Press.

Kotter, J (1982). *The General Manager*. New York: Free Press.

Lave, J (1988). *Cognition in Practice*. Cambridge: Cambridge University Press.

Lave, J and E Wenger (1991). *Situated Learning, Legitimate Peripheral Participation*. New York: Cambridge University Press.

Lawrence, P and J Lorsch (1967). *Organization and Environments; Managing Differentiation and Integration*. Cambridge: Harvard Business School Press.

Leonard–Barton, D (1992). Core capabilities and core rigidities: A paradox in managing new product development. *Strategic Management Journal*, 13, 111–125.

Leonard-Barton, D (1995). *Wellsprings of Knowledge: Building and Sustaining the Sources of Innovation*. Boston: Harvard Business School Press.

Levitt, B and JB March (1988). Organization learning. *Annual Review of Sociology*, Annual Reviews, 319–340.

Lindkvist, L (2004). Governing project-based firms: Promoting market-like processes within hierarchies. *Journal of Management and Governance*, 8, 3–25.

Lindkvist, L (2005). Knowledge communities and knowledge collectivities: A typology of knowledge work in groups. *Journal of Management Studies*, 42(6), 1189–1210.

Lundin, RA and C Midler (1998). *Projects as Arenas for Renewal and Learning Processes*. London: Kluwer Academic.

MBD (1998). *ISDN Revolution* (in Japanese). Tokyo: NTT.

Maccoby, M (1999). Find young leaders or lose them. *Research–Technology Management*, 42(1), 58–59.

March, J (1991). Exploration and exploitation in organizational learning. *Organization Science*, 2(1), 71–87.

Markides, C (1998). Strategic innovation in established companies. *Sloan Management Review*, 39(3), 31–42.

Markides, C (1999). *All the Right Moves: A Guide to Crafting Breakthrough Strategy*. Boston: Harvard Business School Press.

Martines, L and A Kambil (1999). Looking back and thinking ahead: Effects of prior success on managers' interpretations of new information technologies. *Academy of Management Journal*, 42, 652–661.

McKinnon, PD (1987). Steady-state people: A third career orientation. *Research–Technology Management*, 30(1), 26–32.

Mitarai, F and U Niwa (2006). *Company for Whom* (in Japanese). Tokyo: Bungei Shunjyu.

Middleton, CJ (1967). How to set up a project organization. *Harvard Business Review*, March–April, 73–82.

Midler, C (1995). "Projectification" of the firm: The Renault case. *Scandinavian Journal of Management*, 11(4), 363–375.

Mintzberg, H and J Walters (1985). Of strategies deliberate and emergent. *Strategic Management Journal*, 6, 357–372.

Mintzberg, H (1978). Patterns in strategy formation. *Management Science*, 24, 934–948.

Mintzberg, H (1973). *The Nature of Managerial Work*. New York: Harper and Row.

Mintzberg, H, B Ahlstrand and J Lampel (1998). *Strategy Safari: A Guided Tour through the Wilds of Strategic Management*. New York: The Free Press.

Mosakouwski, E and B McKelvey (1997). Predicting rent generation in competence-based competition. In *Competence-Based Strategic Management*, A Neene and R Sanchez (eds.), pp. 65–85. Chichester: Wiley.

Nadler, DA and ML Tushman (1989). Organizational framebending: Principles for managing reorientation. *Academy of Management Executives*, 3, 194–202.

Nadler, DA, RB Shaw and AE Walton (eds.) (1995). *Discontinuous Change: Leading Organizational Transformation*. San Francisco: Jossey–Bass.

Nahapiet, J and S Ghoshal (1998). Social capital, intellectual capital, and the creation of value in firms. *Academy of Management Review*, 23(2), 242–266.

Nelson, RR and SG Winter (1982). *An Evolutionary Theory of Economic Change*. Cambridge: Belknap Press.

Newell, S, L Edelman, H Scarbrough, J Swan and M Bresnen (2003). "Best practice" development and transfer in the NHS: The importance of process as well as product knowledge. *Health Services Management Research*, 16, 1–12.

Nihon Keizai Shimbun. Dynamic collaboration (25 August 2003). p. 8.

Nisbett, R (2003). *The Geography of Thought*. New York: The Free Press.

Nohria, N and S Ghoshal (1997). *The Differentiated Network: Organizing Multinational Corporations for Value Creation*. San Francisco: Jossey-Bass.

Nonaka, I and H Takeuchi (1995). *The Knowledge-Creating Company*. New York: Oxford University Press.

Nonaka, I and R Toyama (2002). A firm as a dialectical being: Towards a dynamic theory of a firm, *Industrial and Corporate Change*, 11, 995–1009.

Nonaka, I (1994). A dynamic theory of organizational knowledge creation. *Organization Science*, 5(1), 14–37.

Noria, N and R Gulati (1996). Is slack good or bad for innovation? *Academy of Management Journal*, 39, 1245–1264.

Nutt, PC and RW Backoff (1997). Organizational transformation. *Journal of Management Inquiry*, 6, 235–254.

Okazaki–Ward, L (1993). *Management Education and Training in Japan*. London: Graham & Trotman.

Omta, SWF and JML van Engelen (1998). Preparing for the 21st Century. *Research–Technology Management*, 41(1), 31–35.

Orlikowski, WJ (2000). Using technology and constituting structures: A practice lens for studying technology in organizations. *Organization Science*, 12(4), 404–428.

Orlikowski, WJ (2002). Knowing in practice: Enacting a collective capability in distributed organizing. *Organization Science*, 13(3), 249–273.

Orr, J (1996). *Talking about Machines: An Ethnography of a Modern Job*. Ithaca, NY: ILP Press.

Osterlof, M and B Frey (2000). Motivation, knowledge transfer, and organizational forms. *Organization Science*, 11(3), 538–550.

Ouchi, WG (1980). Markets, bureaucracies and clans. *Administrative Science Quarterly*, 25, 120–141.

Ouchi, WG (1981). *Theory Z: How American Business Can Meet the Japanese Challenge*. Reading: Addison-Wesley.

O'Reilley III, C and M Tushman (2004). The ambidextrous organization. *Harvard Business Review*, 82, 74–82.

Otsubo, F (2006). Interview (in Japanese). 11, 153–158, Voice.
Pascale, RT (1985). The paradox of corporate culture: Reconciling ourselves to socialization. *California Management Review*, 27(3), 26–40.
Pascale, RT (1990). *Managing on the Edge: How the Smartest Companies Use Conflict to Stay Ahead*. New York: Simon and Schuster.
Peirce, CS (1898/1992). *Reasoning and the Logic of Things*. Cambridge: Harvard University Press.
Pettigrew, A (2003). Strategy as process, power and change. In *Images of Strategy*, S Cummings and D Wilson (eds.). Blackwell: U.K.
Porter, M (1985). *Competitive Advantage*. New York: Free Press.
Prencipe, A and F Tell (2001). Inter-project learning: Processes and outcomes of knowledge codification in project-based firms. *Research Policy*, 30, 1371–1394.
Priem, R and JE Butler (2001). Is the resource-based "view" a useful perspective for strategic management research? *Academy of Management Review*, 26(1), 22–40.
Quinn, RE and KS Cameron (eds.) (1988). *Paradox and Transformation: Toward a Theory of Change in Organization and Management*. Cambridge: Ballinger.
Reberto, AM (2005). Why great leaders don't take yes for an answer: Managing for conflict and concensus. Pearson Education, Inc., Publishing as Wharton School Publishing.
Reckwitz, A (2002). Toward a theory of social practices: A development in cultural theorizing. *European Journal of Social Theory*, 5(2), 243–263.
Rond, M and H Bouchikhi (2004). On the dialectics of strategic alliances. *Organization Science*, 15(1), 56–69.
Rosenberg, N (1982). *Inside the Black Box: Technology and Economics*. Cambridge University Press.
Rosenbloom, N (2000). Leadership, capabilities and technological change. *Strategic Management Journal*, 21, 1083–1103.
Sanchez, R (1995). Strategic flexibility in product competition. *Strategic Management Journal*, 16, 135–159.
Sanchez, R (1996). Strategic product creation: Managing new interactions of technology, markets, and organizations. *European Management Journal*, 14(2), pp. 121–138.
Sanchez, R (2000). Modular archtectures, knowledge assets and organizational learning new management processes for product creation. *International Journal of Technology Management*, 19(6), 610–619.
Sawhney, M and E Prandelli (2000). Communities of creation: Managing distributed innovation in turbulent markets. *California Management Review* 42, 24–54.
Shannon, C and W Weaver (1949). *The Mathematical Theory of Communications*. Urbana: University of Illinois Press.

Shapiro, C and HR Varian (1998). *Information Rules*. Boston: Harvard Business School Press.

Simon, HA (1996). The architecture of complexity: Hierarchic systems. In *The Science of the Artificial*, 3rd Ed., HA Simon (ed.). Cambridge: MIT Press.

Spender, C (1990). *Industry Recipes: An Enquiry into the Nature and Sources of Managerial Judgement*. Oxford: Basil Blackwell.

Star, SL (1989). *The Structure of Ill–Structured Solutions: Boundary Objects and Heterogeneous Distributed Problem Solving*. In *Residing in Distributed Artificial Intelligence*. Menlo Park: Morgan Kaufman.

Star, SL (1992). The Trojan door: Organizations, work and the "open black box". *Systems Practices*, 5, 395–410.

Stewart, T (1997). *Intellectual Capital: The New Wealth of Organization*. New York: Doubleday.

Sull, DS (2005). Dynamic partners. *Business Strategy Review*, 16(2), 5–10.

Sydow, J, L Lindkvist and R DeFillippi (2004). Project-based organizations, embeddedness and repositories of knowledge: Editorial. *Organization Studies*, 25(9), 1475–1489.

Teece, D, G Pisano and A Shuen (1997). Dynamic capabilities and strategic management. *Strategic Management Journal*, 18(3), 509–533.

Thompson, JD (1967). *Organizations in Action*. New York: McGraw–Hill.

Tichy, NM and E Cohen (1997). *The Leadership Engine: How Winning Companies Build Leader at Every Level*. New York: Harper Collins.

Tidd, J (1994). *Home Automation*. Imperial College of Science and Technology.

Turner, JR (1999). *The Handbook of Project Based Management*, 2nd Ed. London: McGraw-Hill.

Turner, JR and R Miller (2003). On the nature of the project as a temporary organization. *International Journal of Project Management*, 21, 1–8.

Tushman, ML (1977). Special boundary roles in the innovation process. *Administrative Science Quarterly*, 22, 587–605.

Tushman, ML and P Anderson (1986). Technological discontinuities and organizational environments. *Administrative Science Quarterly*, 31, 439–465.

Tushman, ML and CA O'Reilly (1997). *Winning through Innovation*. Cambridge: Harvard Business School Press.

Tushman, M and D Nadler (1978). Information processing as a integrating concept in organizational design. *Academy of Management Review*, 3(3), 613–624.

Tushman, M and E Romanelli (1985). Organizatinal evolution: A metamorphosis model of convergence and reorientation. *Research in Organizational Behavior*, 7(2), 171–222.

Ulrich, HP and JB Gilbert (1984). *Self-Organization and Management Social Systems*. Berlin: Springer Verlag.
Utterback, JM (1994). *Mastering the Dynamics of Innovation*. Boston: Harvard Business School Press.
Van de Ven, AH and MS Poole (1995). Explaining development and change in organizations. *Academy of Management Review*, 20(5), 510–540.
Vangen, S and C Huxham (2003). Nurturing collaborative relations, building trust in interorganizational collaboration. *The Journal of Applied Behavioral Science*, 39(1), 5–31.
Watts, J (2003). *Six Degrees The Science of a Connected Age*. W.W. Norton & Company.
Weick, KE (1969). *The Social Psychology of Organizing*. Reading: Addison–Wesley.
Weick, KE (1979). *The Social Psychology of Organizing*. 2nd Ed. Reading: Addison–Wesley.
Weick, KE (1989). Theory construction as disciplined imagination. *Academy of Management Review*, 14(4), 516–531.
Wenger, EC (2000). Communities of practice: The organizational frontier. *Harvard Business Review*, 78(1), 139–145.
Wenger, E (1998). *Community of Practice: Learning, Meaning and Identity*. Cambridge: Cambridge University Press.
Wernerfelt, B (1984). A resource-based view of the firm. *Strategic Management Journal*, 5, 171–180.
Whittington, R (2003). The work of strategizing and organizing: For a practical perspective. *Strategic Organization*, 1(1), 117–125.
Whittington, R (2004). Strategy after modernism: Recovering practice. *European Management Review*, 1(1), 62–68.
Whittington, R (2006). Completing the practice turn in strategy research. *Organization Studies*, 27(5), 613–634.
Williamson, OE (1975). *Markets and Hierarchies: Analysis and Antitrust Implications*. New York: Free Press.
Williamson, OE (1981). The economics of organizations: The transaction cost approach. *American Journal of Sociology*, 87(3), 548–557.
Windeler, A and J Sydow (2001). Project networks and changing industry practices: Collaborative content production in the German television industry. *Organization Studies*, 22(6), 1035–1060.
Yano, K (2006). Interview (in Japanese). *Voice Journal*, 11, 159–164.

Index

abduction 55
abrasion 12, 20
absorptive capability 106
Alcatel 85
ambidextrous organization 200, 228
AMD 144
Apple 198
Aquos 73
architectural competence 105
architectural innovation 15
architectural knowledge 105
architecture 17
architecture development 57
ASPs (Application Service Providers) 94
AT&T 198
Au 60
automobiles 3

black box 76, 165
black box strategy 72
boundaries penetration 13
boundaries synchronization 20
boundary innovation 57
boundary networks 4
boundary objects 130
boundary spanners 106, 255
broadband 84
BUG 203
business model 1

Canon 5
career path 9
Carlos Ghosn 252
CCD 65
cdma 2000 60
cell 133
cell production 164
chemical reactions 248
c-HTML 43
CMOS 65
collaborate leadership 224
collectivity of practice 7
common determination 179
common interest 180
communal knowledge 7
communications 3
community 6
community knowledge 29
community knowledge creating cycle 29
community of practice 6
company-wide organizational learning 21
competency traps 13
competitive advantage 20
components 17
conflict 12
construction 3
constructive dialog 224
consulting 3

Content Providers (CP) 37
core competencies 2
core rigidities 13
corporate strategy 21
corporate ventures 20
CPUs 88
creative abrasion 116, 224, 254
creative collaboration 12
creative destruction 24
creative dialogue 39
cross-functional teams 115, 252
crossover 18

decentered knowledge 6
destructive technology 92
dialectical dialog 53
dialectical leadership 53
dialectical thought 112
different corporate cultures 11
DIGA 166
digital appliance products 20
digital appliances 151
digital camera 58, 151
disciplined imagination 24
DNA 71
domain-specific knowledge 6
DSPs (digital signal processors) 90
DTC (Desk Top Conference) 88
dual ladder system 9
dual networks 25
DVD 96
DVD recorder 151
dynamic capabilities 216
dynamic chain 220
dynamic collaboration 232
dynamic view of strategy 4

e-business 2
emergency project teams 72–74
emergent strategies 52
Emotion Engine (EE) 140
enabler 115
Enoki 36
entrepreneur strategy 219
episodes 236
Ericcson 60
events 236
explicit knowledge 8
exploitation 23
exploitative networks 19
exploitative practice 70
exploration 23
exploratory activity 4, 16
exploratory networks 19
exploratory practice 23
external integration capability 108
external integrative competencies 229
external knowledge 216
extra-organizational activities 238

Fastweb 85
FeliCa chip 46
FeliCa Network 46
Fixed Mobile Convergence (FMC) 85
flat & web 169
FOMA 26
Fujio Mitarai 171
Fujitsu 15
Fumio Ohtsubo 161
functional organization networks 49
game business 20
gatekeeper 106, 255.
Gateway Business Division (GBD) 37
General Magic 198
Google 205
Graphics Synthesizer (GS) 140
Great Leap 21, 157
GrR Home net corporation 204
G-square 204
GUIs (graphical user interfaces) 90

hardware 17
harmonized knowledge 11
harmony 76
Hayakawa 71
hidden competitive power in the enterprise 245
hierarchical organizations 2
horizontal integration network 109
HTTP 103
human knowledge 12

IBM 144
IC 65
IC chip 46
ICT (Information & Communication Technology) 1
Idei 46
Ikeda 196
imaginative capability 24
i-mode 15
improvised mutual learning 15
incremental innovation 23
incubations 67
industry boundaries 14
informal networks 4
informal projects 75
Inktomi 198
innovate leadership 68
innovation 1
integration of boundaries 21
Integrative competencies 83
Intel 88, 144
internal corporate venture 219
internal integration capability 108
internal integrative competencies 225
internal knowledge 217
inter-organizational networks 3
inter-project collaboration 11
inter-project learning 14
inter-project ToBs 181
intrinsic motivation 180
IP 84
IP-based videoconferencing systems 84
ISDN 84
IT 1
IXY Digital 177

Japanese company 18
Java applications 58
joint development 63
joint ventures 46
J-phone 58
J-SKY 58
Junichro Miyazu 196

Kameyama factory 79
Kaoru Yano 244
knowledge boundary 4
knowledge difference 105
knowledge in practice 16
knowledge integration 2
knowledge sharing 5
knowledge transfer 5
knowledge-based economy 1
knowledge-based service 68
knowledge-based society 255
Konami 126
Konosuke Matsushita 152
Kunio Nakamura 152
Kutaragi 46
Kyocera 62

leadership 21
Leadership Team (LT) 70, 110
Leadtek 85
learning community 6
LSI 46, 70
Lucent 85

Machida 62
macro-micro linkages 242

Market-adaptive strategies 213
Market-creating strategies 213
marketing innovation 24
marketing knowledge 24
Masashi Kojima 194
Masaya Maeda 179
matrix form 3
Matsunaga 37
Matsushita Electric 4
Matsushita Semiconductor 160
MCUs 93
Mebius 73
mental models 13
mental walls 249
micro strategy 217
Microsoft 198
middle managers 75
Mitsubishi Electric 18
MN 128, 203
mobile communications business 23
mobile e-commerce 46
mobile internet service 26
mobile phone 19
mobile phone system 70
mobile telecommunications 13
mobile wallet 46
modular innovation 90
module development 57
morning meeting 185
Movie Sha-mail 58
MPU 90
Oboshi 28
MSN network 204
M-Stage Visual Net 109
Multi-layered LT networks 253
multi-layered LTs 252
Multimedia Business Department (MBD) 196
multimedia communication system 83
multinational corporations 2
mutual knowledge 11
mutual learning 5

Nakamura 152
Nakamura Reform 157
Namco 126
Natsuno 37
NEC 61
network competencies 70
network connectivity 25
network mindset 220
network strategy 21
networked ToBs 20
new concept 18
new organization 18
new product development 15
new products and services 2
Nintendo 117
Nissan Motors 252
NTT 4
NTT DoCoMo 4

OEM (Original Equipment Manufacturer) 99
Ohga1 18
only one device 71
only one product 71
only one strategy 72
only one technology 76
organizational behavior 6
organizational boundaries 12
organizational learning 5
organizational slack 202
organizational walls 249
overall optimization 173

paradoxical organization 200
path dependencies 13, 17
path dependent knowledge 13
path-breaking resources 217
path-dependent resources 217
path-dependent technology 23
PAVC 160

PC 90
PCI 90
PHOENIX project 205
PHS (Personal Handyphone System) 62
picture messaging 58
PictureTel 88
PlayStation Portable 126
PlayStation 2, 20, 126
PM division 155
PMBOX 247
political negotiating practice 76
Polycom 91
pragmatic boundaries 81
pragmatic boundary 110
product architecture 85
product development 17
productive friction 12
professional services 3
project culture 249
project leader 9
project learning 75
project management 3
project management institute 247
project manager 9
project members 3
project networks 3
project startup 234
project strategies 20
project-based organizations 1
projects 2
ProShare 88
PSX 126

Qualcomm 60

R&D 99
radical change 24
radical innovation 18
Radvision 85
recursive interplays 19
reflective practitioners 235
resource-based view 216
reverse marketing 159
RNESAS 144

SCE 116
S-curves 46
Sega enterprises 120, 204
service architecture 102
set-top box (STB) 90
Sha-mail 58
shared thought worlds 11
Sharp 4
Siemens 85
Silicon graphics 122, 198
Skype 92
Softbank Mobile 58
software 17
software-based architecture 90
Sony 5
Sony Computer Entertainment 46
Sony Music Entertainment (SME) 119
spiral strategy 77
square 126
stability were constant 87
stechnological innovation 20
strategic alliances 20
strategic communities 15
strategic intent 24
strategic knowledge networks 30
strategic outsourcing 32
strategic positions 23
strategy as action 21
strategy dynamics 220
strategy formulation and implementation 12
strategy practices process 233
strategy praxis 233
strategy-making process 21
subsystems 17
Susumu Koike 165
switching circuit technology 87

synergies 20
systems architecture 103
systems LSIs 88

T.120 88
tacit knowledge 12
Takao 60
Tandberg 92
Tatami project 73
teams 2
Teams Boundaries (ToB) 14
technological boundaries 58
technological change 13
technological domains 57
technological innovation 20
technology architecture 83
technology integration 15
telecommunication 2
telecommunications carries 15
temporary organization 4
The horizontally-integrated ToB 110
third-generation mobile phone service 26
time-pacing strategy 20
tipping point leadership 46
ToB network 14, 80
top management 79
Toshiba 61
Toyota Motors 110
TQM 110
transaction cost 216
trial and error 15
TV conferencing 99
TV phone 62

V products 156
value chains 79
value from volume 34
value network 24
value-chain integration 77
vertical integration network 109
vertical launch strategy 151, 160
vertically-integrated networked ToB 111
Victor 204
video chat 99
video messaging 58
videoconferencing systems 84
video-on-demand 85
visual communication systems 84
Visual FMC 94
Visual phone 63
Vodafone 19
VoIP [Voice over IP] 85
V-shaped recovery 153

Waku-Waku project 161
WBS 247
W-CDMA 60
web conferencing systems 84
WiMax 94
Windows 95 90
win-win 129
wireless LANs 85

Yahoo 205
Yamaha 204

Zaurus 65